NORTH AMERICAN INDIANS: AN ANTHROPOLOGICAL PERSPECTIVE

GOODYEAR REGIONAL ANTHROPOLOGY SERIES

Edward Norbeck, Editor

ANTHROPOLOGICAL PERSPECTIVES OF:

MODERN EUROPE
Robert T. Anderson

INDIA
Stephen A. Tyler

INDONESIA
James L. Peacock

CIRCUMPOLAR PEOPLES
Nelson H. Graburn and Barry S. Strong

NORTH AMERICAN INDIANS
William W. Newcomb, Jr.

Additional Volumes Forthcoming:

Southeast Asia

China

Africa

Philippines

Polynesia and Micronesia

Middle East

Latin America

NORTH AMERICAN INDIANS: AN ANTHROPOLOGICAL PERSPECTIVE

WILLIAM W. NEWCOMB, JR.

TEXAS MEMORIAL MUSEUM

GOODYEAR PUBLISHING COMPANY, INC.
Pacific Palisades, California

FOR BILLY

**Library of Congress
Cataloging in Publication Data**

Newcomb, Jr., William Wilmon, 1921–
   North American Indians.

   (Goodyear regional anthropology series)
   1. Indians of North America. I. Title.
E77.N54 1974   970.1   73-88990
ISBN 0-87620-624-0
ISBN 0-87620-623-2 (pbk.)

Library of Congress Catalog Card Number: 73-88990
(Paper) Y-6232-6
(Cloth) Y-6240-4
ISBN: 0-87620-623-2 (P)
     0-87620-624-0 (C)

Current printing (last digit):
10 9 8 7 6 5 4 3 2 1

Printed in the United States of America

CONTENTS

PREFACE

This book was written to provide students and
general readers with a concise introduction to the
Indians of North America. Between the Rio Grande
and the Arctic and the Atlantic and Pacific coasts
were thousands of more or less distinct Indian
groups in 1492, ranging in size and social complexity
from simple, family-sized groups to highly structured
and relatively immense tribes and confederacies.
Living as wandering gatherers, hunters, fishermen,
settled farming villagers, and various combinations
of these, they sprang from a variety of backgrounds,
spoke a large number of languages, and had long
since inhabited every corner of the continent. They
would constitute a confusing jumble of peoples were
it not that those groups sharing common pasts and
dwelling near one another tended to share similar
ways of living. I have endeavored to describe the
principal features of each of these cultural patterns
or systems, traditionally designated as culture areas.

In order to grasp their variety and nature, it
seemed advisable to include some background
material. Thus, the origins and cultural
development, biological nature, aboriginal
population, and languages of North American
Indians are briefly touched on in the introductory
chapter, as is the concept of culture. In subsequent
chapters the environmental setting, prehistory, and
history of each culture area is sketched in before
the salient features of its cultures are summarized.
The chapters are roughly ordered geographically,
proceeding from the eastern part of the continent
westward. This has the merit of allowing such
related cultural provinces as the Eastern Woodlands
and the Plains to be grouped together.

Each generation of Americans rediscovers
America's natives, and this is as true for the
anthropologist as for the layman. It is partly a

matter of the accumulation of data leading to a revision and adjustment of an older picture, but it is also due to the different angle of vision our particular moment in history affords us, or forces upon us. The Indian as seen from the last third of the twentieth century is not the Indian as viewed from its first third, and both are far different from the Indian as pictured in the nineteenth century. Despite the staggering amount of information now available, in many ways today is a particularly difficult time to write about American Indians. The small, scattered, but very visible Indian minority and its varied partisans have found their voices and have sometimes engaged in desperate acts. Though their words may be strident and their actions sometimes serve their cause badly, Indian grievances are real, injustices deep-seated, and inequities vicious. The anthropologist, whatever his own heritage, is almost invariably a sympathetic partisan. But to become partisan participant here serves knowledge and its interpretation poorly; to become propagandist for a new view of Indian history distorts that history as badly as the Indian aspect of American history has often been traduced. Even though this book is not concerned with the current Indian scene, it remains inescapably a product of its parlous time.

I have attempted to present the major and minor disputes and the interpretations and opinions about various aspects of Indian culture and history fairly and objectively. I have made no particular effort to muffle my own views, but I have endeavored to provide the reader with the various sides of controversies and the sources concerning them. In a single volume devoted to such a tremendously broad subject, only sketchy and shallow descriptions are possible. Many fascinating and important aspects of life have to be neglected or omitted; games, amusements, mythology, art, and music, to mention a few, are short-changed. I can only hope that curious readers will consult the bibliography in order to pursue these and other subjects.

To single out all the people who over a good many years have contributed directly and indirectly to this book is impossible, but a few of them must be mentioned. My mother and father first kindled a boyhood interest when they sent me on a hunt for an elusive Indian campground on a southern Michigan farm. Mother could describe the camp of the "old ones" exactly; I have been searching for it one way or another ever since. The staff of the Texas Memorial Museum has been patient when, perhaps too frequently, I have been preoccupied with the writing of this book. Among them, Mrs. Willena C. Adams, Technical Reports Editor, has read the entire manuscript several times, volunteered many practical suggestions, and given me continual help and encouragement. Mrs. Mary Louise Glass, the museum's Administrative Assistant, has promptly and efficiently supervised the typing of various drafts of the manuscript. I could not have completed this work without the encouragement and forebearance of my family, including my son, to whom this book is dedicated. Finally, I am deeply indebted to the various Indians I have worked with off and on over the past twenty years, and to all those, whites and Indians, who have labored to understand the native Americans, and who in consequence have given me so much.

ONE

INTRODUCTION

ORIGIN AND DEVELOPMENT[1]

When man first entered the North American continent, he was modern in a biological sense and heir to hundreds of thousands of years of painfully won cultural experience. But from the perspective of modern civilization, he was woefully equipped to survive in the rich, unspoiled, often demanding wilderness of America. Yet those pioneer hunters and those who soon joined them, as few as they must have been and as scant as was their equipment for coping with a new land, prospered mightily and were the seed from which sprang the tremendously diverse, inventive, and fascinating cultures and civilizations that are the subject of this book.

Serious students of Indian origins are agreed that the earliest migrations to America were by way of the Bering Strait between Siberia and Alaska before 11,500 years ago, probably several thousand years earlier, and possibly many thousands of years before that. Ocean-going vessels had not yet been invented, and a glance at a map quickly reveals that there was no other practicable route into America from the Old World. The Bering Strait is about fifty-seven miles wide today, but this expanse is broken by the Diomede Islands, and the longest water gap is about twenty-five miles, so land is normally in sight at all times for those who make the crossing. Eskimos in recent times have not found the strait to be a barrier, and they and other peoples also may have crossed when it was choked with ice. But there is every reason to believe that the earliest migrants were not even faced with the problem of a water barrier; they crossed to the New World on dry land.

A dry-shod crossing was possible during long periods of the Pleistocene, the last great geological epoch, because a land connection joined the two continents. The Pleistocene was an epoch of climatic turmoil, a period of awesome glaciations that at times buried much of the northern half of North America under thousands of feet of snow and ice. There were four major Pleistocene glaciations, each separated from the others by longer or shorter interglacial periods during which the climate warmed and glaciers receded. The glacial periods themselves were also marked by fluctuations of glacial advance (substages) and intervals of warmer climate and retreating glaciers (interstadials). There were two major centers of glaciation in North America. In the West a Cordilleran ice mass centered in British Columbia and extended to the Columbia River valley in the south, and in the north to the Brooks Range in Alaska; the Laurentide ice centered in the Hudson Bay area and at its maximum extended to the Arctic in the north and the Atlantic Ocean in the east. Its southern border stretched from northern New Jersey westward, down the Ohio Valley and up the Missouri River valley, joining the Cordilleran ice in Alberta and British Columbia. Glaciers also formed in the higher elevations of the Sierra Nevada and the Rocky Mountains, as they did at high elevations in Mexico and South America.

The glaciations rearranged the landscape of North America in a massive way, drastically affected the composition and distribution of plant and animal communities, and locked up immense quantities of the earth's water, substantially lowering sea levels. The Bering and Chukchi seas, which today separate Asia from North America, are shallow, and if the sea level in the Bering Strait were lowered 150 feet, a bridge nearly 200 miles wide would connect the two continents. Should the sea level drop 450 feet, about the maximum fall during the Pleistocene, a land mass 1,300 miles wide would join them. Since times when the land connection was greatest were also periods when glacial ice was at its maximum, one might suppose that migrations of men and animals might be blocked by ice. Yet this was not the case. Neither the Chukchi or Seward peninsulas, large areas of central Alaska, or the spasmodically dry Bering land mass were glaciated during the 70,000 or so years of the Wisconsin, the last major glacial epoch. In effect, then, a portion of North America was attached to Siberia and at least for a short time isolated from the interior of the continent by a formidable ice barrier.

A number of animals migrated to North America from Asia at various times during the Wisconsin, including mastodons, mammoths, musk oxen, bison, moose, elk, mountain sheep, bears, wolves, and foxes. Before the Wisconsin had run its course, man, very probably following the game animals on which he depended, also had entered America and breached the glacial barriers.

It was shortly after one of the last Wisconsin substages, the Mankato, and during the Two Creeks interstadial or shortly after it, some 11,500 years ago, that man unquestionably established his presence in the heart of North America. For the preceding 15,000 years, the way south may have been blocked by ice, but now an ice-free corridor opened up between the Cordilleran and Laurentide ice masses, leading from the Arctic into the plains of North America. Hunters of big game animals in central Alaska, the Bering Strait land mass, and eastern Siberia appear to have quickly taken advantage of the corridor to burst into the virgin heart of North America.[2]

Before turning to the rather considerable amount of information available about these early Americans, mention must be made of the possibility that the first penetration and occupation of America occurred much earlier. The evidence for men having entered America in the middle or early Wisconsin, or perhaps even in the Sangamon interglacial that preceded it, is based on the discovery at many places in North and South America of very crude stone tools—percussion-flaked scrapers, choppers, and flakes—sometimes with geological or faunal associations that seem to imply great antiquity. But in general it is the crudity of the stone tools at these sites and the lack of bifacially flaked knives and projectile points that are their main claim to antiquity. At none of the supposed "pre–projectile point" sites in the United States—from the Lewisville Site and Friesenhahn Cave in Texas, to the presumed hearths dating from more than 30,000 years ago on Santa Rosa Island off the California coast, or the even older flaked cherts found near the Calico Hills in California, or others—has the presence of man before about 12,000 years ago been convincingly demonstrated or proved.[3]

The only sites in North America with apparently good claims to great antiquity are in Mexico, but they were relatively recently discovered, and it is as yet difficult to give them a fair evaluation. At Tlapacoya in the State of Mexico, crude stone tools and man-made hearths, associated with the remains of Pleistocene animals, were buried by volcanic ash that yielded radiocarbon dates of 24,000–20,000 years ago. Nearby, in Puebla at Valsequilla, other roughly chipped stone artifacts have been discovered under a bed of volcanic ash, radiocarbon dated at between 40,000 and 19,000 years old, although the dated ash at this site did not come from the immediate vicinity of the artifacts. It would appear, then, that man may have been in Mexico 20,000 years ago, and perhaps earlier.[4]

Several other considerations support the possibility that men found their way into America on the order of 20,000 or 40,000 years ago. At such a time level, the people of eastern Asia did have a crude and meager stone technology, and those who might have found their way into the New World would presumably have had the kinds of stone tools that are found in pre–projectile point sites. Climatically considered too, some of the earlier intervals of the Wisconsin were apparently conducive to migration. Nevertheless, technologically sophisticated peoples continue to use simple and crude tools, and the way was open into the heart of North America during the Two Creeks interstadial.

Other lines of evidence cast considerable doubt on the reality of early-early man equipped with a pre–projectile point tool kit. Since his remains are so scarce and ephemeral, to use Martin's word,[5] population would have had to be scant and its growth very slow. While there might conceivably be some ecological reason for such a state of affairs, it seems highly unlikely. Martin suggests that the only reason he can envision for such a lethargic population growth would be that "the earliest early man came over the Bering Strait without early woman."[6] The probabilities are that there would be a population explosion once man gained the virgin continent and had access to its abundant animals, which had never been hunted by man. Actually, the earliest well-validated Paleo-Indian populations in North America did, it seems certain, undergo just such a population explosion. In sum, until a pre–projectile point complex is found to underlie a Paleo-Indian cultural horizon, or until more early-early sites are thoroughly confirmed by association or radiocarbon dating, and until their rare occurrence is satisfactorily explained, its existence will continue to be regarded as possible, but unproven.

Paleo-Indian Stage[7]

Archeologists have devised a number of classificatory schemes by which the nature, extent, and sequence of prehistoric cultures in North America may be more readily grasped. In order to keep the narrative simple and uncluttered, a minimum of terminology is used here. Following Krieger, who employs a series of developmental stages, "Paleo-Indian stage" is used to designate the earliest authenticated American cultures.[8] The earliest Paleo-Indians to indubitably inhabit North America were primarily hunters of big game animals, particularly the mammoths then widely distributed in the grasslands of North America. E. H. Sellards[9] proposed that the term "Llano complex" be used to designate the tools associated with these hunters, and "Llano culture" is employed here for this widespread and apparently quite homogeneous way of life. The distinctive tool of the Llano culture is the Clovis fluted point, an elongated leaf-shaped point from 2½ to 4½ inches long. One or more flakes have been detached from one or both sides of the base, leaving a channel, or flute, extending up to as much as a half of the point's length. Unfluted points, flint scrapers, gravers, knives, hammerstones, tapered bone shafts that may have tipped spears, and a few other tools also have been discovered in Llano sites. Among these are long, prismatic flint blades, produced by an indirect percussion or punch technique and used with no retouching. This particular tool, which is duplicated in Upper Paleolithic sites in the Old World, is seen by some as an indication of Siberian origins of the Llano culture.[10]

Clovis fluted points are frequently found in association with mammoth bones, the original "Clovis" site, now known as Blackwater Draw No. 1, located between Portales and Clovis, on the Llano Estacado of eastern New Mexico, being one such case. Blackwater Draw was at that time a marshy lake, and other "kill sites" in the Plains and Southwest are also in situations that suggest that the mammoths were surprised at watering places or perhaps were driven or stampeded into marshes or bogs where hunters could more easily kill them. The Clovis fluted points must have been hafted to lances or spears, but whether the weapons were used at close quarters, hurled, or propelled by spear throwers (atlatls), with which the striking power of a spear is enhanced, is not clear.

Radiocarbon dates from a number of sites reveal that the Llano culture existed for a relatively brief span of time, between 9500 and 9000 B.C.[11] Although the stratified sites are situated and radiocarbon dates have been obtained principally from sites in the Plains and the Southwest, Clovis fluted points have been found throughout the contiguous United States, and in Alaska and Mexico. In eastern North America, many more Clovis points have been discovered than in the Plains, but they have been mostly surface finds, and their relationship to the Llano culture in the west is not well understood. The proposal that big game hunters spread to the east from the Plains, perhaps following the retreating ice, and in this more forested country hunted the browsing mastodon instead of the increasingly scarce mammoths, is an appealing one, but one that has not been conclusively demonstrated.[12]

Clovis points are obviously rather specialized tools and must have had a developmental history of considerable length. There is substantial agreement that they developed from the Levallois-Mousterian bifacial flaking tradition of the Old World, but whether in Asia, Alaska, or the heart of the North American continent is a matter of doubt. None of the Llano sites overlies earlier evidence of human occupancy, and no precursors of Clovis points have been found in the Americas, with one possible exception. In Sandia Cave in the Sandia Mountains of New Mexico, underlying a Folsom cultural occupation and a sterile yellow ocher stratum, nineteen whole or broken projectile points were recovered. Known as Sandia points, they are percussion-flaked with a single, small shoulder on one side of the base, giving them an odd, asymmetrical appearance. Some of the points are vaguely Clovis-like, with thinned and somewhat concave bases. No reliable radiocarbon dates have been obtained for the Sandia or Folsom levels in the cave, or for the nearby Lucy site, which also yielded Sandia points. The known dates of the Folsom culture at other sites (9000–8000 B.C.) and the sterile layer overlying the Sandia artifacts would seem to suggest that they might predate the Llano culture. Reinvestigation has indicated, however, that the Sandia points may have been redeposited from the Folsom level, and the general consensus seems to be that the people who made the Sandia points were provincial outliers or offshoots of the Llano hunters of the Plains.[13]

The hypothesis is quite appealing, then, that when the Two Creeks glacial retreat opened up an avenue between the Cordilleran and Laurentide ice masses, Llano men, or perhaps big game hunters who were their immediate ancestors, passed through this corridor into the Plains of North America. The warm Two Creeks interval lasted only a century or two before the onset of the Valders advance, but no more than this brief interlude would have been necessary for man to establish himself in the heart of the continent. Haynes, arguing from cautious and conservative figures, has estimated that in the 500-year span of the Llano culture, the descendants of a single original band of 30 hunters could have occupied much of North America, numbered as many as 425 bands, and constituted a population of 12,500.[14] Considering the likelihood that a number of migrating bands were involved, that their size may easily have been double the 30-member figure, and that their rate of increase may have been higher than that calculated by Haynes, the rapid occupancy of North America from Canada to Mexico and from coast to coast becomes eminently reasonable. That Llano hunters spread rapidly through North America also favors their being the continent's first humans. Earlier residents would surely have hindered their advance, however primitive their culture.

It can hardly be coincidental that the extinction of the large Pleistocene animals of North America—some thirty-one genera, including mammoths, mastodons, camels, and horses—occurred almost simultaneously with the arrival of Paleo-Indian hunters. Sudden environmental changes may have been partially responsible, but the onslaught of these new human predators seems to have been an important and perhaps critical factor in their disappearance.[15] In the Plains heartland of North America, perhaps as early as 9000 B.C. and almost surely by 8000 B.C., the mammoth had become extinct, and the Llano culture disappeared with it. It was succeeded by the well-known Folsom culture (termed "Lindenmeir culture" by Krieger[16]). Folsom men were specialized hunters of an extinct species of bison *(Bison antiquus and/or B. occidentalis)*, whose principal concentrations were in the High Plains country.

The Folsom culture is the best known of the Paleo-Indian cultures by virtue of being the first of the early man sites in America to be authenticated. In 1926, paleontologists from the Colorado Museum of Natural History discovered near Folsom, a little town in northeastern New Mexico, a distinctive type of projectile point in association with fossil bison bones. The discovery of man-made tools with a long-extinct bison came as something of a shock to those who believed that man was a recent migrant to America. Acceptance was slow to come, but by the third year of excavation and the discovery of additional tools associated with bison bones, the evidence was overwhelming, even to the most skeptical. The nineteen projectile points found in three seasons of work were all of a distinctive type. Skillfully and artistically made, most of these Folsom fluted points are about two inches long, somewhat leaf-shaped, with concave bases from which short projections or ears extend. They are more precisely flaked than Clovis points, and their most distinguishing feature is the longitudinal flutes of the blade faces that extend almost to their tips. They are unquestionably related to and developed from the Clovis fluted points of the Llano tradition. A number of other stone and bone tools have been found in Folsom sites, all of the kind one would expect of a hunting people. As has been noted, radiocarbon dates at various sites fix the time span of Folsom from about 9000 to 8000 B.C.[17]

In recent years another Paleo-Indian culture with few, if any, connections to the Llano and Folsom cultures has come to light. Known as the Old Cordilleran culture, it was widely distributed throughout the plateau and mountain country of the Pacific Northwest and was, at least in part, contemporaneous with the Llano culture to the east. The Old Cordilleran culture is distinguished by a well-chipped, bifacial projectile point, pointed at both ends, and known as a Cascade point. Also found in Old Cordilleran sites are several kinds of knives and heavy chopping tools. Unlike the Paleo-Indian big game hunters of the Plains, a rather unspecialized hunting, fishing, and gathering existence was pursued.[18] Major Old Cordilleran sites excavated so far include Flint Creek and Fort Laird in the Yukon, the Yale site in British Columbia, Five Mile Rapids and Indian Well on the Columbia River, and Fort Rock Cave in Oregon. Perhaps of considerable significance, Cascade points or Cascade-like points have a tremendous distribution from Alaska and the Pacific Northwest into the Southwest and beyond, perhaps even into South America.[19]

Archaic Stage

With the recession of the great continental glaciers and the extinction of mammoths, mastodons, and other mammals, the Paleo-Indian cultures disappeared and were replaced, and in part developed into, the regionally diverse Archaic cultures of eastern North America. They pursued a more balanced wild food economy than their predecessors, and relatively full usage of natural resources allowed a semisedentary and in some particularly favored regions, a sedentary way of life to develop. Archaic cultures were characterized by and distinguished from Paleo-Indian cultures by the appearance of food-grinding implements—manos and milling stones and, to some extent, mortars and pestles. No doubt, wild plant foods had been utilized by the big game hunters, but now, as indicated by these implements, seeds, nuts, roots, berries, and other plant products became a much more significant part of the diet. A wider variety of projectile point types also occur in Archaic culture sites, as do a diversity of other stone and bone tools—awls, drills, eyed needles, shaft smoothers, and the like. Caves and rock shelters were frequently utilized as campsites, and the dead were, at least sometimes, buried in graves, a custom that seems not to have been practiced in earlier times.

In the Plains, what has come to be known as the Plano culture succeeded the Folsom tradition, and it was an outgrowth and development from it. Some, with considerable justification, prefer to regard the Plano as the last of the Paleo-Indian cultures.[20] Plano peoples were primarily hunters of the giant bison, which was soon to become extinct, and many of the varied projectile point types bear a close relationship to the old fluted point tradition. Lanceolate in form, most were skillfully and carefully chipped, usually by pressure-flaking. Food-grinding implements also occur in many Plano sites, however. Dating from about 8000 to 6000 B.C., major Plano sites include the Cody complex at the Horner and Eden sites in Wyoming; the Agate Basin sites in eastern Wyoming; the Meserve, Scottsbluff, Red Smoke, and Lime Creek sites in Nebraska; the Portales complex at Blackwater Draw and Milnesand, New Mexico; and the Plainview and Bonfire Shelter sites in Texas.

In eastern North America the old Paleo-Indian hunting tradition gave way to a variety of local Archaic cultures, differing from one another regionally as they adapted to local environmental conditions. Subsistence was based on a variety of game animals, on fish and shellfish, and on wild plant foods. In terms of the remains found by archeologists, an array of stemmed, notched, sometimes barbed, and often broadbladed projectile points were employed. Milling and grinding stones were used, and ground and polished stone tools and art objects appear. Ground stone axes, adzes, and similar tools indicate considerable work in wood. In some marginal areas, what were essentially Archaic cultures persisted into historic times.[21]

Encompassing a tremendous area in western North America, from the eastern slopes of the Rockies to the Pacific, and from Oregon to the Valley of Mexico and beyond, another distinctive cultural type appeared. Known as the Desert culture and first defined by Jennings and Norbeck,[22] its origins are obscure, though they seem to lie with the Old Cordilleran culture. Radiocarbon dates indicate that this culture appeared about 9000 B.C., and in some areas—southern California, the Great Basin, southern Texas, and elsewhere—it lasted, with very little change, into historic times. There was considerable regional diversity, but all manifestations of the Desert culture were alike in their relatively full utilization and expoitation of the available resources of the arid lands. They hunted and fished when such pursuits were profitable, but everywhere they depended heavily on harvesting seeds, roots, tubers, and other plant foods.

Archeologically, Desert cultures are characterized by grinding implements, typically flat milling stones and manos. A wide variety of generally small projectile points are found, in addition to a variety of chopping, cutting, and scraping tools. Because Desert culture sites are frequently located in rock shelters or other dry places, many perishable objects have been preserved, including a large assortment of basketry, matting, netting, cordage, sandals, wooden artifacts, and even human feces. Of critical importance, the venerable and widespread Desert culture was the substratum from which developed the great agricultural civilizations of Mesoamerica.

Agriculture and the Rise of Civilization

If the native cultures of America had remained at a hunting and wild plant gathering level, the story of the American Indian would be much simpler to relate, his numbers would have been far fewer, and the influence of his diverse cultures on the modern world might well be negligible. But advanced Indian civilizations did develop in the New World, based, as elsewhere, on the cultivation of food plants.

The beginnings of agriculture in the New World long posed a problem for archeologists and botanists, but in recent years answers to many fundamental questions have been found. Though it may seem unlikely at first glance, the regions in which various plants were domesticated were not rich natural regions where men lived bountifully on the wild products of the land. On the contrary, many and perhaps all of the major domesticated plants originated in regions and at times when the wild food resources were poor and men hard put to eke out a bare subsistence.[23] The origin of the major American cereal grain—maize, corn, or Indian corn (Zea mays)—posed a particularly difficult problem because no wild corn had ever been found growing anywhere, and as a result there was much speculation about whether it had evolved from a wild grass in Mesoamerica or South America, or even from a grass of Southeast Asia. But in the summer of 1948, small, primitive corn cobs were recovered from Bat Cave in New Mexico by archeologist Herbert Dick, and in the following year, other remains of an ancient variety of corn were recovered from the La Perra Cave in Tamaulipas by Richard MacNeish. Radiocarbon dates at both sites indicated that the cobs were between 3,000 and 5,000 years old. Subsequently Mac-Neish and his colleagues discovered in the caves and rock shelters of the Tehuacan Valley, in the arid highlands of Puebla, Mexico, a tiny primitive corn that was dated to about 5000 B.C. The cobs represented either a wild variety of maize or an early domesticated form, and their early date suggests that corn was indeed domesticated in the southern Mexican highlands. Of equal importance, a sequence of cultural development was revealed there that covered a span from the first ancient occupancy of the valley to historic times, and well illustrated the development of agriculture and the evolution of New World civilization.[24]

The sparse early population of the Tehuacan Valley followed a variant Desert culture tradition, pursuing small mammals and birds and the few remaining Pleistocene antelopes and horses, and gathering many wild plant foods. Between 7000 and 5000 B.C., the emphasis on wild plant foods increased; in this interval domesticated squash (*Curcurbita moschata* or *C. mixta*) may have made its appearance, and wild maize may have been one of the grasses utilized. Population had increased, but it remained seasonally nomadic. In the next millennia, though only a relatively small percentage of the diet was based on domesticated plants, a number of cultivated plants appeared, including the ears of podlike corn already mentioned, bottle gourd (*Lagenaria*), amaranth, tepary beans, avocados, and peppers. By about 3400 B.C., almost a third of the food supply is estimated to have been derived from agriculture, and by this time small pit-house villages appeared, indicating a more settled life. A more productive hybrid maize had been developed, and pumpkins (*Curcurbita pepo*), the common or kidney bean (*Phaseolus vulgaris*), and cotton (*Gossypium*) were cultivated. The importance of agriculture subsequently increased; better, more productive varieties of maize were planted, and pottery was introduced. In short, 4,000 years ago the basic foundation of civilization had developed in the Tehuacan Valley, as it had in many other parts of Mesoamerica.

The more plentiful and assured food supply fostered sedentary life, population increase, accumulation of wealth, and the appearance of villages and, ultimately, cities. It released some people from the burden of subsistence activities to busy themselves with others—to govern an increasingly complex society; to deal as specialists with the supernatural world; to become artisans and artists, soldiers and philosophers; and to pursue many other occupations and specialties. The two regions in which agriculture had its origins, in Mesoamerica and in the central Andes of South America, also were the regions in which the consequences of the agricultural revolution were the greatest and most striking. In Mesoamerica, from central Mexico to Honduras, Nicaragua, and Costa Rica, a complex of civilizations developed, independent of one another, yet sharing a number of basic similarities. Characteristic of the great civilizations of Mesoamerica, in addition to their common agricultural base, were masonry temples; step pyramids; well-developed stone sculpture; a precise ritual calendar; a sophisticated mathematics, including the concepts of zero and position numerals; a form of writing, a richly developed symbolic art; human sacrifice in bloody rituals; and conquest states governed by exalted, sometimes deified rulers.

Here peoples and states arose to flourish and conquer, then to fail and be succeeded by others. Included were the great early Olmec civilization of Veracruz and Tabasco, the Maya of southern Mexico and Guatemala, the Mixtecs and Zapotecs in Oaxaca, and a sequence of predominant civilizations centering about the Valley of Mexico. There, in what is known as the late Pre-Classic Period (300 B.C. to A.D. 300),[25] the great civilization of Teotihuacán had its beginnings. By the Classic Period (A.D. 300–900), Teotihuacán, situated northeast of modern Mexico City, had become the principal ceremonial center and probably the political capital of a great state. The awesome and spectacular ruins of Teotihuacán cover seven square miles of palaces, houses, ceremonial mounds, and pyramids. About A.D. 600, Teotihuacán was destroyed, in all probability by northern barbarians, and after several centuries of strife and political turmoil throughout Mesoamerica, the Toltecs arose at Tula, north of Mexico City, to be ultimately destroyed, in turn, by others about A.D. 1160. From a group of competitive states, the Aztecs ultimately emerged as the last of the great pre-Columbian powers in central Mexico, to be defeated in 1519 by the Spaniards under Cortez.

These great "nuclear" civilizations of Mesoamerica, to use Kroeber's term,[26] influenced the peoples of adjacent regions to the north directly and indirectly and over a span of many millennia. The precise nature of these influences has not yet been worked out, but its major outlines are fairly clear. In the Southwest, Mesoamerican influence was felt early and continued sporadically until almost historic times. The early appearance of corn at Bat Cave has already been mentioned, and other items, such as ceramics, also spread into the region at an early date. Between A.D. 500 and 1000, a number of items—including those necessary to support village life, ball courts, certain decorative traditions in ceramics, copper bells, and, apparently, loom weaving of cotton—had diffused into the area. After A.D. 1000, Mesoamerican influences continued to be felt, particularly in architecture and in religious cults.[27]

The influences that penetrated what is now the eastern United States were of a different kind or kinds, and they began somewhat later than in the Southwest. In about 1000 B.C., what is known as the Woodland tradition appeared in the East. Partly developed from the Archaic, it added pottery, ceramic figurines, mortuary mounds, extensive earthworks, and the cultivation of plants, including corn, all of which apparently were derived from Mesoamerica. The time and place of origin of the Woodland is in dispute, but the Mississippi and Ohio valleys seem to have been its centers. By about A.D. 700, another strong Mesoamerican impulse began to be felt in the Eastern Woodlands. Known as the Mississippian tradition, it first appeared in the lower and central Mississippi Valley and was a composite of the Old Archaic and Woodland traditions, to which had been added intensified cultivation of corn, large permanent villages, and flat-topped earthen mounds on which were constructed temples or other ceremonial structures. Mounds were sometimes arranged around plazas, and these traits, in addition to art styles, details of form and decoration of pottery, and others, clearly were derived from a Mesoamerican source. The Mississippian tradition spread widely in the Eastern Woodlands and, as will become evident, gave a distinctive character to the historic tribes and confederacies of the Southeast culture area.

The route or routes by which these influences reached the Eastern Woodlands and their nature are a matter of speculation and dispute. One hypothesis favors a migration from some undisclosed point in northern Mesoamerica by way of northeastern Mexico and Texas into the Eastern Woodlands. But the formidable barrier of the extensive and forbidding semidesert of northeastern Mexico and southern Texas, coupled with the lack of any concrete evidence, seems to render this hypothesis untenable. For various other reasons, routes from the Southwest across the Plains and through the West Indies into Florida also seem unlikely, leaving some kind of seaborne contact across or around the Gulf of Mexico as the most likely route of diffusion.[28]

BIOLOGICAL AFFILIATIONS[29]

There is no reason to believe that the first people to inhabit North America were racially or genetically different from the population of northeastern Asia from which they had sprung. Unfortunately, this Asiatic population is not yet well known, but the Tzeyang skull from a site west of Chungking, the so-called Liukiang man found in a cave near Liuchow, and the three skulls from the Upper Cave at Choukoutien in northern China are similar to American Indian skulls and would not be regarded as out-of-place had they been discovered in America.[30]

These late Pleistocene remains, as the earliest known in America, are wholly modern. The last of the more primitive men, Neanderthal man (*Homo sapiens neanderthalensis*) disappeared 35,000 to 40,000 years ago, and though present in Siberia, there is no evidence that he found his way into America. Similarly, there is not the slightest scrap of evidence that earlier, more primitive types of man entered America. Since there were no higher primates in the Americas from which men might have arisen, no remains of near-man or more primitive forms of humanity have ever been discovered in the New World.

Indubitably, early human skeletal remains are rare in the Americas, about two dozen finds having respectable claims to antiquity.[31] Their scarcity is attributable partly to a relatively sparse population and quite possibly to treatment of the dead. If the dead or dying were abandoned in places where scavengers could get at them, for example, chances of preservation would be poor. It seems likely too that some earlier investigators, who often believed that Indians had only recently inhabited America, rejected or disregarded skeletal remains that may have been ancient.

Among the discoveries generally regarded as ancient is Midland man, or, more accurately, Midland woman, for the skull (a calvarium) appears to belong to an adult individual of that sex. Found in a blowout in 1953 near Midland, Texas, the site was meticulously excavated, and the cranial and other fragmentary remains were subjected to searching analysis.[32] The remains were associated with an extinct fauna, including a horse, four-horned antelope, and mammoth, and they appeared to underlie a Folsom cultural level. The investigators believe the Midland skull antedates the Folsom time level, but the dating of specimens found in blowouts is a hazardous business at best, so that there will always be some doubt about its antiquity. The age of the find aside, the skeletal remains are those of a fine-boned, long-headed person. The long-headed skull is characteristic of what Neumann[33] terms the "Otamid variety" of Indian, and which is still characteristic of some American Indian groups.

In 1947 near the railway station of Tepexpán, between Mexico City and the massive ruins of Teotihuacán, Helmut De Terra discovered the skeleton of an Indian who had apparently drowned in the swampy muck at the edge of a glacial lake. Nearby were the skeletons of two large mammoths, perhaps mired in the mud during the incident that claimed the human. The body, which lay face down, was picked at by vultures or other scavengers after death so that the skeleton is incomplete, but the round (mesocephalic) skull is well preserved and has no characteristics that would distinguish it from modern Indians. The investigators, relying on geological and radiocarbon evidence, set its age at about 10,000 B.C.[34]

Another victim of drowning was uncovered by a road grader in 1931 near Pelican Rapids, Minnesota. The skeleton was of a fifteen-year-old girl who apparently had fallen or was pushed into a glacial lake. Unfortunately, the grader, in cutting the ten-foot-deep trench, had removed all of the overburden, so that there was no way of knowing whether the soil was undisturbed. The gravel close to the skeleton showed the typical varves, or layered bands, that result from seasonal melting of glacial ice, and there were no traces of pollen in the soil around the skeleton, possibly reflecting the paucity of flowering plants at the edge of a glacier. On the other hand, a shell ornament found with the skeleton originated in the Gulf of Mexico and did not appear to be ancient. Some bones of small animals still found in the region, which apparently were the contents of the girl's medicine bag, also appeared to be recent. The skeleton, whatever its age, is modern, as are all of the other reputedly ancient remains of man found in the Americas, whether found in Florida, Arizona, Ecuador, Brazil, the Strait of Magellan, or elsewhere.[35]

Modern Indians resemble the peoples of Asia more closely than those of any other continent, but are less similar to the more extreme variety of Mongoloids of Mongolia, China, and Japan than they are to the peoples of Southeast Asia, Tibet, and other outlying Asiatic areas. It appears that the classic, possibly cold-adapted Mongoloids, with pronounced epicanthic eye-folds, extremely broad, flat faces, broad, low noses, and yellowish skin tones, arose from an older, more generalized population, and that it had not appeared or had not spread to Northeast Asia when men first entered America. In later times this physical type did make its appearance in America, and the Eskimos, Aleuts, and some of the Athapaskan-speaking Indians, who are believed to be descendants of relatively recent migrants, often evince these characteristics.

The low-key debate about the homogeneity or heterogeneity of American Indians seems to be mostly a matter of semantics, perspective, and emphasis. American Indians are very much a single entity in the sense that they generally have medium-brown skin, dark eyes, black, straight head hair, modest amounts of face and body hair, and large, broad faces with high cheekbones. Their general homogeneity, the Eskimos, Aleuts, and some Athapaskans excepted, extends to their blood types, American Indians being monotonously limited so far as the better known serological reactions are concerned, to O, M, and Rh-positive blood. The case for Indian homogeneity was somewhat overstated by the old cliché that he who has seen one Indian has seen them all; it is much less of an overstatement to say that he who has blood-typed one Indian has typed them all.

One of the first classifications of American Indians was proposed by R. B. Dixon,[36] and a number of others have been made since then.

J. Imbelloni[37] refined the Von Eickstedt classification, dividing the natives of North and South America into eleven subvarieties. Based mainly on living Indians, but deducing their chronological order of entry into the New World from it, the classification is not generally accepted by American physical anthropologists.[38] Georg K. Neumann,[39] utilizing more and better data than Von Eickstedt or Imbelloni, classifies the Indians of North America into eight subvarieties. He believes that all but one of his varieties represent separate migrations from Asia to North America.

Those who view American Indians as racially varied point out that some groups are tall, others short, some lighter or darker than others, or differ in details of facial and cranial anatomy. Such differences do not necessarily have to be attributed to genetic differences of the ancestral migrants. If the migrants were relatively homogeneous genetically, their subsequent dispersion to different environments in the New World, their isolation from one another, mutations arising among them, selection, and random genetic drift, all operating over 10,000 or more years, would be more than sufficient to account for their present variability. Nevertheless, it seems probable that the first American Indians were racially something of a "mixed bag"[40] of nondescript Mongoloids. In time, with the arrival of new migrants and minor changes in the descendents of the early arrivals, some variability in American Indian populations appeared. But as Stewart has said, "No population of comparable size has remained so uniform after expanding, in whatever time has been involved, over such a large land area."[41]

POPULATION

For many years estimates of the population of preconquest North America varied so widely that it was apparent that either the data they were based on or the methods of estimation, or both, had major faults. James Mooney, in a posthumous publication edited by J. R. Swanton, made the first widely accepted estimate of the aboriginal population of North America. Working with totals from tribe-by-tribe estimates, in what has been termed a "dead reckoning method," he estimated the population north of Mexico, including Greenland, to be 1,153,000.[42] At the same time, William Christie MacLeod, by projecting population estimates for localized, intensively studied areas to wider regions, estimated the aboriginal population of the United States to be 3,000,000. If he had followed his own method more faithfully, however, his total population would have been 4,000,000.[43] Low population estimates bottomed with Kroeber, who relied heavily on Mooney's estimates. After noting that Mooney had apparently been reducing his tribal estimates as his work progressed and that Swanton also felt that Mooney's estimates were too high, Kroeber estimated a population for all of North America, excluding Panama and Costa Rica, of 4,200,000.[44] For America north of Mexico, Kroeber estimated a population of 1,026,000, noting, however, that his estimates were "approximate and preliminary."[45]

These population estimates were seriously flawed in several ways. There was much blind reluctance to credit early eyewitness population figures with much veracity, assuming that soldiers, missionaries, and other contemporary sources invariably exaggerated native populations. Such was the case sometimes, but populations also were underestimated and occasionally were quite accurate, as cross-checking of sources has often revealed. Low estimates also were based, in part, on data that postdated European-introduced epidemics that had devastated native populations. Anthropologists vastly underestimated the tremendous population decline that was caused by introduced diseases. Smallpox, measles, whooping cough, scarlet fever, and other diseases, for which mortality rates were comparatively low among Europeans, were terribly lethal to Indian populations. Often sweeping ahead of advancing frontiers before an accurate idea of population could be recorded, entire tribes were all but wiped out. Apparently the bitterly cold climate of northern Asia and America through which the ancestors of historic Indians had to pass served as a barrier to many kinds of disease germs, and as a consequence, Indians were peculiarly vulnerable to many diseases introduced by Europeans.[46]

In all candor, it also should be pointed out that the earlier, low population estimates had the effect of making the European conquest of North America more palatable to white Americans. Displacing a million or so Indians north of the Rio Grande and ultimately reducing their population to half that number is far easier to rationalize or ignore than is the extirpation of ten or fifteen times that number. This is not to imply any conscious manipulation of population figures in an earlier day, but only to suggest that demographers and social scientists were not sufficiently conscious of the social forces and the intellectual milieu within which they worked.

Disbelief in the old, entrenched population estimates was no doubt widespread, but it was not until 1966 that Henry F. Dobyns summarized the growing body of evidence enumerating the many deficiencies of the traditional estimates. He also proposed another method of reckoning pre-Columbian Indian populations. Using a projection technique, he attempted to establish a depopulation ratio by comparing a "known or confidently estimated preconquest population" to the minimum or nadir population of the same area after conquest.[47] This ratio is then compared against other comparable ratios in order to arrive at a ratio that might be employed for areas where data are deficient or lacking. Using this technique and depopulation ratios of 20 to 1 and 25 to 1,

Dobyns estimates a hemispheric population between 90,043,000 and 112,553,750, a population of the "Mexican civilization" of 30,000,000 to 37,500,000, and a population north of Mexico of 9,800,000 to 12,250,000.[48]

Dobyns's projective technique has been criticized as yielding excessively high figures for peoples who subsisted on a wild food economy, but fairly accurate estimates in regions where population was densest and population decline the greatest.[49] That depopulation of cultures with wild food economies was less than others has not been established, however. Driver has also argued that Dobyns's estimate of the population of Mexico is too high on the grounds that the modern population of Mexico has only surpassed Dobyns's minimum figure since 1940.[50] But to argue that the population trends of a modern industrial nation can be applied to a preconquest, preindustrial situation is not persuasive.

Much work obviously needs to be done before complete reliance can be placed on any of the population estimates for America north of Mexico. But the old fiction of a ludicrously low native American population has been shattered, and the means are at hand to confirm or revise more recent estimates. By combining projective techniques and estimates derived from resource potential, and by utilizing much more fully the documentary data, there is every reason to believe that reliable estimates of Indian populations are attainable. For America north of Mexico, estimates are unquestionably far higher than traditionally believed. They may not be as high as Dobyns put them, or they may be higher.

In relative terms, the greatest population density in North America occurred where intensive agriculture was practiced, which is to say from the Valley of Mexico southward. North of the Rio Grande, the Southeast culture area, considering its relatively well-developed agricultural base, probably had a greater population than any other North American area. The Puebloan peoples of the Southwest must also have been numerous, but their total population probably fell well below that of the Southeast. The Northeast Woodlands, including the prairie region to the west, likely had a somewhat lower population density. The arid lands of the West and the northern subarctic were undoubtedly rather sparsely populated. Native population of the Columbia-Fraser Plateau would have been somewhat higher, and the extremely bountiful environments of California and the Northwest Coast supported large populations for cultural systems based on wild food economies.[51]

CULTURE AND CULTURE AREAS

Men are rather unexceptional animals physically; in an intellectual sense they are unique. Their mental qualities and peculiarities have been the subject of much discussion and debate, but for our purposes it is sufficient to point out that the gulf which separates man from other animals stems from his capacity to arbitrarily assign meaning to or bestow value upon anything. It is termed the "ability to symbol."[52] It finds most frequent expression verbally through articulate speech, but men are inveterate symbolizers in other ways, letting colors, actions, objects, and events "stand for" all sorts of things. No other animal can symbol; none can freely and habitually invest things with arbitrary meanings. No other animal can let the sound "ko" stand for sin, or uncle, or democracy, or, in fact, grasp its meaning at all. It is this ability that has provided man with the means to be human, to possess and be possessed by culture.

Social scientists embrace an assortment of cultural concepts, and since the cultures of North American Indians are the central subject of this book, a brief discussion of the view taken here of this remarkable human attribute and its consequences is necessary. For our purposes a culture is regarded as the total way of life of a definable group of people—band, tribe, or nation. "Way of life" is meant to include language, knowledge, beliefs, habits, customs, institutions, rituals, games, tools, dwellings, and all those other things that are dependent upon the ability to symbol.[53]

When an insignificant ape became human, which is to say when through the natural processes of evolution man developed the faculty to symbol, his culture or cultures were at first meager and weak in that they did not provide the knowledge, tools, or other means to distinguish him very dramatically from other animals. But the ability to symbol allowed men to cooperate efficiently, to communicate effectively with one another, and it permitted men to pass on to their children the knowledge, techniques, wisdom, mythology, misinformation, customs, habits, and other things that they and their forefathers had accumulated. In brief, every culture became and is a cumulative continuum, the culture of one generation passing to its successor in an ever-lengthening stream.

In a general, overall sense, culture has been progressive in that it has evolved from poorer to better methods of exploiting the earth for man's benefit. But for much of the human career, for hundreds of thousands of years in fact, progress was painfully slow. Metaphorically, it was only yesterday that man learned to be a food producer rather than a forager and hunter, limited by and dependent upon the largesse of nature. He learned to tap the sun's energy in the form of fossil fuels a few hours ago; he harnessed the atom a moment ago. Culture, then, has been technologically progressive, and its rate has accelerated.[54]

Many peoples in different places and at different times have contributed to or been in the forefront of cultural progress; others, because they were isolated, lived in restrictive environments, or for other reasons were never able to participate in or contribute to the mainstreams of world culture. North and South America are particularly pertinent here in that they were isolated from the rest of the world and, as we have seen, were uninhabited until relatively recent times. Some of their cultures also underwent a food-producing revolution, which bears on the problem of the inevitability of cultural development, and a considerable and important part of the modern world's agricultural wealth is based on plants originally domesticated by American Indians. Not all native Americans were affected by the civilizations that arose as a consequence of the food-producing revolution, however, and as a result, some of the hunting and gathering cultures duplicated in an approximate and rough way the cultures that must have characterized mankind during most of his past existence.

While culture in the general sense has been progressive, and individual cultures are often described as dynamic (though the dynamism of many often seems close to that of a millpond), cultures are also inherently conservative. They must be, of course; individuals become habituated to patterned ways of thinking and acting. To change habits is difficult, if not impossible; to behave in customary ways is personally efficient and collectively necessary. Once established, various institutions, whether economic, political, or religious, are, by their nature, persistent and apt to thwart or hinder change in themselves and in other aspects of culture. In essence, then, what a tribe or nation is today is essentially what it was yesterday, and what is new today is largely a developmental consequence of yesterday. A tribe or nation is perpetually a becoming, foreshadowed today by its yesterday, and its tomorrow is but its lengthened shadow. Cultures are often likened to rivers flowing down through the ages. They dig their own channels, you might say, and they must flow in them. Rivulets join them here and there; their currents speed up at times, slow down at others; old elements drop out, new elements are added. But even during times of revolutionary change, when many novel elements are entering a cultural stream and old ones are being discarded, many more elements are being retained and transmitted than are being newly introduced.

Cultures are also systematic; each one is a more or less self-consistent organization of related parts—material, mechanical, economic, social, political, ideological, linguistic, artistic, and so forth. To describe cultures coherently, one must break them down into their component parts, even though in their actual functioning no such compartmentalization exists. That is, almost every cultural activity can be referred to more than one aspect of culture. Thus, bison hunting on horseback was a characteristic subsistence habit of Plains Indians, but it took place in a social context, often with religious sanctions. In the following chapters, technological systems are described first, followed by discussions of social and political organizations, then ideological components, primarily supernatural beliefs and behavior.

No segment or component of culture floats free; each is responsive to and is affected by other segments, as it, in turn, affects them, often in intricate ways. As Leslie White[55] has noted, however, the interaction is not equal. The technological aspect of cultures, that is, the material, mechanical ways in which they are articulated with their environments, is basic and primary. In a general way at least, they determine the nature of other aspects of cultures. Peoples with relatively unproductive, bare subsistence technologies have similar and characteristic types of social systems that differ from those typifying more productive systems, and so on. While the range of technological systems of North American Indians was quite wide, and their corresponding social systems diverse, all of their societies were organized on the basis of kinship. Had they experienced an industrial revolution, the story would have been quite different. Other intracultural relationships will be pointed out or will become evident in the following pages.

Although cultures are systems, their components are seldom, if ever, in perfect adjustment in the sense of being composed of totally harmonious parts. Droughts occur, game animals become extinct, crops fail, and new technological and other adjustments are made, necessitating changes and adjustments in other cultural segments. Cultural innovations, both indigenous and borrowed from others, may lead to a train of internal changes and to stresses and strains. In an overall sense, some North American Indian cultures in isolated regions, before they were interrupted by Western civilization, probably came as close to a state of harmonious balance as human societies can, in contrast to modern industrial nations in which technological and other changes occur so rapidly and regularly that their segments are continuously in a state of stress and change.

Every person is introduced at birth into an already made, functioning cultural system. Actually, whether conception or birth is permitted, how the mother behaves during pregnancy, and birth itself are all heavily conditioned by cultural practices, so that even a newborn baby already has been physically influenced by the culture that comes to envelop him. But a baby is not born with a culture; he does not come equipped with a language, a set of beliefs, customs, and morals, a religion, or any other of culture's many segments. He is introduced, instead, into a world of human beings who possess or, more accurately, are possessed by a culture. He can, of course, learn only that of which he is a part. If the language of the cultural world into which he has been thrust is English, that is what he learns; if it is Choctaw, that is what he comes to speak. If his mother's sister is called mother and is accorded the behavior appropriate to mothers, this is what he terms her and how he behaves toward her. So it is with other aspects of culture; it cannot be otherwise. Most men are unaware that they are engulfed, directed, and managed by their culture, that it pervades and permeates every nook and cranny of their conscious being, and that they can never escape it even in dreams, delirium, or insanity. So overwhelming, so powerful is culture's grip on man that, paradoxically, it may cause him to deny or thwart the most basic urges of his organic being. It may lead him to mutilate his body in excruciating ways; it may cause him to deny, pervert, or repress his sexuality; it may drive him to suicide, or it may prevent him from even contemplating self-destruction. And it may lead him to sacrifice his life in countless other ways.

Since it is learned, not only do those born into a culture become its carriers and heirs, but others may borrow from it too. The interchange of elements and complexes between tribes and nations, particularly those occupying adjacent and similar environmental regions, is apt to be quite extensive. In North America, though there were literally thousands of distinct bands and tribes, those occupying the same kinds of natural regions were apt to adjust to them and exploit them in similar ways. Consequently, a number of more or less successful classifications have been devised to order them. Before the turn of the century, Otis T. Mason had described thirteen "environments," or "culture areas," for North America very similar to those in vogue today. In 1917 Clark Wissler allotted eleven culture areas, based on six food regions, to North America, in large part coinciding with Mason's. A. L. Kroeber, following Wissler in emphasizing the role of the natural environment in shaping culture areas, refined his scheme, setting up seven major culture areas in North America, with a large number of subareas. In 1961 Harold Driver modified Kroeber's classification, establishing fifteen major culture areas north of Mesoamerica.[56]

This multiplicity of classifications illustrates the tremendous diversity of Indian cultures, but it also reflects the varying interests and aims of those who establish them. They are, as most anthropological systematists are at pains to point out, only cataloguing devices—a means to an end, not an end in themselves. But it should also be emphasized that the nature of a classificatory scheme drastically affects how cultures and their relationships are viewed and understood. In brief, all culture area classifications distort the cultural realities in one way or another. Thus, to establish two culture areas for the Arctic and but one for Mesoamerica, as one classification does, magnifies the picayune differences separating Arctic peoples and minimizes the substantial differences present in the Mesoamerican area. Similarly, naming and implicitly giving equal rank to seven, eleven, or seventeen culture areas distorts and blurs their nature since they are not, by any means, equivalent or coordinate entities. To put the civilizations of the Valley of Mexico on the same footing as the Shoshones of the Great Basin, for example, obscures the tremendous differences that distinguish them—in population, means of exploiting their environments, complexity of social groupings, formal mechanisms for dealing with the supernatural world, and so forth. It is something like saying that basketballs and oranges are equivalent because they are round, thereby minimizing the important and distinguishing characteristics of each.

Kroeber, who felt it was "subjective" and "unscientific"[57] to consider differences in cultural levels, attempted to deal obliquely with such obvious disparity by resorting to what he called "intensity of culture," which consists of two elements, "special content" and "special system." He seems to have been attempting to contrast and compare culture areas first by cultural level, as judged by technological productivity, and second by the distinctive constellation of cultural elements that serve to set apart certain culture areas. Here, in the concluding section, an attempt is made to compare and contrast various culture areas primarily on the basis of their technological productivity and the many other differences that result therefrom.

Culture area concepts are also static; they freeze the peoples of a region at a particular time, and in North America the time is not equivalent for all areas. The culture area (or areas) of the Eastern Woodlands, for example, is normally portrayed at a time just before European contact, while the Plains culture area did not come into existence until the eighteenth century, and is often described as it was in the last decades of that century, or even later. Cultures change through time, of course, and culture areas wax and wane geographically and in their cultural natures. While a vertical time dimension cannot be or has not been grafted to a horizontal classificatory system, temporal considerations are frequently reflected or implied in such terms as "cultural climax," introduced by Kroeber.[58] Culture area classifications also suffer from the necessity of drawing boundary lines. Inevitably, some tribes or peoples share more or less equally the characteristics of two or more cultural provinces. Since the focus of this book is on the major aboriginal cultural types of North America, these marginal or transitional tribes have had to be neglected.

In this volume a modified and somewhat simplified culture area approach has been adopted. Nine major North American cultural types or systems are discussed. Settling on nine culture areas rather than seven, eleven, or some other number is a matter of judgment and emphasis. This is so because some culture areas are not very distinctive, or are said not to be, and are often merged with others. Thus, the Indians east of the Mississippi and generally south of the Great Lakes and the

St. Lawrence may be lumped together in a single culture area or, as is done here, split into two separate culture areas. Since another volume in this series will deal with the circumpolar peoples of the world, and so will include a discussion of the Eskimos and Aleuts, they are omitted from this book. This estrangement is a realistic one in the sense that they are racially, linguistically, and culturally distinct from American Indians.

LANGUAGE

There have been many misconceptions about American Indians, none more prevalent than those concerning language. A surprising number of people, for example, believe there was one Indian language and are apt to ask such questions as "What is the Indian word for cradle?" The facts are that American Indians are tremendously diverse linguistically, many languages being as different from one another as they are from English, or as different from English as English is from Chinese. In America north of Mexico, in a recent classification by the Voegelins,[59] well over 200 languages are listed, and there would be more were they well known enough to be classified. About 350 languages are spoken in Mexico and Central America, and a babel of about 1,450 are spoken in South America.[60]

Nor are Indian languages primitive or more animal-like than English or any other language. They may differ by utilizing sound units (phonemes) that are absent from European languages, or so rare that it is extremely difficult for a person habituated to English or other European languages to learn them. Glottalized consonants, for example, are exceedingly difficult to learn, and others, such as whispered vowels, are not apt to be even heard by English speakers. Similarly, the use of tones in some Indian languages (in which the meaning of a word is altered by changing the pitch of a vowel) is confusing to English speakers whose use of phonemic tone is negligible. Even if many familiar sound units were used in an Indian language, they may be used in places or in combinations that are inadmissible in English or other Indo-European languages. Thus, the name of the Northwest Coast tribe known as the Tlingit is difficult for English speakers to pronounce, not because the *tl* combination of sounds is unknown in English ("little," for example) but because it does not occur initially in English words. As the phonology of Indian languages differs from European languages, so too does their grammar, syntax, and general structure. Nouns and pronouns may be combined in one word, the subject or object of a sentence may be contained in a word that English speakers would call a verb, and, in general, the structure and philosophy may be radically different from anything encountered in a European tongue.

There is, of course, no necessary correspondence between the language of a people and the form of their culture. Speakers of the Algonquian family of languages, for example, followed a diversity of life styles. Some, like the Crees and Montagnais, were hunters of the northern coniferous forests; some, like the Delawares on the Atlantic Coast, were semisedentary farmers, hunters, and fishermen; while others, such as the Blackfeet, were bison-hunting plainsmen. Most often cited as examples in this connection are the rich, powerful, and complex culture of the Aztecs of Mexico and the impoverished gleaners of the deserts of Utah and Nevada, the Gosiutes and Paiutes, all of whom speak Uto-Aztecan languages. On the other hand, there is nothing to prevent peoples who speak unrelated languages from sharing a common culture in other respects, and many examples are found in North America, from the Northwest Coast to the Southeast.

The first attempt to classify and determine the relationships among North American Indian languages was made in 1891 by Major J. W. Powell, the explorer of the Green and Colorado rivers who subsequently became head of the Bureau of American Ethnology of the Smithsonian Institution. His work, the result of twenty years of labor in which he was assisted by many other people, established fifty-eight language families north of Mexico.[61] Considering the fragmentary word lists and the generally incomplete data at his disposal, it was remarkably accurate. With more precise and extensive knowledge, many of his language families have been merged with others, but none of his major groupings has been subdivided.

Grouping dialects and languages into more inclusive clusters of linguistic families and superfamilies implies, of course, that related languages have diverged from a common ancestral language sometime in the past. Since 1950 the development of the statistical comparison of the relationships among language vocabularies (lexicostatistics) by Morris Swadesh and other linguists has enhanced knowledge of the relationships among Indian languages, and progress in relating larger and larger clusters of languages has been rapid.[62] Joseph H. Greenberg,[63] for example, has suggested that there are but eight superfamilies of languages in Central and South America, and that all the languages of the Americas, with the exception of Eskimo and Nadene (to which Athapascan belongs), probably are members of a single language phylum. If this suggestion is confirmed, it would add much weight to those who have proposed that there was a single, early migration of men to America.

The most controversial aspect of lexicostatistics has been the development of glottochronology, "the study of the rate of change in language, and the use of the rate for historical inference, especially for the estimation of time depths and the use of such time depths to provide a pattern of internal relationships within a language family."[64] Glottochronology stems from a study by Morris Swadesh,[65] who alleged that "fundamental vocabulary" changes at a constant rate. Glottochronologists have used a basic or core vocabulary of from one hundred to about two hundred terms that are thought to be present in virtually every language, whether the culture of its speakers is literate or nonliterate, primitive or advanced, relatively stable or changing rapidly. The list is made up of body parts (head, hand, breast, nose, etc.), pronouns (I, thee, we), low numbers, universal natural objects (sun, moon, earth), common animals and plants and their parts (fish, bird, dog, tree, skin, flesh, blood, bone, egg, hair, feather), common actions (eat, bite, see, hear, know, die, sleep), and the like.

In a study by Robert B. Lees[66] of 13 languages whose rate of change was known, it was found that the rate of retention of some 200 core items of vocabulary was about 81 percent per millenium. Despite the relatively small number of control languages used and the fact that all but two of them were Indo-European languages, it was postulated that the basic vocabulary of all languages changes at this rate. If such a rate of change could be convincingly demonstrated, it would be as important to linguistics and historical anthropology as radiocarbon dating has been to archeology and geology. But the promise of glottochronology has not been fulfilled. Subsequent studies, particularly one by Bergsland and Vogt,[67] have demonstrated that the basic premise of the method is in error, that not all basic vocabularies change at the postulated rate.

NOTES

[1] Literature dealing with the peopling of the New World and its early inhabitants is extensive. See Sellards (1952); Wormington (1957); MacGowan and Hester (1962); Krieger in Jennings and Norbeck (1964); Willey (1966); Mason (1962). Other pertinent sources are cited below. Wright and Frey (1965) are helpful in understanding the Pleistocene.

[2] Haag (1962); Müller-Beck (1966); Haynes (1964; 1967); Martin (1973). The issue of how long the continental ice masses were joined, and whether or not there may have been a route or routes around them is a matter of some dispute.

[3] Krieger (1964) is one of the chief exponents of a "pre–projectile point stage." For various publications dealing with these sites, see Evans (1961); Orr (1956); Crook and Harris (1957; 1958); Martin (1973); Leakey, Simpson, and Clements (1968); Heizer and Brooks (1965).

[4] Mirambell (1967); Haynes (1967); Lorenzo (1967); Irwin-Williams (1969). Radiocarbon dating rests upon the fact that every living organism absorbs, along with its normal complement of carbon, a radioactive isotope of carbon,

called carbon 14. It is thought that carbon 14 is formed by the reaction of cosmic rays with atmospheric nitrogen, and that a constant amount is present in the atmosphere. Since living organisms constantly exchange carbon with the atmosphere, their carbon 14 content is also constant. But following death, no more carbon—and consequently no more carbon 14—is ingested by an organism. Instead, the radioactive carbon 14 atoms in the organism begin to decay, or disintegrate, at a known constant rate. Thus, by measuring the remaining radioactivity of an organic sample, it is possible to compute the time elapsed since death.

[5] Martin (1973, 973).

[6] Ibid.

[7] Mason (1962) contains a good review and includes an extensive bibliography.

[8] Krieger (1964); other more or less synonymous names for this developmental level are Paleo-American stage (Suhm, Krieger, and Jelks, 1954), a portion of the Upper Lithic stage (Willey and Phillips, 1958), and the Big Game Hunting tradition (Willey, 1966).

[9] Sellards (1952).

[10] Green (1963).

[11] Haynes (1964; 1966).

[12] Willey (1966, 48–49).

[13] Hibben (1941); Roosa (1956); Mason (1962); Krieger (1964); Haynes and Agogino (1960); Willey (1966, 40–42).

[14] Haynes (1966).

[15] Martin (1973).

[16] Krieger (1964, 52).

[17] Sellards (1952).

[18] Butler (1961).

[19] Krieger (1964).

[20] Mason (1962, 231).

[21] Willey (1966, 60–64).

[22] Jennings and Norbeck (1955).

[23] Willey (1966, 78ff.) contains pertinent comments.

[24] See Byers (1967), and particularly MacNeish's Introduction, for the story of these discoveries.

[25] Willey (1966, 90–91).

[26] Kroeber (1948, 787).

[27] Wauchope (1956).

[28] For varying viewpoints, see Beals (1932, 149–50); Krieger (1948; 1953, 253); MacNeish (1947); Mason (1935; 1937); Newell and Krieger (1949, 224–32); Newcomb (1961, 20–22); Kelley (1955); Willey (1966, 336–37); Ekholm (1944); Caldwell (1958).

[29] See Howells (1967, 293–309) for a review of the origins and biological nature of the American Indians.

[30] Stewart (1960).

[31] Stewart (1960); Vallois and Movius (1952); Comas (1955).

[32] Wendorf et al. (1955); Wendorf and Krieger (1959).

[33] Neumann (1952).

[34] De Terra, Romero, and Stewart (1949).

[35] Jenks (1936).

[36] Dixon (1923).

[37] Imbelloni (1958).

[38] Von Eickstedt (1933–34); see Newman (1951) for a summary of criticisms of this classification.

[39] Neumann (1952).

[40] Howells (1967, 296).

[41] Stewart (1960, 260).

[42] Mooney (1928).

[43] MacLeod (1928).

[44] Kroeber (1939, 166).

[45] Ibid., p. 131.

[46] Stewart (1960, 265–66).

[47] Dobyns (1966, 412).

[48] Ibid., p. 415.

[49] Driver (1961, 63).

[50] Ibid., p. 63.

[51] These estimates fly in the face of tradition, but they make more sense than those which would have the California acorn-eaters the most populous people north of Mexico. See Kroeber (1939).

[52] White (1940). Reprinted in White (1949) and elsewhere.

[53] See Kroeber and Kluckhohn (1952) for a review of concepts of culture. For a concise summary, see White and Dillingham (1973).

[54] For the evolution of culture, see White (1959); Childe (1946); Vaillant (1962); Adams (1966).

[55] (1959, 18–28).

[56] Mason (1895); Wissler (1938); Kroeber (1939); Driver (1961).

[57] Kroeber (1939, 222).

[58] Ibid., pp. 222–28.

[59] Voegelin and Voegelin (1946).

[60] McQuown (1955).

[61] Powell (1891).

[62] Hymes (1960).

[63] Greenberg (1960).

[64] Hymes (1960, 4).

[65] Swadesh (1952).

[66] Lees (1953).

[67] Bergsland and Vogt (1962); also see Chretien (1962); Van der Merwe (1966).

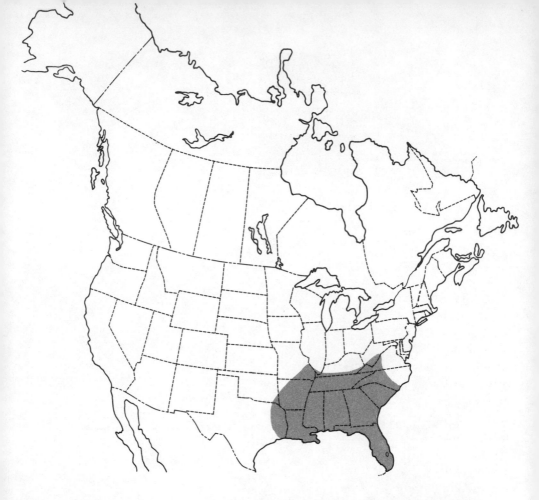

1. Catawba
2. Creek
3. Timucua
4. Koasati
5. Chickasaw
6. Alabama
7. Chatot
8. Apalachee
9. Pensacola
10. Mobile
11. Biloxi
12. Chitimacha
13. Atakapa
14. Avoyel
15. Natchez
16. Choctaw
17. Tunica
18. Quapaw
19. Yuchi
20. Cherokee
21. Calusa
22. Caddo
23. Hichiti

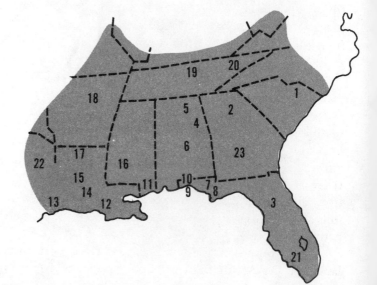

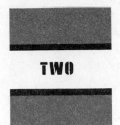

TWO

SOUTHEASTERN FARMERS

It is difficult to imagine the magnificence of the forests and the wealth of wildlife that characterized the primeval eastern woodlands of North America. Stretching southward from the coniferous forests of Canada to the Gulf of Mexico, and westward from the Atlantic seaboard to east Texas, the Ozarks, and the prairies of Illinois, the eastern woodlands covered about a third of the continent. Predominantly a land of forests, the woodlands counted about 130 species of deciduous trees, from the birch and poplar of the North, through the oak, hickory, beech, maple, and chestnut of the Northeast, to the magnolia, cypress, sweet gum, and live oak of the South. Included on its northern fringe were evergreen white pines and hemlocks, in the South the loblolly and pitch pines and other scattered evergreens. It is an exaggeration to claim that a squirrel could scurry through the trees from the Atlantic to the Mississippi without once setting foot to the ground, but it puts the immensity of the forests in proper perspective.

This great forest blanket was made possible by relatively heavy precipitation, generally averaging about forty inches a year, and fairly evenly distributed throughout the year. In the northern reaches of the woodlands, winters were long and severe, and snowfall was particularly heavy on the southeastern or lee shores of the Great Lakes. The short growing season in the northern part of the area hampered the productivity of Indian horticulturalists, whose principal crops were derived from the tropics. But much of the Eastern Woodlands had rich, fertile soils and a long growing season, and they were highly productive under native cultivation.

The two outstanding physiographic features of the eastern woodlands are the Appalachian Mountains and the Great Lakes. The low

Appalachians, geologically ancient and much eroded, extend from New-foundland and the Gaspé Peninsula southwestward to central Alabama. The heavy forest, dense underbrush, and rugged passes of the Appalachians confined the European settlements to the coastal fringes of the continent for many years, but they were only a minor hindrance to native peoples who had no wheeled vehicles and were not burdened with bulky possessions, but who did have an ancient, intimate knowledge of the land. Nor were the five Great Lakes and connecting waterways a barrier to the Indians. Instead, they served the Indian and the fur trader, who followed his well-worn routes as easy avenues of communication.

These largest of the world's fresh water lakes and the St. Lawrence drain the northern portions of the eastern woodlands, and the Ohio-Mississippi river system drains much of the region west of the Appalachians. Relatively short rivers drain the eastern and southern slopes of the mountains and the coastal plain, and in a number of places they have cut water gaps in the rugged uplands, allowing access to the interior. The absence of natural barriers that might have isolated the eastern woodlands from the rest of North America, and the lack of formidable obstacles within the region had a considerable effect on the development and nature of its cultures. Open to external influences by land and by sea, and with easy internal communication, its past was complicated by the comings and goings of many peoples and its historic tribes linked by many shared cultural traits.

The forests, meadows and openings, streams, lakes, and marshes of eastern North America supported a diverse and plentiful assortment of animals. Larger game animals included elk, woodland bison, woodland caribou, white-tailed deer, and black bear. North America's two great predators, the timber or gray wolf and the cougar or mountain lion ranged throughout the region. Bird life was varied and astonishingly plentiful, from wild turkeys and passenger pigeons to Carolina parakeets and Great Auks. The Atlantic and Gulf coasts and the rivers that flowed into them were well stocked with fish, shellfish, manatees, and whales and other marine mammals. Fish and shellfish of many kinds were also abundant in the Great Lakes and other inland waters.

The stone-age, digging-stick technology of the Indians of the eastern woodlands did not substantially alter the original forest cover, although slash-and-burn agricultural techniques and annual firing of meadows and brushland were probably more widespread than has been realized. But with the coming of Europeans, the massive, wholesale reduction of the forests for their timber and to clear the land for farms was begun immediately. Considering the extent of the forests, they were demolished in an incredibly short time. Their destruction was paralleled by the extirpation of many animals, partly as a consequence of the alteration of the forest habitat but also as a result of their indiscriminate slaughter. The woodland bison, woodland caribou, and elk were early casualties, and many other animals were much reduced in numbers or exterminated. A few, such as the white-tailed deer, raccoons, and foxes, benefited from the clearing of the forests. The total impact of this assault on the land and its fauna is impossible to precisely judge today, but it must have involved, directly or indirectly, virtually every living organism. That much of it remains verdant, fertile, and beautiful is mute testimony to one of the earth's most magnificent and amply endowed regions.

Before Europeans reached its shores, this vast land was inhabited by several hundred different Indian tribes, speaking a number of different languages and following many somewhat different life styles. These peoples have been classified—combined with one another or subdivided, lumped together or split apart—by anthropologists in a variety of ways.[1] Actually, two broadly similar but readily distinguishable and geographically separate cultural provinces occupied the eastern woodlands. The tribes and confederacies of the Southeast culture area, treated in this chapter, may be characterized as possessing productive horticultural technologies, relatively complex social and political institutions, elaborate ceremonial and religious lives, and, in all likelihood, the heaviest concentration of population of all the culture areas north of the Rio Grande.[2] Apparently, because many of its tribes were soon destroyed or changed greatly under European impact and so are inadequately known, and because much that characterizes Southeastern cultures is alien to what Indians are popularly supposed to be and so has not engaged the public attention, the region often has been slighted. But obviously the cultures of the Southeast warrant separate and extended discussion. The Northeast Woodlands culture, discussed in Chapter 3, is unquestionably more heterogeneous and less distinctive than the Southeast, but the adaptation of its peoples to a colder climate, their relationships to the hunters and fishermen farther north, and their differing past combine to warrant a separate discussion.

In broad terms the Southeast may be distinguished from the Northeast by its greater reliance on domesticated crops, fields being communally cultivated by men and women. The ability of Southeastern towns to feed De Soto's army through the winter from stored crops without undue hardship indicates the productivity of this horticultural system. While men cleared the fields in the Northeast, gardening was primarily a feminine activity, and hunting and fishing played a correspondingly larger part in subsistence. The peoples of the Southeast were sedentary, remaining in their villages and towns throughout the year, in contrast to many of the northerners who deserted their villages for hunting, fishing, and foraging expeditions of considerable duration. Villages and towns, often palisaded, were characteristic of both cultural provinces, but in the Southeast there were also great ceremonial centers, with plazas around which were arranged earthen mounds. On top of these were temples with perpetual, sacred fires, dwellings of priests, and other ceremonial structures. The ranked social classes of the Southeast, with hierarchies of secular and religious officials, were absent in the Northeast. And there were many other social and political differences. Perhaps these kinds of differences are best epitomized by the priestly chiefs of the Southeastern Natchez who arbitrarily might have their followers put to death. Such autocratic power was unheard of in the North, whether among the Delawares, Hurons, Winnebagos, or others. Confederacies or incipient confederacies were common in both North and South, but only in the South were theocracies common and widespread. Other lesser but also distinguishing differences in house types, clothing, ornaments, tools, ceramics, and artistic traditions could be mentioned.

Tribes of Southeastern culture inhabited an extensive sweep of the eastern woodlands from the Atlantic Coast westward across the Mississippi to the blackland prairies of east Texas, and from the Gulf Coast and the Florida peninsula northward into Illinois, Kentucky, and Virginia. There has been considerable discussion about which tribe or group of tribes should be regarded as "typical" and which represented a distinct "climax" culture in the Southeast.[3] Suffice it to say that a number of cultural differences distinguished various tribes, but apart from a number of geographically marginal peoples, they were not of tremendous magnitude.

Many different languages were spoken in the Southeast, the most widespread being Muskogean languages of the Gulf linguistic stock. The Muskogean languages are subdivided into a western division, composed of Choctaw-Chickasaw, and an eastern division made up of Alabama-Koasati, Hitchiti-Mikasuke, and Creek-Seminole.[4] Other Gulf languages related to Muskogean were spoken by the now-extinct Calusas of southern Florida, apparently the Timucuas of northeastern Florida, the Natchez (including the Taensa and Avoyel) of Mississippi, and the Tunicas (Tunica proper, Koroa, Yazoo) and the Chitimachas and Atakapas of Louisiana and Texas. It is now recognized that there is an ancient connection between the Gulf languages and Algonquian, and there is a strong presumption that speakers of Gulf languages were original, or at least very ancient, inhabitants of the Southeast.[5]

In a broad sense, speakers of Gulf languages occupied the geographical heartland of the Southeast; speakers of other languages inhabited its periphery. On the western borders of the Southeast, in adjoining sections of east Texas, southeastern Oklahoma, southwestern Arkansas, and western Louisiana were about two dozen Caddoan-speaking tribes. Mostly linked together in one or another of three confederacies, the Hasinais, Kadohadachos (or Caddo proper), and Natchitoches spoke dialects of a common language. Caddo, together with the languages of the Plains-dwelling Wichitas, Kichais, Pawnees, and Arickaras, constitutes a Caddoan family of languages. The Caddoan languages are distantly related to the Iroquoian languages and are now joined together in an Iroquois-Caddoan linguistic family. Of the Iroquois branch of Iroquois-Caddoan, the Cherokees of North Carolina and Tennessee are the best known in the Southeast, the others being the Nottoways and Tuscaroras of the Carolinas.

Speakers of Siouan-Yuchi languages are widely scattered in the Southeast: the Biloxis on the Gulf coast in Mississippi; the Quapaws (or Arkansas) in Arkansas, bordering Siouan-speaking relatives in the Plains; and the Catawbas and Tutelos in Virginia and the Carolinas. The Yuchis, speaking a language now regarded as affiliated with Siouan, inhabited the southern Appalachians in northern Georgia. On the northern, coastal fringes of the Southeast were the Pamlicos, Pamunkeys, and others, and in the Ohio Valley, the Shawnees, all of whom were speakers of Algonquian languages.

PREHISTORY

As mentioned in the Introduction, the peoples of the Southeast were historic representatives and descendants of one of the most grandiose, intriguing, but, in some ways, still mysterious archeological complexes ever to exist in the United States. Named Mississippian for the river valley that nurtured its greatest expressions, it took root there sometime after A.D. 500. Whether it developed from a single source in the central Mississippi Valley, or from several interdependent subcenters is still in dispute. The probabilities favor three centers: one in the central Mississippi Valley at the confluence of the Mississippi and Ohio rivers; a second, eastern center on the headwaters of the Tennessee River; and a Caddoan center in the vicinity of the big bend of the Red River.[6] The ultimate origins of the Mississippian culture pattern are undeniably Mesoamerican, as we have seen, but the details of how and when influences and people reached the Southeast are in doubt. There appears to have been intermittent contact, probably over a period of many centuries, and apparently some immigration, though no mass movements of Mesoamericans into the region.[7] Not only did the Mississippian pattern spread up the river valleys to pervade the Southeast, but its influence spread into the Plains as the Plains Village tradition (see Chapter 4) and affected cultures in the upper Mississippi Valley and, to various degrees, those of all the Northeast Woodlands.[8]

The greatest "flowering" and "climax" of the Mississippian is often said to have occurred between A.D. 1200–1400, implying that Southeastern culture was decadent and in decline by the time Europeans arrived. There is, actually, little to support this view, particularly if general cultural collapse and decline are distinguished from social and political revolution or from changes in ceremonial and religious practices. When De Soto led his expedition through much of the Southeast in 1540–42, its tribes and confederacies were vigorous and flourishing; most, probably all, of the great ceremonial centers, including Cahokia near East St. Louis, Etowah and Lamar in Georgia, Moundville in Alabama, and others, were in use. On the other hand, what has come to be known as the Southeastern Ceremonial complex, represented archeologically by a complex of art motifs that were almost surely the material trappings of a widely shared religious tradition, may well have been undergoing radical change or decline by historic times.[9]

HISTORY

Spaniards had some knowledge of Florida by about the beginning of the sixteenth century, and in 1513 Juan Ponce de León, traditionally said to be searching for the marvelous fountain of youth but probably more interested in conquest and slaves, explored portions of both Florida coasts. Near St. Augustine, on the northeast coast, the expedition was attacked by Indians who must have been the Timucuas. Sailing south close to the coast, Ponce rounded the tip of the peninsula, and in a bay on the west coast had another clash with Indians, this time Calusas. In 1517 Ponce's pilot brought the harrassed and thirsty expedition of Hernández de Córdoba into what was probably this same bay (San Carlos), and it was driven away by the natives.[10] In 1519 Francisco de Garay sailed along the Gulf coast west of the Florida peninsula, and in 1521 Ponce de León unwisely returned to found a colony on the Gulf coast of Florida. Soon after landing, the expedition was attacked by Calusas, defeated, and driven off. Ponce, suffering from an arrow wound, died soon afterward in Cuba. Farther north, in 1526, Lucas Vazquez de Ayllón attempted to plant a colony on the Savannah River below modern Savannah, Georgia. But Ayllón soon died, strife broke out among his followers, and less than one-third of the 500-man force returned to Española.[11]

In 1528 the ill-starred expedition of Pánfilo de Narváez landed some 400 men and 80 horses at the head of Tampa Bay, avoiding the warlike

Calusas to the south. Though the local Timucuas were poorly treated by the Spaniards, they did not attack the gold-crazed invaders. After two weeks the main body of the expedition marched northward, their ships departing, never to be seen again. By the time the expedition reached the main Apalachee town of Apalachen, in the vicinity of modern Tallahassee, dreams of gold were turning to thoughts of survival. The Apalachees were unfriendly, the Spaniards having occupied their town, and they killed stray Spaniards and horses whenever possible. After about a month the expedition marched westward to an Indian town near the sea. There, in the vicinity of Panama City, the expedition built barges in an attempt to reach Mexico by sea. Two of the barges were eventually cast up on the Texas coast. Of those who survived the voyage, only four men, including the hardy treasurer of the expedition, Cabeza de Vaca, reached Mexico.

By far the most extensive early contact with Indians of the Southeast was that of the brutal, plunderous expedition of Hernando de Soto.[12] Landing in Tampa Bay in the spring of 1539 with a force of over 500 men, 200 horses, vicious dogs, a herd of hogs, and collars and chains for the captives they intended to take, the expedition marched northward farther inland than had Narváez. The army also occupied the main town of the Apalachees and spent the winter there. Though the Indians, who had abandoned their town, managed to burn about two-thirds of it during the five-month occupation, it still supplied ample food for the army, its horses, dogs, hogs, and captives. And when the Spaniards departed in the spring, each man left with a load of maize. This was a pattern repeated over and over, and it leaves no doubt about the productivity of Southeastern horticulture.

De Soto had heard tales of a great queen who lived to the north and of vast tribute, including gold, she had amassed. By the end of April the army had crossed Georgia and reached the Savannah River. Here, some 25 miles below Augusta, it entered Cofitachequi, a capital of the Creek Nation. The queen, borne on a litter, placed a string of freshwater pearls around De Soto's neck, and before departure (with the queen as a captive), he had acquired a chest-full. Tales of Indians in the mountains who possessed gold drew De Soto north through the Piedmont of South Carolina through country later inhabited by Cherokees, but perhaps then occupied by a Siouan group, to the town of Xuala at the foot of the Blue Ridge. Pushing on, the army crossed the mountains to the Hiwassee Valley and the Cherokee town of Guasili, near what is now Murphy in western North Carolina. Marching westward, they reached the Tennessee River, followed it past present Chattanooga to Chiaha, an Upper Creek town. They spent the summer moving south through Alabama in Creek territory, looting and pillaging as they went. In August, the army passed the last Upper Creek village of Talisi, east of Selma. They had found no riches in the mountains or in the lands of the Creek Nation.

Continuing south, they entered territory of the Mabila (or Mobile) branch of the Choctaws. At the great town of the Mabila, just above the junction of the Alabama and Tombigbee rivers, the Spaniards were accorded a dance in the plaza, but it abruptly turned into an all-day battle. The town was burned and a great quantity of the Spanish gear was lost, including De Soto's looted pearls. About two dozen Spaniards were killed as well as 7 horses, and almost 150 men were wounded. The Spaniards estimated that 3,000 Indians had been killed. In November, after recovering from their wounds, De Soto and his men again turned inland, ascending the Tombigbee River, leaving Choctaw country and entering the lands of the Chickasaws. The army wintered in two Chickasaw towns in what is now northeastern Mississippi, near Tupelo. In March, 1541, the Spaniards were again assaulted by Indians, losing a dozen men, over 50 horses, 300 pigs, and much of their baggage. The natives apparently suffered small loss. It was not until late in April that the army could be on its way. De Soto led it westward, crossing the Mississippi on barges into Arkansas. Much of the summer was spent in northeastern Arkansas between the St. Francis and Mississippi rivers. Here, utilizing rich alluvial soils, was a large native population living in large towns, some with moats and palisades. The identity of these Indians is in doubt; Swanton[13] suggests that they were Muskogeans, perhaps related to the Natchez.

Late in the summer the expedition marched west to the Arkansas River, followed it up from Pine Bluff to Little Rock, and on to the native town of Caligua. In September they turned southwest into the Ouachita Mountains and by November were in southern Arkansas, going into winter quarters in an Indian village, near modern Camden. In the spring of 1542 they descended the Ouachita River, and late in May De Soto died of a fever; his weighted body was dropped into the Mississippi near Natchez. The survivors under Luis de Moscoso made an unsuccessful attempt to reach the Spanish settlements by land, but they turned back after crossing the Caddo country of east Texas. Returning to the Mississippi above Natchez, they spent the winter building barges, and in the spring of 1543 descended the Mississippi and ultimately reached Pánuco.

It was an incredible odyssey by determined, resourceful men, but the murders, massacres, rapes, and kidnappings of natives regularly practiced by the Spaniards are testimony of the grotesque behavior men have too often reserved for other men unlike themselves. Not only did the expedition leave a trail of bloodshed, pillage, rape, and probably political and social upheaval, but it introduced new diseases throughout the Southeast. When De Soto visited Creek towns on the middle Savannah River, some already had been abandoned because of a recent epidemic, probably originating in the Ayllón colony downstream. Elsewhere De Soto seems to have been responsible for the introduction of the terribly lethal European diseases.[14]

It was not until the seventeenth century that European settlement of the Southeast began in earnest. Spain had founded St. Augustine, Florida, in 1565 and was well entrenched by the time the English, in 1673, established their first colony in South Carolina. A few years later the French were on Mobile Bay on the Gulf, and the Indians of the Southeast found themselves very nearly encircled by the competing, aggressive Europeans. As was the case elsewhere, the Europeans allied themselves with nearby tribes, the natives soon becoming dependent upon European goods for which they traded furs and, in this region, slaves as well. Intertribal warfare often instigated by rival European powers, tribal dispersal, social and political breakdown, and epidemic diseases devastated the natives. Many tribes had been wiped out by the beginning of the eighteenth century, and some soon afterward; others were much changed; and a new one, the Seminole, incorporating remnants and refugees from a number of tribes, came into being. A group of Creeks, Hitchitis, and Yuchis from Alabama and Georgia fled to the Florida swamps where, from time to time, they were joined by runaway Negro and Indian slaves and other Indian refugees. They came to be known by their Creek designation, Seminole, meaning something similar to "wild men" or "men of the forest who live by hunting."

In the west the once great Caddo confederacies had sunk into numerical insignificance before the nineteenth century, apparently as a result of epidemics. Most tribes in the lower Mississippi Valley were quickly exterminated or dispersed. The Natchez, for example, who in De Soto's time had been known as the most powerful people in the lower valley, appear to have declined drastically in the century and a half prior to French occupation of their country. When first met by the French in the last years of the seventeenth century, they lived in nine villages along a creek that flowed into the Mississippi, near present Natchez, Mississippi. They were completely crushed in wars with the French by the middle of the eighteenth century. Four hundred survivors were sold into slavery in the West Indies; the remainder sought refuge among the Chickasaws. The Natchez decline seems to have been fairly typical for the tribes of the lower valley, but it was not representative of all the Southeast.

To the north and east, English traders settled among the Cherokees, Chickasaws, and Creeks, often marrying Indian women, with the result that there was considerable adoption of white customs and traits, from log cabins, peaches, and cows to political institutions and Christianity.

Although the French and Indian War was fought to the north and west, the treaty concluding it in 1763 left only England in control of the Southeast. The Creek Confederacy, in particular, waxed powerful under the British, but with the success of the American Revolution a few years later and the tremendous expansion of the new nation, dark and bitter days lay ahead for the still surviving Southeastern Indians.

By the nineteenth century the Choctaws, Chickasaws, Creeks, Cherokees, and Seminoles had come to be known as "the Five Civilized Tribes" because they had adopted so much from the white invaders. Many of them had large farms; had adopted white housing; raised cattle, pigs, and other introduced livestock; dressed as whites; possessed slaves; and, in some cases, had become Christians. In 1821, Sequoyah, a Cherokee, invented a syllabary in order to write his language, and it is alleged that within a few months all of the Cherokees were literate. The Cherokees drew up a constitution modeled after that of the United States, and the Choctaws and Creeks put their laws into writing.

But the acculturation of the Five Civilized Tribes was of little benefit in their struggle to hold on to their ancient lands. Americans coveted the lands, and the government forced the tribes' removal west of the Mississippi in the 1820s and 1830s to what is now Oklahoma. The ruthless removal of the Five Civilized Tribes cannot be recounted here; suffice it to say that, sparked by naked avarice, it was one of the more ignoble deeds in American history.[15] It marked the end of the Southeast as a distinctive cultural province, although some Cherokees in the mountains of North Carolina, some Seminoles in Florida swamps, and scattered groups elsewhere managed to survive in their old homelands, where their descendants may be found today.

CULTURAL SUMMARY

Subsistence and Material Culture

The Indians of the Southeast were primarily a riverine people, tied to the easily cultivated bottom lands and terraces of rivers and streams by the crude digging sticks and hoes they had to work the land. Despite their primitive equipment, they were extremely productive farmers. They grew several varieties of corn in extensive gardens, and in much of the Southeast, because of the long growing season, they raised several successive corn crops on the same ground. In addition to the staple corn, they grew beans, squash (and pumpkins), tobacco, and gourds. Sunflowers may have been domesticated in the eastern woodlands, the oil from the seeds being used both for food and for cosmetic purposes.

Another secondary crop of the Southeast was *Chenopodium*, commonly known as pigweed, whose small seeds were used in porridge and stews.

Gangs of men and women planted and tended the fields, the heavier work of clearing new fields falling to the men. Public plots and fields allotted to priest-chiefs were prepared and planted first, then the other tracts of land according to the particular social hierarchy of the tribe. Corn was pounded into meal in wooden mortars with wooden pestles, and depending upon the fineness of the meal desired, was passed through cane sieves or winnowed in small baskets. Corn was stored in baskets, and special granaries were erected to hold surplus crops. The old log corn crib of the American farmer appears to have been but a slightly altered version of the aboriginal model. The various kinds of corn were prepared in a wide variety of ways. It was roasted green; used alone or with beans, squash, and meat in stews, soups, and gruels; or steeped in ashes and made into hominy; and the meal was baked in the ashes as a kind of unleavened bread.

Despite reliance on these crops, game, such as deer, bear, bison, turkey, and wildfowl, was avidly pursued by hunters, often in communal hunts. Bows and arrows were the chief weapons of the men, and the testimony of the chroniclers of the De Soto and Narváez expeditions leaves no doubt but that they were accurate archers who possessed powerful bows. The blow gun with an unpoisoned dart was also in use in the Southeast. Fish were taken with hooks, traps, and weirs, shot with bow and arrows, and also stupefied in shallow pools with a root poison so that they could be easily caught. The only domestic animal was the dog, used to some extent for hunting, and, among the Natchez, consumed by warriors prior to going on the warpath.[16] The De Soto expedition, during its peregrinations in the Southeast, was often presented with gifts of packs of small, fat dogs. The Spaniards promptly ate them, but the natives seem to have reserved them for sacrificial and ceremonial use, at which times they also may have consumed them.

The Indians of the Southeast made intensive and extensive use of the rich and diverse flora of the region. Several species of grapes were native to the eastern United States, for example, and the Indians not only gathered the ripe fruit, but apparently cut back, cleared the ground around, and otherwise nurtured particularly productive or fla-vorful vines. All of the native grapes have cultivated varieties, some dating to at least colonial times, and there is a strong presumption that Indians initiated this domestication. Similarly, a number of species of wild plums native to eastern North America were gathered by the natives. Coronado, De Soto, and other explorers made frequent reference to the fine quality of both the ripe and the dried fruit. Since the origins of the plums planted in colonial orchards are obscure, it is also possible that the domestication or incipient domestication of some of our plums should be attributed to the natives of North America.[17] Many other wild fruits, including persimmons, raspberries, and mulberries, were gathered and either eaten fresh or dried for future use. West of the Mississippi, pecans were an important wild food, as were walnuts to the east; acorns, other nuts, and various seeds, roots, and tubers were also utilized.

Despite the decline and disappearance of the ancient ceramic traditions of the Southeast soon after the advent of European metal utensils, undoubtedly the pottery of the area and the artistic styles associated with it and various shell and stone ornaments, were elaborate, highly distinctive, and set the area apart from other regions north of the Rio Grande. The mortuary and ceremonial pottery of the Mississippian cultures was varied and included bottles, jars, bowls, and other forms. A wide assortment of handles, straps, bases, spouts, and the like were added, and particularly fascinating are human, animal, and plant effigy motifs that were employed. Ceramics were decorated in many ways, including incising, polishing, slipping, engraving, painting, punctating, and marking with fabrics. There was considerable areal variation in Mississippian ceramics, some for example, revealing continuation of older Woodland traditions, some being an abrupt departure from older styles.

The spectacular grave offerings that have been recovered from major ceremonial centers in the Southeast and attributed to the Southern cult or Southeastern Ceremonial complex also need to be considered in this connection. Although, as has been noted, the Southern Cult may have been in decline by historic times, it persisted, as Howard[18] has observed, as the Busk, or Green Corn Ceremony, of historic tribes, and its art motifs and artifacts have also persisted. The grave offerings of the Southern Cult, which include pottery, copper and shell gorgets, conch shell masks, stone palettes and statues, and pipes, are decorated with certain motifs—weeping or forked eyes, sun circles, crosses, rattlesnakes, and others. The resemblances to Mesoamerican art forms and motifs are impressive, but it cannot simply be dismissed as provincial Mesoamerican. Esthetically considered, in fact, the clean, relatively uncluttered lines of many Southeastern ceramic vessels are more pleasing to present-day tastes than the busy, cluttered nature of many Mesoamerican pieces.

In addition to ceramics, baskets, mats, and other containers were woven out of a variety of plant materials, including cane. The inner bark of the mulberry was utilized for clothing. Although a complex wood technology was hampered by the lack of metal tools, basic tools and utensils such as digging sticks and hoes, mortars and pestles, were fashioned of wood. Dugout canoes were laboriously made by alternately

charring and scraping out tree trunks that had been felled with stone
axes and fire.

There is considerable variation in settlement patterns in the Southeast. At some archeological sites, the ceremonial complex of mounds and plazas was separated from the villages that were located some distance away. But at others, dwellings and the ceremonial structures are contiguous. Some sites were strongly fortified with palisades and earthworks, while others were not. Some centers were densely populated, but there were also many small settlements. At one of the largest sites, Cahokia in East St. Louis, Illinois, for example, there are eighty-five mounds of assorted sizes and a village area that stretched for six miles along a tributary of the Mississippi.

The striking feature of Southeastern settlements and doubtless the focal point of social and ceremonial life were the mound complexes. The construction of earthen mounds was a monumental task for people who possessed no metal tools, wheels, or draft animals. They laboriously built the mounds by scraping up earth into baskets, carrying the baskets to the mound site, dumping them, and returning again and again for more loads. "Borrow pits" from which the earth was taken are present near many mound sites, and the remnants of baskets in which the earth was transported also have been found. The enormity of the task is appreciated when it is realized that Monk's Mound in East St. Louis was originally about 100 feet high, 1,080 feet long, and 710 feet wide, and covered about 16 acres.[19] Most mounds were considerably smaller, but even one 15 feet high and two hundred feet long represents a good many man-hours of labor and the concerted, coordinated efforts of many people.

These earthen mounds, like the stone-faced prototypes of Mexico, were platforms on which were built ceremonial structures and at which the great ceremonial activities took place. Both the Mexican and Southeastern mounds are truncated, or flat-topped, and ramps or steps lead to their tops. Like the Mexican pyramids, many in the Southeast were periodically rebuilt or added to, and there were a number of other similarities. There is no doubt but that those of the Southeast are provincial expressions of those to the south.[20] Often the square or rectangular mounds were grouped around open plazas or squares in a rectilinear arrangement. The plazas were kept clear and clean for public ceremonies. The houses or temples erected on the mounds were similar to ordinary houses, usually being somewhat larger and apparently with more ornamentation.

Ordinary houses were rectangular to oval, from 10 to about 25 feet in length or diameter, with gabled or conical thatched roofs. Built on a foundation of poles to which were tied smaller branches and laths, they were ordinarily plastered with clay. Fires were built in the center of the floor of these nuclear family dwellings, the smoke finding its way out through the thatch. Platforms for sleeping were placed around the walls, and apart from wooden stools, which were reserved for high ranking people, there were few other furnishings.

The appearance of Southeastern Indians was often a decided shock to the first Europeans to see them, and their clothing and bodily ornamentation were at wide variance from today's Indian costume. Men wore breechcloths, leggings, sleeveless shirts, and moccasins, but in hot weather discarded most clothing. In cold weather a fur robe and feather mantles were added. Women wore hide or woven grass skirts and, sometimes, loose shirts or blouses. The Southeast was one of North America's great centers for artificial cranial deformation, although among historic tribes it was not universally practiced and it was sometimes associated with social station. Tattooing and painting of the body were also widespread. Among the Natchez, for example, heads of infants were deformed on their cradleboards, and both boys and girls were tattooed across the nose. As they grew older, and depending upon their rank and exploits, other tattooes were added so that a warrior's entire body might be covered with designs of various kinds.

Facial and body hair was plucked out, and head hair was treated in many ways. Among the Caddoes, for example, a popular male style allowed the hair to grow to a length of about two inches, except for a small patch on top of the head, which was encouraged to grow to waist length, this queue being decorated with feathers. Roached styles were common, and many styles appear to have been associated with rank and age. Both sexes also ornamented themselves with earrings and necklaces. In general, Southeasterners paid considerable attention to their appearance, clothing, and bodily ornamentation. Besides being deemed attractive, they signalized much about a person's age, accomplishments, and social standing.

Social Organization

Apart from some of the regionally peripheral tribes, there was a good deal of similarity in social organization throughout the Southeast. It was an area in which descent was reckoned through the women, no doubt a reflection of their important contribution to subsistence. The maternally oriented families were, throughout much of the area, organized into clans, theoretically descended from a remote ancestress and, of course, forbidden to marry among themselves. Clans were named after animals and plants, such as bear, deer, or corn, but the association was not pushed to the point that members of a bear clan, for example, were forbidden to kill or consume bears. Clans were not localized, and members of many or all of them could be found in each village or town.

Tribes were divided into halves, or moieties, which functioned in the playing of games and in government. But the basic governmental unit of the Southeast was the town or village, usually linked with a number of others in loose alliances. Confederacies, often composed of tribes of somewhat varying language and culture, also existed. The Creeks, for example, in the early part of the eighteenth century were scattered out over much of Alabama and Georgia. Those who called themselves Muskogee, and who were located mostly in the northern part of the region, believed that they had settled there first, and were known as the Upper Creeks. Other later comers, such as the Alabamas and Hitchitis, who varied somewhat from the Upper Creeks culturally and linguistically, became known as Lower Creeks. The Muskogee called themselves White People and the Lower Creeks, People of Alien Speech. They all felt themselves friends and allies, and a number of complementary activities grew up which served to hold them together. The White People, or the People of Peace, did not take the initiative in warfare, and their towns served as sanctuaries for murderers and even enemies. The People of Alien Speech, also known as the Red or War People, were considered to be aggressors, and did not provide sanctuary.

Among the Natchez and related people such as the Chitimachas, a hereditary class system existed, and it has been the source of much discussion and speculation. The Natchez had developed two classes: a graded class of nobility subdivided in descending order into Suns, Nobles, and Honored Men who claimed descent from the Sun; and a class of commoners.[21] The commoners were referred to as Stinkards, although not in their presence since it was a term of opprobrium. Differences between classes were observed by the marked deference paid Suns, particularly the Great Sun, in clothing, housing, and other ways. In this matrilineal society the mother of the Great Sun, known as the White Woman, occupied a high position and one of considerable authority. She and other female Suns selected the successor to the position of Great Sun, the office ordinarily falling to the White Woman's eldest son. The Great Sun, no doubt with the advice and consent of his mother, selected other officials from among the members of the Sun class, including the Great War Chief, who was normally his next eldest brother. The descendants of male Suns regressed in rank each generation, so that the son of the Great Sun was a Noble, his grandson an Honored Man, and a great-grandson a Stinkard.

The most curious aspect of this class system was the rule that forced the nobility to marry Stinkards. In their matrilineal system this meant that the offspring of women belonging to the nobility, who had married

Stinkard men, belonged to the nobility. The children of men of nobility, except as noted above, were like their mothers, Stinkards. With each of the noble classes required to marry Stinkards, it is obvious that the Stinkard class would have disappeared were there not some compensating mechanism in the system. There were far fewer nobility than commoners, which served to slow the drain on the lower class, but the fact that the Stinkard class was replenished by the conquest of neighboring peoples apparently kept the system functioning.[22] It is tempting to equate the class system of the Natchez with European royalty of an earlier day, or with various caste societies. Such comparison is revealing, not because of the similarities but because of the basic differences. The Natchez marriage rules kept it an open, mobile system involving all the people, whereas in a true caste society, endogamous rules keep the various social categories separated. Though superficially disguised, Natchez society remained one organized around kinship, functioning on the basis of kin relationships.

In the Southeast, birth usually took place in an isolated hut on a riverbank, especially built for use during menstruation and childbirth. Immediately after birth, a woman washed herself and the infant in the stream, and then, as among the Natchez, fixed the child to a cane or wooden cradle board to begin the process of flattening the head. Natchez babies were allowed to suckle as long as they liked or until the mother again became pregnant. Girls seem to have received most of their training from their mothers at home; boys came under the tutelage of an old male clansman who taught them archery, held running, swimming, and other contests, and generally trained them to become good Natchez. It was regarded as particularly important that boys learn to live harmoniously and peacefully with others.[23] Besides the threat of ostracism, scratching the back and flanks with garfish teeth was used as punishment and as a means of hardening and toughening youths.

Among the Natchez, Creeks, Caddoes, and apparently most Southeastern peoples, premarital sexual experimentation was looked upon favorably. In fact, among the Natchez it was virtually demanded since it was thought that a woman at death could not pass over the bridge to the afterworld unless she had been free with her sexual favors while a girl. In contrast to the sexual freedom of the unmarried young people, adultery after marriage was frowned upon and seems to have been rare. Among the Caddoes, marriages seem to have been brittle and divorce easy, but among the Natchez, on the other hand, divorce was rare.

Marriage throughout the area, as in most kinship societies, was an arrangement between families and clans rather than a romantic match between couples. Among the Natchez, a man gave appropriate gifts to his prospective father-in-law, asked for permission to marry the girl, and if the girl's family agreed to the match, it was formalized by a ceremony and feast in her parents' house. Residence of the newly married couple might be in the groom's home, or a new house might be built for them. Ordinary Natchez seldom had more than two wives, but Suns often had a number of spouses.[24]

Of life's major crises, death was paid more attention than any other by the natives of the Southeast, and this was particularly so for religious leaders. Among the Natchez,[25] for example, the death of a Great Sun or a White Woman were occasions for spectacular sanguinary rites. When a Great Sun died, his wives, guards, and various other officials were put to death, and other volunteers also might accompany their leader to the afterworld. In the four days or so after the death of a Great Sun, those who were to accompany him to the afterworld took their places on scaffolds erected in the plaza, where they were waited upon by their relatives, and from time to time they danced in the plaza. On the day of the funeral, the body of the Great Sun was carried on a litter to the temple in a procession that included placing the bodies of strangled infants before the procession so that the body of the Great Sun would pass over them. Those who were to join the Great Sun in the afterworld were given balls of tobacco to eat. Stupified by the tobacco, a deerskin was placed over their heads, and relatives quickly strangled them with bowstrings. The cabin of the Great Sun was burned and all fires in the village extinguished. When the flesh of the Great Sun had rotted away, generally after several months, his remains were exhumed, put in a woven container, and placed in the temple with the bones of his ancestors. At this time the temple guards might also be strangled.

Among the Natchez, the Great Sun, believed to be a descendant of the sun god, wielded virtually absolute power and was the principal religious leader of all the Natchez towns. Similarly, in the Caddo confederacies, the hereditary confederacy leader was also the voice of the gods and resided in a sacred temple. These political and religious leaders were assisted by a corps of officials, varying somewhat from tribe to tribe, but most formed a hierarchy with specific duties. Among the Creeks, political organization was in some respects unique, although they shared with other Southeasterners a tendency to form loose alliances and confederacies. Creek towns, varying somewhat from one another in origin, dialect, and other respects, were essentially autonomous political subdivisions. But the towns recognized one another as friendly, shared various ceremonial activities, and often aided one another against enemies. The result of European presence was to encourage the strength of the confederacy.

The *miko*, or town chief, of the Creeks was normally selected from the membership of his predecessor's clan, and in the Red towns was usually from a Red clan, in White towns a member of a White clan. Despite the deference paid a town chief, he did not have absolute power but was advised and assisted by a group of counselors, some of whom were drawn from his clan. A group of "beloved men," actually retired warriors who might have any clan affiliation, made up a council, and matters of importance were decided by these officials.

Warfare

Throughout the Southeast, warfare was an important, heavily ritualized, and honored and highly esteemed activity. It was the principal way for men to gain prestige, and among such people as the Natchez, it was the sole way a man had of advancing from one class to another. Thus, a lowly Stinkard, through his prowess as a warrior, might advance to Honored Man, and his wife was elevated with him. It was apparently more difficult to advance from Honored Man to Noble, and few, if any, men appear to have advanced more than one step in rank. The advance of a Stinkard man to the Honored category was symbolized by additional tattooing and the bestowal of a new name.

Preparations for war were usually elaborate, and among the Caddoes, for example, feasts, dances, prayers, and other ceremonial and ritual activities might consume a week's time before the departure of a war party. As excitement mounted, new recruits were caught up in the emotional frenzy and joined the party. Finally, before departure, the quarters that the warriors had occupied were burned. Most war parties throughout the area were small, perhaps averaging two dozen warriors, although much larger ones were sometimes raised, particularly under the influence of Europeans. The intent of war parties was to strike stealthily, usually at dawn, kill or capture a few of the enemy, and withdraw without casualty. Warriors employed bows and arrows, axes, and clubs as weapons, and carried small hide shields for defense. As has been noted, many villages were palisaded for defense against surprise attack.

Those enemies who were killed were scalped; captured warriors were brought back to the captor's village, where they were often required to dance and sing in the plaza for several days before they were tied to frames and tortured to death by fire. The flesh or blood of these enemies was often consumed in ritual cannibalism. The torture of captives on a frame, practiced by the Natchez, Caddoes, and other Southeasterners, almost certainly had its origins in Mesoamerica.[26] Captive women and children were frequently adopted, and occasionally men were saved by widows as replacements for husbands lost in battle.

Throughout the Southeast, religious beliefs centered around an omnipotent celestial deity, usually the sun, or the sun as the principal manifestation of this supreme power. The sun and fire were believed to be intimately connected, fire being regarded as the earthly representation of the sun or as a spouse or other close kin. As a consequence, sacred fires maintained in the temples were characteristic, and among some tribes, particularly the tribes of the Creek Confederacy, the annual extinguishing of the old fire and the lighting of a new fire constituted the ceremonial and religious climax of the year. Among the Natchez and Caddoes, the emphasis was on maintaining perpetual fires. Among the Natchez, the Great Sun, regarded as a descendant of the sun or a descendant of *The* who had been dispatched by the supreme deity, was a part of this sun-fire identification and, as with the Caddo priest-kings, served as the sacred channel of communication between man and the supernatural powers.[27]

The fire temple of the Natchez was a two-room, rectangular building situated on a mound. One room was a ceremonial storeroom, the other a repository for the bones of the Great Suns and their families; the perpetual fire was also located in this room. The identification of the Suns with the perpetual fire was so close that it was believed that should the fire go out, the Suns would also die. Should the keeper of the fire allow it to be extinguished, he and his family were put to death.

Great public religious rituals were conducted by priests in the ceremonial centers in an annual round closely geared to the agricultural cycle. The climax of the religious year among the Creeks, Seminoles, Yuchis, and other tribes was a Green Corn Ceremony, or "Busk," held in July or August after the main harvest of corn. Busk is a corruption of the Creek word *poskita*, which means "to fast," and it conveys but imperfectly the significance of this complex religious festival. Basically, the Green Corn Ceremony was a rite of renewal and renovation, a way of discarding the old and impure, and beginning the new year pure and spotless. In material terms, the concept was symbolized by throwing away, breaking, or burning old clothing, tools, pottery, and other utensils. The town and its dwellings were swept clean and all fires extinguished. To climax the varied activities of the Busk, a new sacred fire, laid with four logs oriented to the cardinal directions, was lighted in the square ground or plaza. From it the new household fires were lighted. The population attained bodily purification by purging themselves with an emetic, the widely used black drink, concocted from the leaves of the yaupon holly (*Ilex cassine*),[28] by fasting, and by ritual bathing. The idea of starting afresh was so strong that past sins were washed away and all crimes, save that of murder, were forgiven. The Busk also marked a time of sexual license, an opportunity for leaders of clan and phratry to lecture their kin, and an occasion for dances and ceremonial ball games. Lacrosse and chunky, the latter played with throwing sticks and rolling stones, were the two great games of the Southeast, and they were played on these occasions. The Busk was brought to a close at sunset of the eighth day in larger towns and the fourth day in smaller towns with an address by the *miko*.[29]

While Green Corn ceremonials were widespread in the Southeast, there were a great many other seasonal ceremonies that, depending upon the tribe, were also of great importance. Among the Natchez, for example, the year was divided into thirteen months, and at each new moon the Great Sun marked the occasion with thanksgiving feasts and other cermonies. The Green Corn Ceremony, while marked by the kindling of a new fire, sexual license of the unmarried, ceremonial ball games, and feasting, was much more of a harvest time thanksgiving ceremonial than one of renewal. Among the Caddoes, harvest ceremonies climaxed the religious year. Their priest-kings were at this time honored with great feasts, dances, and merriment, although for these religious leaders it was a time for fasting and praying to thank the gods for the harvest and to ensure future good fortune.

Throughout the Southeast there were a remarkable number of specialists who dealt with the supernatural world, from the priestly leaders who may be best thought of as concerned with the welfare of the people and confederacy as a whole, and who presided over the great public ceremonies—the planting and harvesting ceremonies—to the part-time shamans who labored mostly in private to heal the sick, control the weather, and forecast the future. Guilds or societies of medicine men were common, and among the Caddoes, for example, these societies publicly initiated new members in dramatic pageants. Disease was often believed to be caused by malevolent supernatural beings, as well as by witches. Curing by medicine men was a matter of diagnosing what supernatural force was causal, and then prescribing a course of action. Shamans cured by sleight of hand, sucking, and sweat bathing. The vision quest, so common in other parts of North America, was little emphasized in the Southeast.

NOTES

[1] Mason (1907–1910, 427–30) subdivided the eastern woodlands into three subdivisions: Atlantic Slope, Mississippi Valley, and Gulf Coast. Wissler (1938, 12, 236–41) divided his "Eastern Maize area" into an "Eastern Woodland area" and a "Southeastern area," much as is done here. Kroeber (1939, 60ff.) saw all of the cultures east of the Rockies as "relatively uniform," and in his inclusive Eastern-Northern area, he recognized sixteen subareas. Driver (1961,

20–21) lumps most of the peoples of the eastern woodlands under the rubric of "East," the remainder in "Prairies."

[2] This view of the Southeast is at odds with the traditional anthropological one, particularly as regards population. See especially Kroeber (1939); Driver (1961).

[3] Wissler (1938, 240) views the Yuchis, Cherokees, and Muskogean speakers as being typical tribes of the Southeast. Kroeber (1939, 62) views the Natchez as the "climax" culture of the area; Eggan (1952, 44ff., Fig. 11) finds Kroeber's position unwarranted. Swanton (1928) emphasizes inland tribes, particularly the Creeks.

[4] Haas (1941).

[5] Haas (1958a,b).

[6] Kroeber (1939, 74–76) sets up a "Red River area" for the Caddoes and Quapaws, but agrees that the Caddoes are "basically Southeastern, with affiliations to the Natchez rather than the Muskogian tribes . . ."; Newcomb (1961, 282).

[7] Willey (1966, 293).

[8] Ibid., p. 338.

[9] Waring and Holder (1945); Williams (1968); Howard (1968).

[10] Sauer (1971, 29–31).

[11] Ibid., pp. 69–76.

[12] The route of the De Soto expedition was meticulously traced by the United States De Soto Commission and was published in a volume edited by John R. Swanton (1939). The route as sketched here follows this interpretation. For a discussion of the primary sources of information about the De Soto expedition, i.e., Biedma, Rangel, the Gentleman of Elvas, and Garcilaso de la Vega, also see this volume.

[13] Swanton (1939, 287).

[14] Sauer (1971, 302–3).

[15] Debo (1940).

[16] Swanton (1911, 129–30).

[17] Sauer (1971, 288–91).

[18] Howard (1968, 80ff.).

[19] Ibid., p.5.

[20] See Wicke (1965) for a summary of these similarities.

[21] Swanton (1911) has assembled the basic information available on the Natchez; for their position within the Southeast, see Swanton (1946).

[22] Hart (1943); Quimby (1942;1946).

[23] Swanton (1911, 87).

[24] The original matrilineal kinship terminology of the Natchez has been influenced by the Creeks so that their terminology, which Murdock (1949, 247) terms patri-Crow, may not represent their original state. The distinguishing features of the known Natchez terminology are separate terms for father and father's brothers, and for mother and mother's sisters. This terminological system was shared with the neighboring Chitimachas and may be related to their class systems (Haas, 1939).

[25] Swanton (1911, 138–57).

[26] Kroeber (1939, 62).

[27] Swanton (1911, 171).

[28] Prepared by boiling the roasted leaves, and stirring the concoction into a froth, the black drink was widely used in the Southeast as a purgative and emetic. It was frequently used before ritual activities as a means of attaining spiritual purification.

[29] Speck (1907).

1.	Beothuk	11.	Tobacco
2.	Micmac	12.	Huron
3.	Malecite	13.	Neutral
4.	Passamaquoddy	14.	Potawatomi
5.	Penobscot	15.	Missisauga
6.	Wawenock	16.	Ojibwa
7.	Norridgewock	17.	Menomini
8.	Abnaki	18.	Winnebago
9.	Algonkin	19.	Sauk
10.	Ottawa	20.	Fox

21.	Kickapoo	36.	Wappinger
22.	Illinois	37.	Nipmuc
23.	Miami	38.	Massachus
24.	Erie	39.	Pennacook
25.	Shawnee	40.	Nauset
26.	Wenro	41.	Wampanoa
27.	Seneca	42.	Narragans
28.	Tutelo		Pequot, M
29.	Powhatan	43.	Mahican
30.	Nottoway	44.	Pocumtuc
31.	Tuscarora	45.	Cayuga
32.	Nanticoke	46.	Onondaga
33.	Delaware	47.	Oneida
34.	Conoy	48.	Mohawk
35.	Montauk	49.	Susquehar

THREE

NORTHEASTERN HUNTER-FARMERS

The English, French, Swedish, Dutch, and other Europeans who began to settle the northern Atlantic Coast of North America in the early years of the seventeenth century had the good fortune to encounter natives who initially were usually friendly and divided into many small independent groups, unlikely to come to one another's aid should the occasion arise. In the beginning they neither shared nor comprehended the possessive, acquisitive attitudes Europeans held about land. The disparity between their stone-age possessions and the iron-age technology of the whites was tremendous, and isolated for millennia from the endemic diseases of the Old World, they had neither the biological defenses nor the cultural techniques to combat the epidemics that soon raged among them. They were, in brief, no match for the aggressive, well-organized, commercially oriented, land-hungry Europeans. Within a relatively few years the coastal Indians had been defeated—slaughtered in genodical wars, ravaged by epidemics, besotted by drink, driven from their homes—their ancient cultures corrupted by dependence upon their conqueror's economy. The displacement of their remnants westward and the rapid penetration of North America by hunters, trappers, and traders also quickly affected inland tribes, and their fate was, in its essentials, like that of the coastal Indians. Remarkably, some of the coastal cultures and many of the inland peoples have managed in some degree to survive. But as a result of the early distortion of their cultures, knowledge of the Indians of the Northeast Woodlands at the time of first contact leaves a good deal to be desired. Though often pictured as skulking savages[1] hardly distinguishable from other creatures of the forest, the direct and indirect contributions of the Northeast Woodland Indians to modern American civilization are numerous and important, and their influence on the course of American history has been profound[2]

Broadly conceived, the natural boundaries of the Northeast Woodlands include the lake country of Minnesota, western Ontario, and southern Manitoba, the lake-studded wild rice region west of Lake Michigan, and the scattered tall-grass prairies of southeastern Minnesota, southern Wisconsin, and Illinois. Eastward it encompasses the Great Lakes, the Ohio Valley drainage, the Appalachians, the St. Lawrence drainage, and the Atlantic coastal plain from New Brunswick to North Carolina. Many of the traits that distinguish various peoples of the Northeast Woodlands stem from its environmental diversity. Thus, the wild rice area made possible a subsistence based on it rather than agriculture, with corresponding differences in the cultures of the Winnebagos and Menominis. Similarly, the growing season is too brief to raise corn very successfully in the northern part of the area, so that some of the Ojibwas, Abnakis, and others were limited to a hunting, gathering, and fishing existence.

Even after allowing for the effects of environmental differences, and apart from a few rather general and amorphous similarities, such as the cultivation of crops where feasible, the cultures of the Northeast Woodlands were remarkably heterogeneous. They cannot be characterized in a few sentences; no tribe is typical of the entire area, there was no overriding cultural focus, and many of its tribes shared many traits with peoples of adjacent areas. In Wissler's words,[3] "characterization" of the area "is difficult." In order to reflect this cultural diversity, the Northeast is here divided into three subareas, Coastal Algonkian, Central-Northern Algonkian, and Iroquoian. The major difficulty is not in designating these subdivisions, but in deciding where the external margins of the area should be drawn. The Ojibwas, Ottawas, and Algonkins on its northern fringes share many traits with more northerly tribes, of the Subarctic culture area. Some of the tribes of the midwestern prairies have much in common with the Plains Village peoples to the west, and the southern border of the area is also difficult to trace, the Shawnees, the Powhatan tribes of Virginia, and others sometimes being classified as Southeastern.[4]

Along the Atlantic seaboard from the Gaspé Peninsula, with its Micmac hunters and fishermen, south to the Tuscaroras of North Carolina, and inland to the Appalachians, were a series of predominantly Algonquian-speaking tribes, grouped together as the Coastal Algonkian subarea. Isolated to some extent by the Appalachians to the west, the region had considerable game, locally rich soils, and a wealth of fish, shellfish, and other creatures in its rivers and coastal waters. In the

North, occupying New Brunswick, Nova Scotia, and Maine, were a group of six tribes who were closely related culturally and spoke similar Algonquian dialects. Sometimes known as the Wabanaki,[5] they were the Abnaki, Wawenock, Penobscot (including the Norridgewock, and Aroosaguntacook), Malecite, Passamaquoddy, and the Micmac tribes, the last being somewhat divergent. Being near or beyond the northern limits of maize cultivation, they relied heavily on hunting; and, depending on the particular location, fishing, sealing, and the gathering of maple sugar and other wild plant products were also of considerable significance to subsistence.

To their south, in New Hampshire, were the Pennacooks, with ties in historic times to the Abnakis, but who are generally grouped with other tribes of New England—the Mahicans, Pocumtuks, Nipmucs, Massachusets, Nausets, Wampanoags, Narragansets, Nehantics, Pequoits, and Mohegans. In the lower Hudson River valley, west to the Delaware River, and southward to Delaware Bay and Cape May were the people who became the Delaware tribe, comprised of three divisions: the Munsi, Unami, and Unalachtigo. Corn, beans, and squash were basic to their subsistence; seasonally, hunting, fishing, and gathering were important.[6] To their south, including the lower Potomac and Chesapeake Bay regions, were the Conoys and Nanticokes, both sharing many similarities with the Delawares. To the south, in Virginia, the Powhatan tribes are sometimes considered to belong to the Southeast culture area, as are the more southerly Pamlicos, the poorly known Iroquoian peoples (Tuscaroras, Nottaways), and the eastern Siouan tribes (Monacans, Saponis, Catawbas, Tutelos).

Occupying the lower Great Lakes and upper St. Lawrence region was a block of Iroquoian-speaking tribes that comprised a second linguistic and cultural subarea within the Northeast Woodlands. (Iroquoian is used here to refer to all the speakers of languages of this family; Iroquois is reserved for the tribes of the League.) They are differentiated from most of the other peoples of the Northeast Woodlands by their greater dependence on agriculture, their more formally structured social and political institutions, specifically by supertribal confederacies, and by other aspects of their cultures. Between Georgian Bay and Lake Simcoe, in a region of sandy, easily worked soils, with abundant fish, and ideally situated for trade with the Algonkian tribes to the north and in the upper lakes, was the Huron Confederacy.[7] In the early years of the seventeenth century, there were four Huron tribes, counting between eighteen and twenty-five villages, the larger ones being fortified. South of Georgian Bay, in southern Ontario, were the Tionontatis, also known as the Petun or Tobacco Nation. Living in nine villages, they spoke the same language and were in other respects similar to the

Hurons. Another confederacy, known to the French as the Neutral Nation because they managed to remain uninvolved in the feud between the Huron and Iroquois, occupied the region from the Grand River valley north of Lake Erie, extending across the Niagara River into New York. Their language and some aspects of their culture were slightly different from that of the Hurons. Three of four tribes lived in some forty villages, plus perhaps the Wenros, a tribe who were dispersed in historic times by the Senecas. Southeast of Lake Erie was another Iroquoian-speaking people, the Erie or Cat Nation. To their east, in the Susquehanna Valley, were the Susquehannas, or Conestogas. Across upper New York State dwelled the best known of the Iroquoian-speaking tribes, the Five Nations, later the Six Nations when the Tuscaroras joined them, and also known as the League of the Iroquois. From west to east, the five tribes were the Senecas, Cayugas, Oneidas, Onondagas, and Mohawks.[8]

West and north of the Iroquoians, occupying the lower Ohio Valley and the land surrounding Lakes Michigan, Superior, and the western and northern shores of Huron, was a region of predominantly Algonquian-speaking tribes, set off here as the Central-Northern Algonkian subarea. The only non-Algonquian tribe was the Siouan-speaking Winnebago of the wild-rice area of Wisconsin. Six Algonquian languages were spoken: Ojibwa (of which Ottawa and Algonkin are dialects), Potawatomi (more closely related to Ojibwa than other Algonquian languages), Menomini, Miami-Illinois, Shawnee, and Fox. The Sauk, Fox, and Kickapoo tribes spoke such similar dialects of Fox that their separation must have taken place in late prehistoric times. Shawnee is related to Fox, but the divergence is more ancient. Early in the seventeenth century, these tribes were seriously affected by the expansion of the Iroquois and the inroads of the fur trade economy, with the result that their early cultures are not well known.[9]

On the northern shores of Lakes Superior and Huron, extending to the height of land separating the drainage of the Great Lakes from that of Hudson Bay, were the Ojibwas (for which the corrupted form is Chippewa). A numerous and scattered people, those north and west of Lake Superior are designated as Ojibwas, the bands of Manitoulin Island and the country north of Sault Ste. Marie as Missisaugas, and those north of Georgian Bay as Ottawas. Scattered to the east and northeast of the Ottawas and poorly known, but apparently intermediate culturally between the Ottawas, and the Montagnais of the Subarctic were bands known as Algonkins. The Potawatomis west of Lake Huron in Michigan, who united in a loose confederacy with the Lake Superior Ojibwas and the Ottawas in the eighteenth century, known as the Council of the Three Fires, are also sometimes reckoned as the fourth Ojibwa division.[10] The Ojibwa-Ottawa peoples are often set apart as a distinct "Northern Great Lakes" or "North Central Algonkian" subarea, since a number of differences in material culture, social organization, and mythology distinguish them from more southerly Algonkians.[11] South of the Potawatomis and occupying the remainder of southern Michigan as of about 1600 were the Sauk, Fox, and Kickapoo tribes. Another tribe or subtribal group known as the Mascoutens have disappeared, and their affiliations are in doubt. During this period, the Shawnees occupied Ohio and parts of Kentucky; the Miami-Illinois tribes were to their west in Illinois and Indiana. The Menominis were located from the Green Bay vicinity northward into Michigan's upper peninsula, and the Winnebagos in Wisconsin to their south.[12]

PREHISTORY

The Northeast Woodlands was the heartland of the Algonquian linguistic family, geographically the most widespread of any in North America. Distantly related to the Ritwan languages spoken in northern California by the Wiyot and Yurok, there is also an ancient connection between Algonquian and the Gulf or Great Muskogean family of languages spoken in the southeastern United States, as has been mentioned. This raises the possibility that at some time in the past, the Eastern Woodlands were solidly occupied by speakers of a Proto-Algonquian-Gulf language, who may have shared a common culture.[13] Soon after 5000 B.C., a distinctive Archaic pattern became established in the Eastern Woodlands. Though apparently brought into the area by an invading population, there are some indications of relationships and transition from the earlier Paleo-Indian cultures. These Archaic peoples followed a hunting, fishing, and gathering way of life (as some of the area's historic Algonkians continued to do). There was a considerable degree of uniformity throughout the area, such differences as existed tending to set off the Southeast from the Northeast. Grit-tempered, cord-marked pottery, with apparently northern origins, appeared in the Northeast Woodlands about 2500 B.C., and some 500 years later, fiber-tempered pottery came into existence in the Southeast. The differentiation between the Northeast and Southeast culture areas, and the Algonquian and Gulf languages may well date from this time and these early Woodland cultures.[14]

Shortly after 1000 B.C., a new tradition with Middle American affiliations, apparently brought by migrants, appeared in the Ohio Valley.[15] Distinguished by burial mounds and other earthworks, the Adena culture and the slightly later and related Hopewell cultures of Ohio and Illinois, spread widely in the millenium before A.D. 500. This Burial Mound tradition, and the agricultural complex that seems to have been associated with it, had southern origins and was apparently borne by

Siouan- or Iroquoian- speaking peoples. An old and much repeated belief was that the Iroquoian tribes had driven a wedge into the Algonkian area of the Northeast in the last few hundred years, invading the area from the south or southwest. But archeological investigations have revealed that they were old-timers in the Northeast, that the historic Iroquois emerged from an archeological complex known as Owasco, which occupied central and northern New York, extending into Ohio on the west and Pennsylvania in the south. Owasco beginnings go back some thousand years, and its ceramics appear to have origins in the Ohio Hopewell, adding weight to the supposition that the Hopewell archeological tradition was, at least in part, borne by Iroquoian speakers.[16]

Sometime after A.D. 500, a new wave of influences, probably brought by invaders from the south, began to spread from several centers in the Mississippi Valley, the chief one being in the vicinity of the mouth of the Ohio. Agriculture had assumed greater importance, villages or towns appeared, and flat-topped earthen mounds were erected, on which were built temples and other special structures. Many new ceramic and other traits distinguished this new cultural pattern. This Mississippian tradition spread throughout much of the Northeast Woodlands in various degrees, merging with local cultures. The linguistic affiliations of the original bearers of the Mississippian tradition are unknown, although the probabilities would seem to favor their being speakers of Siouan and Caddoan. Willey[17] seems to favor an actual invasion of such peoples of the Northeast Woodlands, though this would not be necessary to account for their influence in the area.

In sum, since first being occupied by Paleo-Indian hunters about 9,000 years ago, the Northeast Woodlands have had a long history of cultural interchange with other regions. It has been the arena for the comings and goings of many peoples, and the setting for the rise and fall of varied cultural systems. The historic tribes were but the final expression of this ancient and tangled past.

HISTORY

Beginning in the last years of the fifteenth century, the Coastal Algonkians had their first fleeting contacts with Europeans as the ships of Cabot, Verrazzano, Cartier, and others probed the Atlantic coast of North America. In the same period, Basque, Portuguese, Breton, and English fishermen and whalers were using the harbors from Maine to the St. Lawrence, and traders soon followed after them. By 1578 about 150 French ships alone were trading with the coastal natives from Newfoundland to the Potomac, and by 1620, when the *Mayflower* landed at Plymouth Rock, more than 500 voyages had been made to New

England.[18] The details of the many confrontations that took place are unknown, but European diseases had spread to the coastal Indians well before the first permanent settlements were made, and it may be presumed that the insatiable appetite for European goods already had been whetted. The superiority of European metal tools was immediately recognized by the Indians, but in order to acquire them, the Indians had to meet the Europeans' demand for furs. The headlong pursuit of furbearers that resulted sparked drastic changes in native cultures, involved them in bitter conflicts, and precipitated widespread movements and migrations.

The first permanent English settlement, Jamestown, was founded in 1607 in the territory of the Powhatan Confederacy in what is now Virginia. In most early settlements, as at Jamestown, there was a brief period of friendship and mutual accommodation, but once the settlers had become established and the colonies had begun to expand, conflict followed. The coastal tribes were soon defeated and forced westward, although a few harmless enclaves were allowed to remain or managed to do so, and their acculturated descendants survive to this day in scattered communities. Withdrawal westward of expropriated tribes caused conflicts with inland natives, but it was the fur trade, with the intrigues of its traders, and the larger international rivalries that were primarily responsible for the first violent territorial, economic, and political upheavals among the tribes and confederacies of the Northeast.

Central to this early history and profoundly important in the competition between England and France in North America was the League of the Iroquois. Apparently organized in response to the presence and influence of Europeans in the last years of the sixteenth century (see below), the Iroquois were strategically located.[19] They had early been drawn into the fur trade, but by the mid-seventeenth century, beaver and other furbearers had become very scarce in their country. Surrounded by enemies and weakened by epidemics, they faced extermination unless they could obtain furs to trade for firearms with which they could continue to maintain themselves. But to do so meant that they had to challenge the French, who, through their Huron allies, monopolized the fur trade of the Great Lakes and beyond. The Iroquois at first attempted to ally themselves with the Hurons, but the French, unwilling to allow their trade to be diverted, managed to thwart them. The Iroquois turned to strong-arm tactics, and as they flanked the French and Huron routes leading down to Montreal and were supplied with firearms by the Dutch and English, they were in a good position to do so. The raids the Iroquois soon made on the fur fleets were devastating. The Hurons responded in 1647 by making an alliance with the Susquehannas and by dispatching a delegation to the Onondagas and Cayugas, with an eye toward making a separate peace with them, which would split the league. These machinations drove the Iroquois into a new kind of warfare. In March, 1649, well before the customary raiding season, a thousand Mohawk and Seneca warriors—probably a far larger force than had ever before been assembled in their wars—fell on the Hurons. Two towns were sacked and burned, and although the Iroquois retreated before attacking their strongest town, the Hurons were completely demoralized. They fled their villages, burning them as they went. Some joined the Tobacco Nation, some the Eries; one entire village even joined the Senecas; and a group of Christian Hurons settled near Quebec under French protection. Another group, which had sought refuge among the Tionontatis, later fled to Lake Superior with some of their hosts. They are known as the Wyandots (after Wendat, the Huron name for themselves).

The Iroquois defeat of the Hurons set a pattern, and in rapid succession they destroyed the Tobacco Nation in 1649; the Neutrals in 1650–51; the Eries, after a struggle of several years, in 1656; and the Susquehannas in 1675, when Maryland broke her alliance with them. Coastal peoples, such as the Delawares, were made subject to the league, and the Iroquois might was soon felt throughout the Ohio Valley and the Great Lakes. By the beginning of the eighteenth century, the league held the balance of power between the French and the British in North America. They soon realized they could not destroy the French, in fact that the French were needed to counter the growing might of the English and their incessant demand for land. The new relationship was made explicit by the Montreal Treaty of 1701 with the French. The Iroquois were able to maintain their uneasy balance through the French and Indian war, and their strength did not falter until the American Revolution, during which the league was finally split. Their military power broken, they were soon engulfed by the advancing frontier.

In the west the Central-Northern Algonkians were drawn into the fur trade in the first years of the seventeenth century, but lacking sufficient firearms, they were no match for the explosive expansion of the well-armed Iroquois. Before mid-century the Sauks, Foxes, Kickapoos, and Potawatomis had fled to Wisconsin where the epidemic-weakened Menominis and Winnebagos could not prevent their settlement. The Shawnees, Miamis, and other Central Algonkians were also displaced during this period, and the need to exploit new fur-bearing areas, the concentration of tribes in the vicinity of trading centers, the conflict between tribes, and the displacement of eastern tribes into the area kept it in a constant state of ferment. In response to the expansion of the fur trade under the French, the Ojibwas moved westward along the north shore of Lake Superior and came into contact and, soon, conflict with the Eastern Dakotas, who they ultimately forced out of Minnesota. In the last years of the eighteenth century, the Battle of Fallen Timbers and the subsequent Treaty of Greenville established American control of the Northwest Territory. The indigenous tribes and the refugee tribes from the east who had settled there were finished as independent peoples. Most of them were moved across the Mississippi in the early decades of the nineteenth century, conquered pawns swept under by the tide of western expansion.

CULTURAL SUMMARY

Subsistence and Material Culture

Throughout the Northeast Woodlands, slash-and-burn agriculture was pursued wherever it was productive, corn, beans, squash, pumpkins, sunflowers, and tobacco being raised in carefully tended gardens. The term "garden" may be misleading, since in the early historic period, the Powhatan, Delawaran, Iroquoian, and probably other tribes had hundreds of acres under cultivation around their villages. Agriculture was then of fundamental importance, particularly to the Coastal Algonkians south of Maine and to the Iroquoian peoples. Agriculture may have been somewhat less important to the Central Algonkian tribes, though no final judgment can yet be made about it, and agriculture was much less important, for environmental reasons, to the Northern Algonkians.[20] Men performed the heavy work of clearing the land, cutting small trees, girdling the larger, and, later, firing the dried brush and trees. Planting and cultivating the crops were primarily women's work. Possessing only crude hoes to work the soil, the people favored river bottom land and sandy river terraces for cultivation, since such soils were generally fertile and easily worked. Dwindling fertility forced abandonment of fields after about a decade of use, and men attempted to clear new ones a year or two before they would be needed. Corn—and most tribes had three or more varieties, including popcorn—was planted in hills, two to three feet apart. Four or more pre-soaked kernels were planted in each hill, and after the corn was well up, beans were also planted in the hills. Squash and pumpkins were planted separately so that they would not be shaded by the corn. The usage of fish for fertilizer by Coastal Algonkians is well known to school children; it seems to have been practiced principally, and perhaps only, by the New England tribes.

Hunting was an important occupation of men, even among tribes that relied heavily on agricultural produce, since skins were needed for clothing. Game was soon exhausted or driven away from the vicinity of villages, so that extended hunting expeditions often had to be made. In some cases, as with the Hurons, there was considerable barter of agricultural foodstuffs with Algonkian hunters to their north for meat and skins. Deer and bear were hunted throughout the woodlands and were, overall, the most important large game animals, although locally others were equally important. Bison were important game animals to prairie tribes, and moose and caribou were hunted on the northern fringes of the area. Elk were present, and smaller mammals from beaver, raccoon, and skunk to squirrel and muskrat were also hunted.

Throughout the Northeast Woodlands with its many lakes and streams, fish and other aquatic foods were an important addition to subsistence, varying, of course, with the locale. Fish were harvested in a diversity of ways: by employing traps, weirs, nets, hook and line; poisoning; spearing; and shooting with the bow and arrow. Oysters, other shellfish, turtles, seals, and other marine mammals were taken by Coastal Algonkians. Fishing, in terms of total available food, was probably more important in the more northern parts of the area where agricultural productivity was low. Fish were taken in winter through the ice, and, seasonally, fish were taken during spawning runs. The Atlantic salmon run, for example, was particularly important to many tribes along New England streams, much of the catch being smoked for future use.

In spring and summer the Coastal and Central Algonkians congregated in small villages, tending their crops. This was also the time of communal hunting when deer and other animals were sought by hunting parties, sometimes using fire, surround, and impounding techniques. If near the sea or a river, the men might also engage in fishing. After the harvest, most Coastal Algonkian villages were largely abandoned as individual families scattered out to their hunting territories for the winter. The men hunted throughout the winter, stalking, trapping, and snaring game. The families returned to their villages in the spring for planting of the gardens.

A great variety of wild plant foods were utilized by the Indians of the Northeast Woodlands, from berries and fruits to roots and tubers. Two plant foods stand out: maple sugar, because it was a unique product; and wild rice, because it assumed a great deal of importance to the subsistence of the Menominis, Winnebagos, and tribes like the Ojibwas who moved into the wild rice region in historic times. While lack of large metal utensils with which to boil down maple sap suggests that it may not have played a large part in subsistence in precontact times, the use of maple syrup or sugar was as widespread as the distribution of the sugar maple. When the sap began to rise in early spring, the trees were tapped by fitting them with flat or grooved pieces of wood from which the sap dripped into bark containers. The sap was collected, boiled down in ceramic vessels to be used as a drink, mixed with other foods, used as seasoning or confection, or reduced to sugar. In solid form it could be stored for long periods of time, and it was an excellent quick-energy, easy-to-carry food for the warrior or hunter.

Wild rice (*Zizania aquatica*) is a cereal grass unrelated to the domesticated rice of the Old World. It grows in shallow ponds, lakes, and swampy places from the Atlantic Coast to the Mississippi Valley. Though used widely in the Northeast Woodlands, it was particularly abundant in the lake country west of Lake Michigan, and the Menominis and Winnebagos depended heavily on it in precontact days. Ripening in the late summer, the wild rice was harvested from canoes. Men poled their craft through the thick rice beds, and women sitting in the bow facing the stern, pulled the heavy heads of grain over the gunwales with a stick, knocking the grain into the boat with another stick. After cleaning the harvest, they spread out the rice to dry, then parched it over a fire to cure it and loosen the husks. The husking process was accomplished by putting the grain in a skin-lined hole, a man then tramping, or "dancing the rice." Among the Ojibwas, family plots were marked off by tying bunches of unripened grain together, and this also seems to have been done to protect the unharvested rice from storms and birds.[21]

The Indians of the Northeast were village-dwelling people, most Algonkian tribes being composed of a number of small, relatively permanent villages or hamlets, which, however, might be partially deserted seasonally as families dispersed to their hunting territories in the winter. The best-known house type of the area was the longhouse of the Iroquoians, which also was adopted, to some degree, by neighboring Algonkians, such as the Delawares. The usual longhouse was some sixty feet long and about eighteen feet wide and high. With gabled or oval roof, the longhouse was constructed on a framework of poles over which were tied slabs of elm or cedar bark. The bark was overlapped and sewed together, so that it may be described as a shingled dwelling. A wide hallway split the interior, with individual families occupying sections, or compartments, along each side. Compartments were furnished with sleeping platforms and shelves, and families opposite one another across the central hallway shared common fireplaces. At the ends of the longhouse were storage areas for the common supply of dried corn, other food, and firewood.

Many Algonkian tribes built round or oval, dome-shaped wigwams, covered with mats by the prairie tribes of the Central Algonkian area, and with strips of bark by the others. Besides central fireplaces, wigwams were furnished with sleeping platforms, storage areas, and the like. Conical bark or skin-covered wigwams were erected as less-permanent structures in hunting camps, and throughout the area a number of other buildings, including ceremonial and sweat lodges, menstrual huts, and summer houses, were constructed. Longhouses and wigwams provided excellent shelter from the elements, but they were not ideal dwellings. They were dark and smoky; they often burned down; and mice, fleas, and body lice plagued the inhabitants.

The Indians of the Northeast Woodlands were adept in the usage of bark, plant fibers, and wood for utensils, baskets, mats, cordage, and other items. Their rather simple pottery vessels and their varied chipped and ground stone tools were quickly replaced by superior European equivalents. But some of their manufactures, such as snowshoes, toboggans, and birchbark canoes, have been taken over by whites and continue to be useful and popular. Birchbark was not available throughout the southern sections of the Northeast, and the dugout replaced the canoe in these regions, although elm and other barks replaced birch bark for some purposes. The bow and arrow, war club, or tomahawk (some with spiked, beaked, and balled heads), and spears were the basic weapons of men. The basic agricultural implements of the women were short-handled wooden, shell, or scapula hoes.

Clothing throughout the region was of skins. Men wore moccasins, leggings, breechcloths, and shirts, omitting everything but the breechcloth in hot weather. Similarly, women wore moccasins, leggings, skirts or shirts, all except the latter being discarded in hot weather. In cold weather both sexes added fur robes, wearing the fur side inside for maximum warmth. Clothing was ornamented with dyed porcupine quills and, with the advent of European traders, glass beads. Decoration of clothing and various objects was generally in distinctive curvilinear floral patterns. Feather mantles were used as robes, and for bedding by the Delawares[22] and other Northeast Woodland people, though the trait is usually associated with the Southeast. Tattooing was practiced principally by men, occasionally by women; and both sexes also painted their bodies in different colors and in varied styles. Facial and body hair was generally plucked out, and a number of hairstyles were in vogue. A scalp lock style, in which all the head hair was removed except for a long lock on the crown, was widespread among warriors. Also common was a roached style in which only a strip of hair was allowed to remain from forehead to neck.

Necklaces, earrings, and wristlets of hair, bone, native copper, colorful stones, feathers, and shell were used for ornamentation, including the small drilled shells that became known as wampum. The term is derived from an Algonquian language of New England and means roughly "strings of white shell beads,"[23] but is employed for both the lighter and darker shells. The advent of metal awls and nails greatly eased the drilling of small cut pieces of shell, and strings or belts of wampum came to play an important role in intertribal affairs, serving as symbols of agreement between Indian tribes and between Indians and whites. The usage of wampum as a medium of exchange was a historic accretion to its precontact ceremonial and ornamental function, hence its modern connotation.

Another accompaniment of all serious political and ceremonial, and most religious occasions was the ritualized smoking of tobacco in pipes. Smoking was generally recognized as a means of communicating with the supernatural world. Europeans first encountered the custom among the Atlantic coastal tribes, but it had virtually continent-wide distribution. In the Northeast area a pipe was also carried by messengers and emissaries desiring to parley with enemies or strangers, serving as a sort of passport. The long stems, often profusely ornamented and painted with widely understood symbolism, were attached to ceramic or soft stone bowls that were often decorated with animals or other figures. These "peace pipes" have come to be known under their French designation, *calumet*.[24]

Social Organization

The varied ways of exploiting the diverse environments of the Northeast Woodlands were reflected in an assortment of ways in which its societies were organized. The seminomadic hunters, gatherers, and fishermen on the northern margins of the area lay at one extreme, the Ojibwas, Ottawas, and Algonkins being subdivided into many autonomous but interrelated bands composed of a number of totemic patrilineal clans. Bands were loosely organized, having little formal structure, their members living together but briefly during the year.[25] At the other extreme were the sedentary villagers of the Iroquoian area, with strong political organizations at the village and tribal level, and often linked with other tribes in confederacies.

The basic unit of Iroquois society was a matrilineal extended family, which occupied a longhouse. Composed of nuclear families related to each other through the female line, the activities of the family were normally directed by an older woman who was a grandmother, mother, older sister, or maternal aunt of the other women. On marriage, men moved into the longhouse of their wives, but remained outsiders in the sense that they acquired no property rights in it, and inheritance of property, goods, and political position was in the maternal line. These maternal households held their agricultural lands in common, the women laboring together in the fields, sharing the fruits of their labor.

Several related households were apt to build their longhouses side by side in a village, but the matrilineal clans of which they were a part were not localized. Each of the clans, and their number varied among the various Iroquois tribes, was usually represented in every village. Most clans, claiming descent from a common female ancestor, were named for animals such as bear or turtle, but clan members did not regard their eponyms as ancestral, nor were they forbidden to eat them. Clansmen aided one another and avenged the murder of one of their members, and each clan had its own council and leaders. Not surprisingly, women played important roles in the management of clan affairs. With the exception of the Mohawks and Oneidas, the Iroquois also possessed moieties, the clans being grouped into one or another of two divisions. Moieties were exogamous and responsible for holding burial rites and the condolence ceremony for members of the opposite moiety. They also had many other competitive and reciprocal functions in games and ceremonies.

Some of the Coastal Algonkians, such as the Delawares, were similar to the Iroquoians in having matrilineal clans, which, in their case, were grouped into three exogamous phratries. Among the Central-Northern Algonkians, before their societies were disrupted by the fur trade, most, if not all, groups appear to have been organized into bands, composed of patrilineal clans. Among some of the more southerly groups, who were more intensive farmers and so more sedentary, "village" rather than "band" may be a more appropriate term. Among some groups, such as the Menominis, clans were linked together in phratries, and moieties were common. Among some of the Prairie tribes, the Sauks and Foxes for example, moiety membership was assigned by order of birth rather than by clan membership.[26]

The Iroquoian peoples and some of the Coastal Algonkians stand apart from others in the Northeast Woodlands by their tendency to form confederacies, the League of the Iroquois being by far the best known. The Huron and Neutral confederacies appear to have been similar to the League of the Iroquois, though historic events and geographic accident combined to magnify the importance and nature of the latter. Some of the Coastal Algonkians also knew confederacies, but their relationships to those of the Iroquoians, if any, are obscure.

Each of the five Iroquois tribes occupied a definite territory separated somewhat from the others, spoke a distinct dialect, and differed from one another in other minor ways. Each had a tribal council representing its clans, which also represented the tribe in the Great Council of the Confederacy. Tribal matters were fully discussed by the council before decisions were reached, and action depended on a consensus of opinion. In addition to the hereditary sachems, there was another class of leaders known as Pine Tree chiefs. These were men who through successful exploits in battle had risen to positions of authority. The advent of white men and the tremendously increased emphasis on warfare enhanced their power, so that at times they were able to challenge the authority of the ancient establishment.

The League of the Iroquois was made up of a council of forty-nine or fifty sachems, the five tribes, however, having unequal representation. The Onondagas, for example, had fourteen sachems, including the head of the Great Council, while the Senecas counted only eight. But since each tribe voted as a unit and all decisions of the council had to be unanimous, the unequal representation was of no great consequence. The sachems were men, although a woman might serve as a regent for a small boy, and they were hereditary within the matrilineages and clans. Some lineages did not have direct representation, though in practice they do not seem to have been disenfranchised. The women nominated the successor to a deceased sachem from among the eligible men of their lineage and clan, the position often falling to a younger brother or to the son of a sister of a former sachem. The role of women in selecting sachems, deposing those who proved unsatisfactory, and, on occasion, serving as regents, gave them exceptional power and authority. The Iroquois probably came as close as any people ever has to achieving a matriarchate.

The Great Council met at Onondaga (near modern Syracuse) at least once a year and more frequently when there was pressing business. It was responsible only for external affairs, each of the five tribes completely controlling their own internal affairs. There are differences of opinion about when the League of the Iroquois was founded, but the probabilities seem to favor establishment in its modern form in the latter part of the sixteenth century.[1] In its essentials the league was an agreement among five tribes to end the chronic feuding among themselves and to establish peace among all Indians on a basis of equality and brotherhood. It was effective in securing peace among the five tribes, but in relationships with others, it ushered in an era of bloody struggle. The Iroquois themselves believed that the league had a divine origin, that the prophet Deganawidah, a Huron refugee born of a virgin mother and an incarnation of the Great Spirit, recruited Hiawatha, a Mohawk chief or shaman, as a disciple and that Hiawatha traveled among the tribes and eventually persuaded them to enter into the Great Peace. Longfellow, incidentally, borrowed the name of Hiawatha for the central character of his famous poem, although it deals with Ojibwa and not Iroquois legends.

The political organization of the Coastal Algonkians was, on the whole, considerably more rudimentary than that of the Iroquoian tribes. Scattered in smaller, more dispersed villages, the appearance of confederacies seems to have been a response to particularly able leaders and, perhaps, to the presence of Europeans. The best known of the early confederacies was that of Powhatan, named for its ruler, who is probably better known as the father of Pocahontas. Powhatan forged a confederacy, or perhaps it shoud be described as a conquest state, that at one time included some 200 villages. But unlike the Five Nations Confederacy, the tributary villages seem to have been linguistically and culturally homogeneous. In 1622 Opechancanough, Powhatan's successor, led a raid that resulted in the death of 350 settlers. The war that followed destroyed the confederacy, and by the mid-seventeenth century only a few Powhatan remnants survived. None of the other Coastal Algonkian confederacies seems to have been older or more durable than that of the Powhatans.

Among the Central Algonkians, political organization was poorly developed in the sense that village-bands of several hundred persons seem to have been the largest grouping attained, tribes existing only in the sense that their members shared a common culture. During the summer gardening season and for a spring buffalo hunt, members of the band were together, separating during other seasons into smaller family groups. Village-bands maintained loosely structured councils, led by chiefs who had little real authority. They were aided by "criers" who made public announcements, presided at various gatherings, and the like. In addition to the civil chiefs, there was also a war chief, the office falling to an eminent warrior. The war chief also had an assistant and commanded a body of warriors who served as police, controlling communal hunts and maintaining order in the villages.

In the Northeast Woodlands, women have often been depicted as experiencing little difficulty in giving birth to children, then quickly resuming their customary activities. Actually, bearing pain stoically was widely admired, and among the Iroquois, the role of women during childbirth was compared to that of warriors in battle. Mortality at birth was apparently high for both women and infants, even though experienced midwives with much practical know-how assisted with the delivery. Soon after birth, Iroquoian mothers gave their babies a name drawn from a stock of clan names. Since names could not be shared with living persons, the child's name was publicly announced at the first opportunity. A new name was assumed at maturity. Among the Delawares and other Coastal Algonkians, adult names were used during important ceremonies, but had limited use otherwise. Adults might also change their names for others they thought more fitting.

Until children could walk they were confined to a cradle board, and they were nursed until they were about two years old. Children were seldom punished physically, and among the Iroquois, men paid little attention to their own offspring. Girls throughout the Northeast Woodlands were isolated at the time of their first menstruation. Boys by the time they reached puberty, particularly among the Algonkians, were under increasing coercion from their kinsmen. Among the Delawares, for example, boys were exposed to increasingly difficult physical ordeals, such as bathing in ice-filled streams, and they were forced to drink noxious and intoxicating concoctions. They were also shamed, ridiculed, and insulted until, ultimately, they were driven from the village to seek supernatural guidance. The belief was that a humbled, miserable boy was better able to induce a supernatural being or to force a supernatural being to feel sorry for him and come to his assistance. Most boys while in this self-imposed exile did succeed in acquiring a guardian spirit, who guided him in his future career and gave him the self-confidence he so badly needed.

Premarital affairs were the usual and expected habit of boys and girls in the Northeast Woodlands. Iroquois marriages were arranged by mothers, without necessarily consulting their children. Soon after a youth had demonstrated his proficiency as a hunter, his mother selected a likely girl of another clan and the opposite moiety, consulted with her mother, and, with an exchange of presents, arranged the match. Feasts in which the bride supplied the cornmeal and the groom the meat or fish sealed the marriage. The Iroquois were monogamous, and marital fidelity was a highly regarded virtue. Although divorce was easy for either partner, it seems not to have been so common as one might think, since it reflected on the wisdom of a couple's mothers.

Unlike some of the northerly Algonkians who sometimes found it necessary to abandon the aged or infirm, the Iroquois were able to care for their old people and those who were ill. Following death, the body was painted and dressed in his best clothing. Members of the opposite moiety carried the corpse to a clan cemetery, where it was interred. The Iroquois believed the ghosts of the dead were dangerous and might cause sickness, or plague the living in other ways, so they placated the spirits with gifts of food. Following a period of mourning, relatives and friends gathered for a feast, after which it was thought that the soul left for a spirit land in the west.

Warfare

Warfare was important and chronic among the Algonkian tribes, but it seems not to have been as central to their cultures or to have had the impact on their lives that it did among the Iroquoians.[28] Woodland warfare originally was waged neither for territory nor for commercial gain. It was, instead, small-scale, seasonal, relatively nonlethal feuding; and its ritualized rules were observed by the combatants. It was not warfare waged by invading Iroquoians against resident Algonquian-speaking peoples, as the older view once had it; much of the Iroquoian feuding was with other Iroquoians, not with the neighboring Algonkians. It was, in brief, a form of primitive warfare that in the early historic period was much magnified and altered by the onslaught of Europeans. The success of the League of the Iroquois from this point of view may be regarded as due to their breaking of the old rules of the game, adopting a more modern, lethal form of war, the principal aim of which was commercial gain.

Among the Iroquoian peoples, boys were expected to become warriors, and from an individual point of view, boys wanted to do so as this was the way to acquire status and prestige. Eminent warriors recruited war parties by going from one village to another, explaining their plans and distributing presents. The purpose of war parties was ostensibly to gain revenge on an enemy for past wrongs, so that Iroquoian warfare may be thought of as a form of feuding writ large. Although five or six hundred Huron or Iroquois warriors were apt to be in the field in the summer, they were usually divided into numerous small parties. Only occasionally were Iroquoian peoples able to generate large-scale attacks in which several hundred warriors laid siege to an enemy village for a week or so. In such cases, after a pitched battle in which both sides suffered a few casualties and lost some prisoners, the attackers withdrew. Ordinarily, small war parties of five or six warriors hid near an enemy's village, hoping to waylay an enemy to kill or capture him. Particularly adventuresome warriors might sneak into an enemy village under cover of darkness in an attempt to set it on fire or to kill someone.

The main aim of warriors, to which attached the most prestige, was the capture of prisoners and, particularly, warriors in the prime of life. Captive women and children, unless needed for adoption to replace losses, were normally killed, their heads or scalps being taken as trophies. Shortly after capture, a ritual was begun that occasionally ended in the escape or adoption of the prisoner, but usually terminated in his lingering death. Normally a prisoner was bound with special thongs brought along for the purpose; his fingernails were pulled out, the fingers used in drawing a bow were bitten or chopped off, and he might also undergo other relatively minor mutilations. His captors lectured him on the wrongs he and his people had committed and ordered him to sing his war song. Each warrior had his own song, and in order to demonstrate his contempt for death and his captors, he often sang it continuously throughout his ordeal. The war chiefs who had organized the expeditions determined to which village a captive should go, and often the captive was put under the care of a family who had recently lost one of their warriors. Among the Iroquois, those male captives whom some family wished to adopt were forced to run the gantlet, a widespread custom in the Northeast. The captive was made to run between two lines of the village's inhabitants, who beat him and attempted to knock him down with whips, sticks, and whatever else came to hand. Those who failed to negotiate the course were killed; those who passed were given new names, were adopted by a family, and ultimately might become tribal members in good standing.[29]

Those captives who were reserved for torture were put through an excruciating series of ordeals, often prolonged for five or six days, fixed to a scaffold, and killed. If the prisoner had been brave, his roasted heart was eaten by young warriors in order to gain his courage, and his body might be cooked and eaten. Torture of prisoners, at least among the Hurons, was a sacrifice to the god of war, and was undoubtedly an attenuated form of a sacrificial cult performed in the Southeast and ultimately traceable to Mesoamerica.[30]

Religious and Ceremonial Life

The religious beliefs and practices of the Iroquoian tribes and confederacies seem to have been quite similar to one another, though they are imperfectly known, and in some respects stand in marked contrast to those of their Algonkian neighbors. The differences follow principally from the more complex, more formally structured society of the Iroquoians involving larger groups of people, which made possible an elaborate round of tribal ceremonies. Many of the Algonkians, on the other hand, lived in smaller, scattered groups, which seldom were able to congregate for prolonged ceremonies. The differences in basic beliefs do not, however, loom so large. Belief in a rather vaguely conceived supreme being, or Great Spirit, for example, was widely held in the Northeast Woodlands by both Iroquoians and Algonkians.

Among the Iroquois the Great Spirit was a creator of other supernatural beings, as well as animals, plants, in fact, the earth and everything on it. The Great Spirit had a twin brother who was his malevolent counterpart, an Evil Spirit who was responsible for the creation of monsters, venomous snakes, obnoxious plants, destructive natural forces, and various misfortunes of the human condition. Among the Hurons, these twins were the sons or grandsons of *Aataentsic*, the first woman on earth and the mother of mankind. She was thought to have many of the evil qualities of her malevolent offspring.[31] Others in the Iroquois pantheon included a rain or thunder being; a sun god associated with war and hunting; a spirit of the wind; and the Three Sisters, known collectively as "Our Life," or "Our Supporters," who represented corn, beans, and squash, and who were thought of as congenial, beautiful women. There were also a great many lesser supernatural beings, including a horde of little people akin to fairies or elves; a group of Stone Giants; various monsters, witches, demons, ghosts of the dead; and others.

The supernatural world of the Coastal Algonkians was, it seems, much like that of the Iroquoians. The Delaware pantheon, for example, was headed by a "Great Power," or "Creator," who was rather remote and somewhat removed from the affairs of mankind. But he had appointed a number of agents, so to speak, who had created the world and all on it. They included celestial, thunder, Earth Mother, and the Four Directions deities. One deity, the Mask Being, was impersonated in an annual or semiannual Big House Ceremony, and the Delawares also recognized a multitude of lesser deities, including Mother Corn, animal and plant spirits, and local genii.[32]

In addition to a teeming world of animistic beings, the peoples of the Northeast Woodlands held rather mystical beliefs in an impersonal, inanimate supernatural force that could permeate nature, animals, and objects. To the Iroquois it was known as *orenda*, and to the Algonkians as *manito*. This force has sometimes been confused with the Great Spirit, and though the Indian seldom quibbled about such fine distinctions, there is justification for distinguishing the two kinds of beliefs.

Reflecting the importance of agriculture in their lives, the Iroquois held six or more great public religious festivals associated with crops and the harvesting of wild fruits and berries. Week-long celebrations were held when corn was planted and again when the green corn was first fit to eat. A brief festival was held when the corn was harvested, and lesser celebrations were held when the beans, raspberries, and strawberries ripened. The Iroquois also held a week-long mid-winter ceremony in which the sacrifice of a white dog played a prominent part. It was basically a ceremony of renewal in which old fires were put out and new ones kindled, and during it individuals were able to ease emotional tensions in a kind of group therapy by asking others to interpret their dreams. They believed that the fulfillment of a person's desires as revealed to him in dreams was essential to well-being, so that men might retire from public office, have themselves tortured, or behave in other extraordinary ways, depending upon their dream experiences.[33] The Iroquois had a number of shamanistic or medicine societies that were concerned with curing, the best known of these being the False Face Society. In spring and again in the fall, members covered their faces with grotesque masks, going from house to house to evict the spirits that caused disease, afterwards holding a dance. There were other equally important medicine societies or lodges, each appealing to certain deities or spirits, each possessing its own songs, dances, rituals, and regalia.

Among the Coastal Algonkians, the Delaware's Big House Ceremony, which was apparently synthesized in historic times from older phratry and family rites, was like the Iroquois mid-winter festival in being, at least in part, a rite of renewal, although its main theme was one of thanksgiving.[34] The major religious ceremony of the Central and Northern Algonkian tribes was the Medicine Lodge Society, or *Midewiwin*. A graded curing society that held meetings annually or semiannually, men joined in order to be cured or in response to a dream or vision. Public dances and ceremonies, which took place in special lodges, involved trances, the "shooting" of one another with shells, or other magical performances. Initiation consisted of receiving instruction, sweat bathing, and being magically "shot" with a white shell.[35]

NOTES

[1] See, for example, Handlin (1963, 16, 64); and Nevins and Commager, (1951, 5). For a review of the portrayal of North American Indians in general American history books and texts, see Newcomb (1971, 45–62).

[2] Hallowell (1957); Josephy (1968, 31–35).

[3] Wissler (1938, 236). In his inclusive Eastern Maize food area, an Eastern Woodland was set apart and further subdivided into Northern, Iroquoian, Central Algonkin, and Eastern Algonkin areas. Kroeber (1939, 88–89) has gone somewhat further, recognizing eight subareas within approximately the same geographical region.

[4] There is no single study of the Northeast Woodlands as a whole, but there is a considerable body of literature dealing with parts of the area and specific tribes. See Ritzenthaler and Ritzenthaler (1970); Flannery (1939); Kinietz (1940); and Quimby (1960).

[5] Speck (1940, 21–24).

[6] Newcomb (1956a).

[7] Tooker (1964); Trigger (1969).

[8] For basic Iroquois works, see Morgan (1851); Beauchamp (1905); Speck (1944; 1955); Fenton (1940; 1941; 1953); Hunt (1940); Noon (1949).

[9] Callender (1962); Kinietz (1940).

[10] Jenness (1934, 277); for Ojibwas, see Landes (1937; 1968); for Potawatomis, Landis (1970) and Ritzenthaler (1953).

[11] Kroeber (1939, 88–97) subdivided the Central Algonkian area into a Wisconsin, or Wild-Rice; Ohio Valley; and Northern Great Lakes. See also Callender (1962, xii–xiii); Skinner (1923); Landes (1937, 52); Fisher (1946).

[12] Skinner (1924, 9–12) claimed them to be Prairie Potawatomis, but others argue that they were Peoria or some other division of the Illinois (Michelson, 1934), or Kickapoos (Wilson, 1956). Basic sources for the Menominis are Hoffman (1893); Skinner (1913; 1921); Keesing (1939); for the Winnebagos, see Radin (1916).

[13] Haas (1958a, b); this linguistic relationship has been examined by Willey (1958) in terms of the archeological knowledge of the region and some intriguing possibilities suggested. Note, however, that he (1966, 294) has retreated

somewhat from his earlier position. For other summaries, see Ford and Willey (1941); Griffin (1946; 1952); Fairbanks (1949).

[14] Willey (1958, 267); Caldwell (1958).

[15] Spaulding (1952).

[16] Willey (1966, 310); Griffin (1944); see also Ritchie (1938; 1961); MacNeish (1952).

[17] Willey (1958, 269–70).

[18] Connolly, as quoted in Wallace (1961, 95).

[19] Hunt (1940).

[20] Kroeber (1939, 148) asserts that for the "East," as a whole, "there is little to argue that the culture was leaning very fundamentally on agriculture."

[21] Ritzenthaler and Ritzenthaler (1970, 22–26); see also Jenks (1898).

[22] Newcomb (1956a, 26).

[23] Hodge (1907–1910, 904–9); see also Snyderman (1955); Speck (1919).

[24] Hodge (1907–1910, 191–95).

[25] For a review of the "atomistic" versus "collective" controversy over Chippewa social organization, see Hickerson (1967).

[26] See Callender (1962) for a study of Central Algonkian social structure.

[27] Wallace (1961, 89) says, for example, "The coming together of these five nations in the Iroquois Confederacy was not a single act of creation at a determinable moment in time. The 'completed cabin' (The Longhouse) was probably the culmination of a long process of development during which smaller leagues had been formed."

[28] A thoughtful review of Iroquoian warfare may be found in Trigger's (1969) monograph on the Hurons.

[29] Morgan (1851, 334).

[30] Knowles (1940).

[31] Trigger (1969, 92).

[32] Speck (1931).

[33] Wallace (1958).

[34] Newcomb (1956a).

[35] Hoffman (1891).

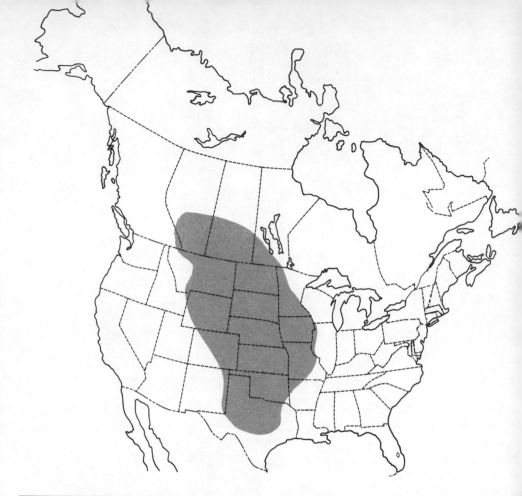

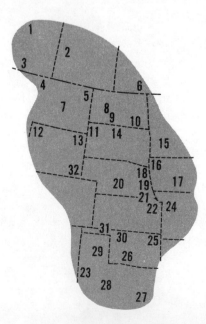

1. Sarsi
2. Plains Cree
3. Blackfoot
4. Gros Ventre
5. Assiniboin
6. Plains Ojibwa
7. Crow
8. Hidatsa
9. Mandan
10. Yanktonai
11. Teton Dakota
12. Wind River Shoshoni
13. Cheyenne
14. Arikara
15. Santee Dakota
16. Yankton Dakota
17. Iowa
18. Ponca
19. Omaha
20. Pawnee
21. Oto
22. Kansa
23. Mescalero
24. Missouri
25. Osage
26. Kichai
27. Tonkawa
28. Lipan Apache
29. Comanche
30. Wichita
31. Kiowa and Kiowa Apache
32. Arapaho

FOUR

PLAINS BISON HUNTERS

Of all the native peoples of North America, it is the Indians of the Plains who have best captured the public's attention, so much so that the war-bonneted Plains warrior has become the epitome of all Indians everywhere.[1] There are good reasons for this: the Plains Indians were among the last natives of the continent to be conquered, and many of them went down to defeat in what has often been described as a blaze of glory. According to the American ethos, if one is to succumb, this is the way to do it. However distorted such an image may be to the Indian whose grandmother was massacred by the cavalry at Wounded Knee, no amount of protest is likely to alter this romantic interpretation. Even if this aspect of Plains Indian life had not excited the public fancy, the nature of their cultures would have. Plains Indians were participants in a tradition that has long been celebrated in the Western world. They were horsemen and warriors, some were among the most skilled and daring riders the world has ever known, and the high career of warrior beckoned every man. It was inevitable that the Plains Indian should be assigned a place in this noble tradition. That the culture exemplified by the mounted warrior was dependent upon animals introduced by Europeans and was thus derivative, that it flourished only briefly, and that some Indians of the Plains followed to the end a different star are really of small consequence. However distorted the stereotype, the Plains Indians will probably remain *the* Indian.

Eastward from the foothills of the Rockies, stretching away to the vicinity of the Mississippi, and from the Canadian provinces of Alberta and Saskatchewan southward almost to the distant Rio Grande and the Mexican border lie the vast interior Plains of North America.[2]

Though more dessicated on the western border and interrupted by the Black Hills of South Dakota and the low Wichita Mountains of Oklahoma, the Plains are primarily a vast, treeless, subhumid or semiarid plain, gently sloping to the east and southeast. The more arid High Plains in the lee of the Rockies average between ten and fifteen inches of moisture annually, but precipitation increases toward the east, the vicinity of the 97th meridian receiving between twenty-five and thirty inches. Periods of adequate or abundant moisture are followed by months or years of fierce droughts, and today, as in the past, these unpredictable extremes have been critically important to human utilization of the Plains.

The northern and central Plains are drained by the Missouri-Mississippi river systems, the Missouri flowing eastward in the northern Plains to be joined by the Yellowstone, then swinging south and southeastward along the eastern margin of the Plains. The Niobrara, Platte, Republican, and other streams flow eastward across the Plains to join the Missouri. To the south, the Arkansas and its tributaries drain much of the south-central Plains, and the Red, Brazos, and Colorado the southernmost Plains. These river valleys act as avenues up which many plants and animals have extended their ranges, and a preponderant share of the cultural influences that affected its prehistoric and historic peoples also came up these river valley highways.

The pioneer distrust of what was known as the Great American Desert was the response of men from the well-watered woodlands of the East to the endless, unfamiliar openness of the Plains. But it was not a barren waste, and for those who could adjust to its violent moods and adapt to its imperious demands, it could be an abundant, rewarding land. Though the short, scattered grama and buffalo grasses of the High Plains might seem inferior to lush eastern meadows, they were highly nutritious, cured naturally, and supported immense herds of bison, pronghorn antelope, and other animals. In the timbered river valleys were deer and elk, and there were black and grizzly bears, wolves and coyotes, jackrabbits and cottontails, many other mammals, innumerable birds, fish in the streams, and a rich variety of other animals as well as plants.

Chief among the grazing animals and crucially important to the Indian occupation of the Plains was the bison, or American buffalo (*Bison bison*), a gregarious relative of domestic cattle and other *Bovidae*.[3] Bison ranged over much of the continent east of the Rockies and north of the Rio Grande, but they were most at home in the Plains. Nobody will ever know how many bison there were, although one expert has tentatively—and by his own admission, conservatively—set the figure at 60 million.[4] During the late summer rut, fantastically large herds congregated to literally blacken the Plains from horizon to horizon. Largest of North America's big game animals, bulls average about 1,400 pounds, with a maximum of 2,000 pounds. They may stand up to 6 feet high at the shoulders. Cows are somewhat smaller, averaging about 700 pounds. Both sexes carry curved horns on massive, low-slung heads, and despite a heavy hump and a body that appears massive and ungainly, bison are not as slow or ponderous as one might suppose. Given a slight lead to begin with, they can outrun good horses and can outdistance an average horse.

Bison are temperamental, unpredictable creatures often described as stupid and obstinate. Hunters were sometimes able to shoot entire standing herds, the sight and sounds of their falling fellows not alarming the unharmed. At other times they stampeded, with no apparent provocation; they were blind, headlong surges, terrifying to those who might be in their path and incredible to those who saw them plunge off cliffs or pass over gullies on the bodies of other fallen or mired bison. Historic Indian hunters, as had generations of their predecessors, took advantage of this characteristic, stampeding bison to reap a bloody harvest. But one characteristic of bison greatly aided his survival, especially before the introduction of horses and firearms. This was the unpredicatable movements of the herds. In winter the entire bison range shifted to the south several hundred miles, then back again to the north in the summer; but they followed no regular migration routes, and their movements can only be described as capricious and erratic. Consequently, hunters could not lay in wait along game trails or migration routes, but had to seek out the sometimes elusive herds.

PREHISTORY[5]

As we have seen, men first had come into the Plains as hunters of large game animals, and until the last wild bison were slaughtered in the last decades of the nineteenth century, men continued to exist there as hunters. Whether this ancient heritage was a direct one may never be known, although historic Indians continued to use some hunt techniques, such as bison jumps, that had been employed a hundred centuries earlier. While the story of Plains prehistory is intimately linked to hunters, and particularly bison hunters, the dominant and most successful prehistoric people in the Plains practiced a dual subsistence of hunting and farming. This adaptation, played out in an environment characterized by recurring cycles of drought, is the essence of the story of Plains prehistory.

About the beginning of the Christian era, influences from the Woodland tradition of the East began to be felt in the eastern Plains, and they ultimately spread up the Missouri River system virtually to the Rockies. Known as the Plains Woodland culture, and varying somewhat from place to place, it was primarily a hunting-gathering culture, though there was some knowledge of corn and squash. Coarse pottery, mostly in the form of undecorated or cord-marked jars with rounded or pointed bottoms, was characteristic, and there are indications of small, semipermanent villages. The dead were sometimes interred in small burial mounds.

In the early centuries of the Christian era, the Hopewell culture reached its zenith in southern Ohio, and its influence carried into the central Plains. Hopewell sites are found on the Missouri River in the Kansas City vicinity, and southward to northeastern Oklahoma. Corn and beans have been found in these Hopewell sites, grown by people who lived in small but relatively permanent villages. The dead were buried in rather crude stone chambers under earthen mounds; storage pits are characteristic of these sites; and pottery and other artifacts indicate affiliations to Hopewell sites in the East.

But it was not until almost a millenium into the Christian era that a widely successful, strongly agricultural way of life was established in the eastern Plains. Known as the Plains Village tradition,[6] it drew heavily on the Mississippian culture to the east, but was a unique adjustment to the Plains environment. Subsistence was based partly on hunting, primarily the bison; and agriculture was of much greater significance than it had been earlier. The principal crops were corn, beans, and squash grown in river bottom gardens and cultivated with digging sticks and bison scapula hoes. Pottery was plentiful and varied, much of it showing affinity to Mississippian forms. Small, scattered villages were located on bluffs or terraces overlooking the fields and were sometimes protected by ditches and palisades. Houses were usually rectangular, earth-covered or mud-plastered structures.

There were a number of varying expressions of the Plains Village cultural pattern, reflecting the diverse origins of the people who had moved into the Plains from the East and Southeast. By the fifteenth century the Plains Village way of life had spread almost across the Plains to the Rockies. But sometime after mid-century a devastating and apparently long-continued drought forced a general abandonment of the western villages. The succession from protohistoric archeological complexes to historic tribes has been somewhat obscured by the migrations and turmoil that resulted, although it is clear that the historic village tribes emerged from this background.[7] The resiliency and success of this kind of adaptation to the Plains environment is indicated by the fact that the village tribes had reached a peak of prosperity, cultural efflorescence, and dominance by the time Europeans arrived in the sixteenth century.[8] The reason for their success is not difficult to find.

It was a more flexible adaptation to the Plains environment than that of the purely nomadic prehorse hunting cultures. If the bison herds could not be located, the hunter faced starvation. But if the Plains villagers had a poor hunt, they could still rely on the produce of their gardens. Or, if their crops did poorly, they could pursue the hunt more diligently.

The prehistoric peoples who followed a purely nomadic hunting career in the Plains are less well known than the semisedentary farmers, because they were less numerous, were scattered, and had few possessions to leave as evidence of their presence. Nevertheless, a considerable number of archeological sites indicate that the ancient bison-hunting life persisted for thousands of years, particularly in the western Plains where farming was difficult or impossible.

HISTORY

In 1541, when Coronado led his expedition from the Pueblo country of what is now New Mexico into the Plains in search of the riches of Quivira, the country from Llano Estacado of northeastern New Mexico and the Texas Panhandle to the Wichita villages (Quivira) of south-central Kansas, was inhabited by pedestrian bison hunters, most, if not all, of whom were Apaches.[9] They knew this immense country intimately, and their culture was well adjusted to its demands. They depended on bison for the bulk of their food and utilized them for tipis, clothing, and utensils. They followed the bison herds with the aid of dogs that transported their meager belongings. It was the ancestral cultural type from which the later horse-using Plains nomadic cultures were in large part descended, though, paradoxically, by the nineteenth century few Apaches continued to pursue it.[10] From 1675 until their dispersal in 1725, these Plains Apaches are known archeologically as the Dismal River Aspect.[11] In this period they inhabited the High Plains from the Black Hills to northern New Mexico and the Texas Panhandle. The identity of the pedestrian bison hunters on the High Plains north of the Plains Apaches is not as well known because by the time European explorers penetrated the region, the natives were already mounted, and tribal movements and migrations may have already been under way. Shoshonis appear to have hunted north and west of the Apaches in Wyoming; and in the far northwestern Plains, the Blackfeet tribes (Piegan, Blood, and the Blackfoot proper) were, it seems certain, among the prehorse bison hunters.[12]

To the east of the Apaches, Blackfeet, and other bison hunters, and concentrated along the river valleys were the Plains Village tribes. Those tribes that had ancient roots in the Plains, and who were generally farther west, may be set apart from more easterly tribes, many of whom were but recently arrived, and who consequently shared many traits with Eastern Woodlands and Southeastern peoples. Thus, the Arikaras, Mandans, and Hidatsas located in the middle Missouri country, stretching from the mouth of the Niobrara to the mouth of the Yellowstone in the Dakotas, were old residents, constituted a cultural or subcultural unit, and are often thought of as the typical Plains Village tribes. To their south, in east-central Nebraska, concentrated a short distance above the confluence of the Loup and the Platte were the Pawnee villages. Caddoan-speaking, as were the more northerly Arikaras, they differed from them in some respects, but were also well-established residents of the Plains. Closely related linguistically and culturally to the Pawnees were the Wichita tribes (Taovaya, Tawakoni, Wichita proper, Waco, and Kichai), in Coronado's time located in central Kansas within the great bend of the Arkansas River[13] and southward into Oklahoma.

On the eastern margins of the Plains, from southern Minnesota through Iowa to the Missouri Ozarks, were a series of Siouan-speaking tribes: the Kansa, Missouri, Oto, Ponca, Iowa, Omaha, and Osage, who still displayed indications of their eastern origins.[14] North and east of the Missouri, where the Plains give way to prairies, and where lakes, marshes, and timber become increasingly common, was the land of the Eastern, or Santee, Dakotas. Composed of a loose confederation of tribes, the Mdewakanton, Sisseton, Wahpekute, and Wahpeton, they depended more on corn, wild rice, and the game of the woodlands than on bison. Their Yankton and Yanktonai relatives migrated to the Missouri River in southeastern South Dakota and took on much of the appearance of the Plains Village tribes.

A common means of communication was needed by the linguistically diverse people who came to inhabit the Plains, and who were in frequent contact with one another. But no one language came to serve as a lingua franca, nor did a trade jargon appear; instead, a unique sign language developed in which a series of gestures, by which lengthy "conversations" could be held, came to be widely shared by Plains tribes.

If ever there was a natural alliance of man and beast, it was that of the nomadic, pedestrian hunter of the Plains and the horse introduced into the New World by the Spaniards.[15] Oddly, horses originated in and much of their evolutionary development had taken place in the Americas, but, as we have seen, they became extinct with the waning of the ice ages. By the time Columbus reintroduced horses into the Western Hemisphere, they had long been domesticated in the Old World, and a rich and complex body of knowledge and habit had grown up concerning their care and usage. The natives of the Plains and adjacent regions were to take over much of this horse complex, fitting it to their particular needs and capabilities.

The horses the Spanish brought to the Americas were strong in Barb ancestry, a breed first introduced into Spain in the eighth century by the Moors. Barbs were a coarser, somewhat larger version of the Arabian and, like them, had long been bred for endurance, hardiness, and swiftness. They mixed with local Spanish stock, and it was the descendants of these animals that were brought to the Americas. The horses the Plains Indians acquired, and those that escaped Spaniard and Indian to become the wild horses of North America—the mustangs—had become, if they were not already, a distinct type. They were small, about 14 hands high, so that some would argue that they should be classified as ponies. Weighing about 700 pounds, with a disproportionately large head, they characteristically had small feet, were well muscled, with a round barrel, and came in every variety of solid and mixed colors. In comparison to the horses brought to the Plains by Americans in the nineteenth century, the appearance of most of them was neither handsome nor promising. But to the chagrin of many who raced their American horses against them, and to the disgust of cavalrymen who pursued them, the performance of Indian ponies was often exceptional. They were fast, enduring, and hardy. Unfortunately, the Indian pony and his feral brother have virtually disappeared. The larger American horse supplanted the Indian pony among most tribes before the pickup truck came along to complete the job. Only a few mustangs survive in remote areas of the west, and they are in danger of extermination from the incessant demands of the pet food industry.

In 1598 Don Juan de Oñate, the colonizer of New Mexico, rode into New Mexico with some four hundred soldiers, priests, and settlers. Among the seven thousand animals they brought were three hundred mares and colts. Within a few years a number of ranches and settlements had been established in the vicinity of the capital of Santa Fe, and the local Pueblo Indians, as well as other natives who had been subdued or enslaved, were put to work on them. Some of these Indians soon escaped with a newly won knowledge of the stock they had been forced to care for, and no doubt many of them rode to freedom on Spanish horses. Such a situation was necessary for the successful adoption of horses by Indians, since they needed to understand the care and maintenance of horses, possess at least rudimentary riding skills, and have the basic equipment necessary to riding, to say nothing of a considerable body of other knowledge and habits.[16]

Soon after the mid-seventeenth century, Apaches from the northeast began to raid the Spanish settlements of New Mexico, carrying off large numbers of livestock; and the Pueblo Revolt in 1680, which succeeded in temporarily driving the Spaniards from New Mexico and in placing much livestock in Indian hands, accelerated the diffusion of horses. All of the Plains Apaches apparently acquired horses before the century was over, and were so well supplied that they traded them to other tribes. All of the Plains tribes south of the Platte probably had some knowledge of horses by 1700, and the horse complex had spread throughout virtually all of the Plains by the mid-eighteenth century.

About the time that the horse complex was spreading north and east, British and French traders in the Great Lakes and Middle West were beginning to draw the natives into trade relationships and were supplying them with firearms and other European goods. The unequal distribution of horses and guns, and the attempts of tribes to acquire whichever they lacked, turned the Plains into a seething cauldron of change, instability, tribal movements, and violence. Newly armed Crees and Ojibwas, for example, attacked their Siouan-speaking neighbors in Minnesota, forcing them westward. Most of these tribes abandoned their semisedentary farming life to become roving bison hunters. In the forefront of this westward march were the Teton Dakotas, a group of seven closely related tribes, whose name for themselves is Lakota. By the nineteenth century the powerful, militant Teton Dakotas were the masters of much of the upper Missouri River region, dominating the once powerful village tribes, often thwarting traders who attempted to ascend the Missouri, and later harassing Americans moving west through their lands. To their east were the Yankton and Yanktonai, who, along with the Assiniboins, referred to themselves as Nakota. Remaining behind were the Eastern or Santee Dakota tribes.

The Algonquian-speaking Cheyennes, originally a settled, gardening people living in the upper Mississippi River valley drainage along the Wisconsin-Minnesota border, were also displaced by the turmoil and upheavals of the seventeenth century. They had moved to the Sheyenne River in North Dakota before 1700 and were in the process of becoming nomadic bison hunters. Well before 1800 the Cheyennes, and the related Sutaios who joined them, had become thoroughgoing mounted bison hunters. They and the Arapahos, who had a similar history, and the Gros Ventres (Atsinas), another Algonquian-speaking people, came to dominate much of the western Plains between the Platte and the Arkansas, west of the Missouri.

Early in the eighteenth century the Comanches, acquiring horses and leaving their Shoshoni brethren in the mountainous country north of the headwaters of the Arkansas, appeared in New Mexico in company with Utes. Before the century was half over, the Comanches had defeated and dispersed the Plains Apaches and were in possession of much of the southwestern Plains. The Plains Apaches who were to become the Jicarillas of modern times retreated into the Sangre de Christo Mountains of New Mexico and the protection of the Spaniards. Others were driven deep into Texas to become the Lipans, and one band, by joining the more powerful Kiowa tribe, managed to survive in the Plains as the Kiowa-Apaches.[17] The Mescalero Apaches, who in prehorse times had occupied the southwestern margins of the Plains, retreated west of the Rio Grande and to southwest Texas beyond the Pecos to escape the Comanche onslaught.

The Comanches also had been at odds with the powerful Wichita tribes to their east. But the two peoples were driven into an alliance, the Comanches by the need to acquire firearms that the Spaniards would not supply, and the Wichitas by their desire for horses and allies to assist in their struggles with the Osages, Spaniards, and other enemies. By the second decade of the eighteenth century, the Wichitas were scattered out in river valley villages from the Kansas-Oklahoma border south through eastern Oklahoma into Texas. Their southward withdrawal was to continue for another century, with villages eventually being established as far south as Waco on the Brazos River in central Texas.[18]

Like other Plains Indian villages, Wichita villages and, particularly, a palisaded village on the Red River known as Spanish Fort, became trading centers. Comanches and other "wild" tribes brought in horses, slaves, hides, and other products of the chase to exchange with French traders or Wichita middlemen for guns, gunpowder, shot, beads, axes, kettles, and other European wares. Farther north the villages on the middle Missouri also became trade centers. About 1775 the Crows split away from their more sedentary Hidatsa relatives to become mounted, nomadic hunters and traders. They obtained horses and mules from the Flatheads, Shoshonis, and, perhaps, Nez Perces on the upper Yellowstone in exchange for items of European manufacture, and these animals brought double their cost at the villages.[19]

By the end of the eighteenth century, the mounted bison-hunting tribes were near the peak of their power. In the south the Wichitas and Comanches had turned back the northward thrust of Spain, and much of northern Mexico had come under their stinging attacks. To the east and north, France was no longer in competition for the furs and trade of the Plains, though her *voyageurs* and *coureurs de bois*, with long experience in the Plains, were to prove invaluable to the victorious English and Americans. Before the eighteenth century was over, the explorer Alexander Mackenzie had crossed the continent to the Canadian pacific, and before the century was a decade old, the American expedition of Lewis and Clark also crossed the Plains and reached the Pacific. Close on their heels followed the free American trappers, the mountain men, to join in a lively competition with the English fur traders, inevitably entangling the Plains tribes in shifting alliances and hostilities.

But by the 1840s, the beaver was depleted and the day of the mountain man was over; the relentless frontier was moving westward, to usher in the years of bitter battles, broken treaties, massacres, and the near extermination of the bison. Several days after Christmas in 1890, it was ended, when at Wounded Knee Creek in South Dakota, the Seventh Cavalry mowed down a band of Hunkpapa Sioux, two-thirds of whom were women and children. It was the last overt massacre of Plains Indians, though more subtle assaults on their lands and persons continued for many decades. This, in fact, sums up fairly accurately the subsequent story of their relationship with the white world.

CULTURAL SUMMARY

Subsistence and Material Culture

The possession of horses was a tremendous boon to pedestrian bison hunters, transforming a life of occasional feast and sometime famine into one in which the food supply was relatively well assured. It even attracted peoples who had followed a more secure life as semisedentary farmers. With horses, hunters could better locate the unpredictable bison herds, and, equally important, they could move their camps and families to the vicinity of the herds with relative ease. The mounted tribes came together in late spring and early summer for large-scale communal hunts, following which they held their important tribal rituals and ceremonies, and engaged in recreational activities. After these, warriors frequently rode off on expeditions to raid for horses or to attack their enemies. With the approach of winter, tribes split into bands and smaller units, finding shelter in protected places and hunting as individuals for the more scattered game.[20]

Acquisition of horses altered hunt techniques considerably, although it is doubtful that ancient practices, such as "jumping" bison over precipices, were forgotten. Now mounted hunters could surround herds, often get them milling, and kill many animals at close quarters. Or, hunters could simply approach a herd as closely as possible and, at a given signal, dash into it to begin the slaughter. Until repeating firearms became available, the lance and the bow and arrow were preferred by hunters. Riding their fleetest and best-trained horses, they approached the bison as closely as possible before driving home lance or arrow. Successful communal hunts were vital to general welfare, and most tribes had special hunt leaders in command of the hunts, and police, who were often members of warrior societies, to see that the hunts were carried out properly. The greatest danger was that eager

young hunters would prematurely stampede the bison, ruining the   **89**
hunt. Such transgressions were apt to be severely punished.

Bison were butchered where they fell by the women. Flesh, internal organs, bone marrow, and blood were consumed; horns and hoofs were fashioned into spoons and other utensils; intestines were used as containers; the dressed skins, with the hair left on, made warm robes; hides were used for tipi covers and bags; the hair might be woven into rope or used to stuff pillows; the sinews served as thread and for bowstrings; and the droppings ("buffalo chips") were used as fuel in a land where wood was often scarce. What meat could not be consumed immediately was dried for future use. Thinly sliced strips of meat were sun- or smoke-dried on racks of sticks, then packed away. Such jerky might also be pounded, mixed with berries, and stuffed into rawhide bags (parfleches), over which was poured grease and marrow. This pemmican kept a long time and was highly nutritious.

Many other animals were hunted, and a number of plant foods were used to supplement and add variety to the diet of the hunting tribes. Antelope were plentiful on the Plains in the early days and were generally hunted by the same techniques as were employed for bison. In the better-watered and better-timbered river valleys, elk, deer, and bear were hunted, usually by lone hunters. Smaller mammals were taken according to need and occasion. Wild plums, grapes, chokecherries, and various other berries and fruits were an important addition to the diet, and were often pounded and dried, seeds and all, for winter use. The wild turnip, where available, was an important root crop that could be dried and preserved for winter consumption. Depending upon the region, agave, prickly pear, wild rice, acorns, and other wild plant foods also supplemented the diet. In times of scarcity, and as the bison range shrank, many other foods were sought. Horses, for example, became an important dietary staple of at least one Comanche band in the nineteenth century. A brisk trade also was maintained between the nomads and the villages, the hunters bartering meat and hides for the corn and other crops of the farming peoples. Few of the nomadic tribes ate fish, though most of the village tribes did.

Among the village tribes, corn, beans, squash (or pumpkins), and sunflowers were grown in carefully tended gardens by women and were, depending upon the particular tribe, region, and time, about as important to subsistence as the game secured by the men. Equipped only with bison scapula hoes, sticks, and crude rakes, the women were forced to plant in the easily worked soils of the river valley bottom lands. Despite primitive equipment, the village peoples were expert farmers, storing their surplus crops in large underground pits, and also bartering surplus produce to hunting tribes. The village tribes raised a number of varieties of flour, flint, and sweet corns, and the Mandans are particularly noted for their quick-maturing and drought-resistant varieties. The village tribes, as well as the Blackfeet, Sarsis, and Crows, also grew tobacco, but among the Hidatsa and probably other tribes, only the older men did so because of the supernatural beliefs associated with it.

After the fields were planted in the spring, the villages were emptied of all but the very old and sick for a bison hunt, during which they lived and hunted like the nomadic tribes. They returned to their villages in late summer for the harvest and to dry part of their crop for storage, after which another large hunt was often conducted in the fall and winter months.

The nomadic tribes utilized the tipi, a conical skin tent apparently derived from those used by northern hunters and perhaps related to similar tents used by northern hunters of the Old World. The advent of horses must have allowed the tipis of the nomadic tribes to be enlarged considerably, since women and dogs would have been hard put to haul the elegant, spacious tipis of later years. Lacking wheeled vehicles, tipi covers and other possessions were transported by the horse-drawn travois, a crude device consisting of two trailing poles on which property was lashed. The travois had been used with dog traction by the prehorse bison hunters, and it was adapted for use with horses.

In the northern Plains, tipis were ordinarily ten to twelve feet high, with a base diameter up to about fifteen feet, and requiring fifteen to twenty hides for their covers. Special-purpose tipis were somewhat larger, and some tribes, such as the Crows who had access to abundant timber, used particularly long supporting poles of thirty feet and more, giving their lodges an hourglass silhouette. In the southern Plains and in areas where the necessary poles were scarce, tipis were smaller. Among some tribes, tipi covers might be painted, often extolling the exploits of their warrior owners, or with various symbolic or magical figures. Fireplaces were located in the center of the tipi, and a space was left at the apex of the structure for a smoke vent. Two poles were attached to flaps that allowed the residents to close or adjust the aperture.

The village tribes used the tipi while on their hunting expeditions, but their primary dwellings were relatively permanent lodges of several types. The Wichitas of the central and southern Plains used grass lodges, and the Osages and related Siouan-speakers built oval, domed houses covered with mats or skins—both types of dwelling originating in the Southeast. The earth lodges of the Mandans, Hidatsas, Arikaras, Pawnees, and Omahas were circular, with flat to almost conical earth-covered roofs. Sizes varied considerably, but the diameter of larger earth lodges was upwards of fifty feet, with ample room for an extended family of forty or more persons, their possessions, and even an occasional horse. Earth lodges were entered through covered passageways, and the floor was normally excavated to a depth of about a foot. A large number of vertical posts formed the outer walls, and a bench of earth was left or a platform of sticks was constructed against them, to be used for sleeping and other purposes. A shallow depression in the center of the lodge served as a fireplace, smoke escaping through a hole in the roof. Four or more stout central posts ten to fifteen feet long supported radial stringers that spanned the distance to the walls. Branches, coarse grass, sod, and finally earth were laid over these, the result being a dwelling that was warm in winter and cool in summer.

The grass houses of the Wichitas were not as flimsy or temporary as the name might seem to imply. Often used for many years, they were built on a sturdy foundation of posts and were from fifteen to thirty feet in diameter and height; they were sometimes plastered with mud. Interiors had much in common with earth lodges, a platform of sticks being built against the walls for sleeping, and a central depression serving as a fireplace. There was no smoke vent, and traditionally there were two entrances: one on the east, the other on the west.

The nomadic tribes typically camped in a circle or semicircle, and each of the divisions had a particular location within the tribal circle. The villages of the farming tribes were located close to water, generally on a bluff above a stream, and were often fortified by a ditch or a ditch and a log palisade. There was considerable variation in the placement of dwellings within villages; apparently they were more regularly planned in early days, but in later years when the life span of a village was apt to be brief, dwellings were scattered about indiscriminately.

The essentials of a man's clothing were a breechcloth and moccasins, to which were added hip-length leggings, buckskin shirt, and a buffalo robe, as the weather or social occasion demanded. Some tribes originally lacked shirts, but their ornamental functions became so important that they were widely adopted. The hallmark of the Plains Indian has come to be the sweeping feather headdress of the warriors. Such headgear was a late development, originating in the northern Plains, although feathers and feathered headpieces were ancient and widespread, as well as often symbolic of individual achievements. Horned and other headdresses of considerable variety were also in widespread use in the Plains. Women's dress varied somewhat, women among such tribes as the Crow wearing a long, sleeveless dress of deer or other skin reaching to the ankles, knee-length leggings, and moccasins. Two-piece dresses were in vogue among the Cheyennes and most southern Plains tribes, and in warm weather the blouses might be omitted.

The manner of dressing hair was highly variable, men generally spending more time and effort with its grooming than women. Styles varied in time and with tribe, from the long, flowing hair of the Crows, whose length might be augmented with horsehair falls, to the Pawnees who favored a roached style. Women commonly braided their hair, and a streak of paint was often applied to the part. Painting of the face and body in a number of colors and a wide variety of styles was widely practiced, and tattooing was in vogue among the Wichitas and other tribes. Men generally plucked out all facial hair, often including the eyebrows. A wide variety of earrings and necklaces of shell, bone, and other materials was worn; and with the advent of traders, silver, copper, and brass ornaments were eagerly adopted. In place of the old porcupine quill adornment of clothing, glass beads quickly attained great popularity. The hair pipe breastplate, composed in later years of tubular bone and shell beads obtained from traders, became an ornate and unique part of the more formal attire of Plains warriors.

The principal weapon of men was the bow and arrows. Because they were easier to use while mounted, Plains bows were generally short. The self-bow, made from a variety of woods, was in widespread use. Derived from Plateau tribes were wooden bows backed with sinew, and compound bows constructed of strips of elk or sheep horn and backed with sinew. At short range, Plains bows were very effective, and a number of accounts record hunters sending arrows completely through bison. Lances, which were thrust rather than thrown, and in historic times tipped with steel blades, were also used effectively by bison hunters. A variety of clubs and knives was also carried by warriors. For defensive purposes Plains warriors carried round, tough bison-hide shields. Often covered with symbolic and magical paintings and ornaments, they were effective in diverting enemy arrows, and unless hit squarely, might even deflect bullets.

Plains Indians relied on skins for all sorts of bags and containers, and they were good skin dressers. Like other Indians, they did not literally tan hides, but their methods of preparation were such that the women were able to produce soft and durable skins. Hides were staked to the ground, hair side down; excess fat and flesh were chopped off; and the hides were left for several days to bleach and dry. After being scraped and, sometimes, after having the hair removed, the rawhide was ready for use. Parfleches, which might be described as rawhide envelopes, were used primarily for food storage, and a number of other containers were manufactured of rawhide. For clothing and many containers, rawhide was further processed by working in fat and brains, rubbing through or over sinews attached to poles, smoking, and other processes. A number of tribes on the Missouri employed hides stretched

over a wooden framework for a primitive, tublike vessel, known as
a bull boat, or coracle.

Social Organization

The nature and habits of the bison, the demands and effects of the
adoption of the horse complex, the fierce competition between tribes
for horses, European goods, hunting grounds, the very considerable interchange of individuals through captivity, and the close association
of many tribes through trade all conspired to have a leveling and unify-
ing effect on the social structure of the tribes that became mounted
bison hunters.[21] Those who had been hard-pressed hunters and gatherers
and who had possessed a correspondingly simple social organization
generally developed more complex organizations. Those who had a farming background, such as the Cheyennes and Teton Dakotas, and those
who probably did, such as the Arapahos, lost or abandoned the clan
organizations they had formerly possessed, or, like the Crows, were on
their way to doing so. As Eggan and Oliver have pointed out,[22] the
demands of the new kind of life in the Plains required a flexible, adapt-
able kind of social structure, not well served by unilateral kinship systems.

The congregation of bison in huge herds in the summer encouraged
large-scale communal hunts. Their dispersal during other seasons meant
that small groups of kindred, sometimes only an individual family,
more often various forms of extended families, or polygynous families,
or combinations of them, camped and hunted together apart from
others. Among the Lipans and Kiowa-Apaches, for example, the basic
social unit was the matrilocal extended family, composed of an older
man and his wife, unmarried children, married daughters and their
husbands, and their children. Several such small, independent, cooperative, mutual-aid units tended to camp together for mutual protection.
In the northern Plains, as among the Blackfeet, the patrilocal analogue
of these extended families was common. Among the Blackfeet, too,
and typical of the Plains, the extended family groups were apt to be
enlarged horizontally by the custom of polygyny, that is, the marriage
of a man to two or more women. Marriage to sisters (sororal polygyny)
was usually the preferred form of plural marriage, but among wealthy
Blackfeet and leading chiefs, for example, there might be ten or more
wives.[23] The widespread practice of polygyny may be viewed both as
a survival mechanism and as an economic asset to husbands. In many
tribes the hazards of war and the chase altered the ratio of the sexes
in favor of women. With polygyny, women were assured of husbands,
and after the advent of fur traders, additional wives were an economic

asset to men as they prepared the hides and skins; in many tribes they were a status symbol.

In summer the scattered family and "camp" groups joined other similar groups to form loosely structured and often transitory bands for the communal hunt and for tribal ceremonies and other activities. Among some of the nomadic tribes, such as the Comanches, band membership was a matter of choice, popular and successful leaders attracting many followers, unfortunate or failing leaders losing theirs. Among others, like the Cheyennes, band members had a feeling of kinship for one another, so much so that marriage within the band was frowned on. Bands were the largest political groupings attained by such peoples as the Lipans and Comanches, and they constituted tribes only in the sense that their members shared a common language and culture. Among most nomadic hunters, however, the bands joined together as tribes in the summer for great communal hunts, recreation, and religious celebrations. The Cheyenne tribe, for example, was composed of ten rather loosely organized bands, each of which possessed its own ceremonies, medicines, and other distinguishing features. When they came together in the summer, they camped in a great circle or semicircle, each band year after year occupying the same position in the circle relative to other bands.

The tribal encampments of thousands of people and the great communal hunts, involving several hundred mounted hunters, obviously required organization, leadership, and control lest the camps be chaotic, bickering mobs, and the hunts ill-coordinated, unproductive wild-goose chases. These needs were met by delegating considerable authority to chiefs or governing councils during this period, and by many clubs and associations (technically known as sodalities) that cut across ties of kinship and band affiliation, and that had administrative, police, and other duties. Formal governmental bodies were quite variable; the relatively formally structured Cheyennes had a tribal council composed of forty-four members, four from each band plus four chiefs. Among the Kiowas, the owner and keeper of the tribally sacred relic, the *taime*, or sun-dance doll, was the nominal head of the tribe during this period. He was advised by the band chiefs and assisted by the men's societies. Among the Comanches, with their simpler background and somewhat different ecological circumstances, band leaders were simply successful, charismatic individuals. They lacked formal councils and had no military or other societies to keep order, but outstanding warriors apparently exercised considerable authority.[24]

Some of the associations and clubs were women's groups, most were men's organizations, many were religious groupings, and a majority of the men's societies were concerned with war or police duties. Among some tribes the clubs were roughly age-graded; membership might be automatic or purchased, and each had its own insignia, regalia, songs, and ritual. The Cheyennes, for example, had six military fraternities that served as tribal police and as fraternities of warriors. Each society had specific duties, such as enforcing regulations during communal hunts, and one of them was an elite society of warriors known as Contraries. This society, and analogous ones among other tribes, often called "Crazy Dogs," did things backwards, behaved abnormally, and wore outlandish clothing. When they said "hot," they meant "cold"; when told to eat, they fasted; more significantly, in battle, when others retreated, they stood firm or advanced. Longevity was not a characteristic of the membership in such societies, nor was it an aim.

Among the semisedentary, horticultural village tribes, with stable concentrations of people and a more assured and regular food supply, social structure was more complex, tightly knit, and less flexible than among the nomadic hunters. The acquisition of horses and trade goods did not necessitate major alterations in social organization. Clan organizations were present; among the central Siouans (Omaha, Ponca, Iowa, Kansa, Oto, and Osage), they were patrilineal, and often several were linked to one another in phratries, or they had a moiety or dual division. The village tribes of the upper Missouri (Mandans and Hidatsas and their Crow offshoots) had matrilineal clans and dual divisions. The Pawnees and Arikaras apparently had the same kind of organization at one time. The Caddoan-speaking Wichita tribes lacked clans and moieties, but they also may have undergone changes in the historic period. Most, if not all, of the villages of these farming peoples were politically independent of one another, with their own particular governing structures of council and chiefs. Though linked together by their various kin groupings, and often brought together for ceremonial and other functions, the villages were the basic autonomous political units, tribes existing in the sense of common culture and sentiment.

Among the mounted hunters, kinship systems changed or were altering toward bilateral systems that were broadly extended on the basis of generation. Thus, there was a tendency to designate all cousins as siblings, and among some of the Blackfeet, sibling terms were employed for all relatives of similar age category, whatever the genealogical connection. Eggan[25] has convincingly argued that the need for the cooperation of "brothers" in hunting and warfare was sufficient for the extension of such terminology to distant relatives and even to friends. The village tribes, on the other hand, had "vertical" systems organized with reference to lineages and clans, and as such were much more exclusive and rigid systems, concerned with perpetuating rights, privileges, and the ownership of property.

Children were named soon after birth, often by older relatives or distinguished warriors. As with many other North American Indians, names were often changed. Boys might take new names as a consequence of visions, and subsequent exploits on the warpath often led a man to adopt a new name. Children who were sickly or ill often had their names changed, and adults might also "throw away" their names if misfortune dogged them. Among some, like the Kiowas, older men near the end of their lives might give their names to promising young warriors. Infants spent much of their time strapped in cradleboards, a serviceable device for nomadic people, but also used by the semisedentary farmers. There was much freedom for and indulgence of young boys whose lives might be brief, particularly among the nomadic tribes. The position of girls and women was inferior to that of males among these tribes, but more nearly equal among the farming people, where women played a very important role economically.

Many of the Plains tribes had more or less formalized age-graded societies, children of roughly the same age belonging to a society of their peers. Among the Blackfeet, Arapahos, and other northern Plains tribes, the rights to regalia, dances, songs, and various privileges were purchased by the children from the next oldest group, which, displaced upward, purchased these things from the next highest grade, and so on throughout life. In the southern Plains, among the Kiowas, all little boys automatically became members of the Rabbit Society. They were instructed and drilled in their future life as warriors, and the society had its own insignia and dances. Boys left the society when they were invited to join one of the adult warrior societies.

Though pubescent girls and menstruating women were generally regarded as unclean and were isolated in various ways, there was no great emphasis on the transition from girl to woman. Boys, as they neared adulthood, sought guardian spirits, but arrival at adulthood was a matter of having participated successfully in a war or raiding party. As a consequence boys married at a somewhat later age than girls. Marriages were normally arranged by the families, accompanied by exchanges between the families of horses and other property. Residence of the newly married couple was variable, but was usually with relatives. Divorce was generally easy; jealous husbands frequently punished adulterous wives by cutting off their noses. The levirate and sororate were common, and often extended to secondary affinal relatives.

The period in a man's life when he was an active warrior was regarded as his best years. While the elderly men played the role of couselors and advisers, it was an age for looking back, not one to savor for its power or prestige. Several forms of burial were utilized by Plains tribes. In the northern Plains, scaffold burial was common, and elsewhere simple interment was the custom, often in an isolated situation. Mourning for warriors in the prime of life was bitter and intense, widows often going about in rags, scratching or cutting their faces and bodies until they bled, cutting the hair, and sometimes maiming or cutting off fingers.

Warfare

The unequal distribution of horses, firearms, and other European goods in the Plains throughout much of the historic period and the necessity to acquire that which was lacking, the competition over good hunting grounds sharpened in the nineteenth century by the declining number of bison, and the struggles between Europeans and Americans over the land and its resources involved the Plains Indians in chronic strife with one another and with the foreign invaders. The historic situation in the Plains demanded that its peoples be warlike, and they were. War, in fact, assumed such importance that it affected virtually every aspect of life. To become a man was to have participated in warfare, and those few who could not assume the role of warrior became women, the well-known *berdaches* who took up the dress and occupation of women. To marry well was to be a successful warrior; to be a leader of men was to have been a proven leader of war parties; and to die well was to die a warrior's death.

The subsistence and manpower limitations of the nomadic Plains tribes, and the absence among them of strong or coercive governmental structures, led to a form of war distinct from that waged by wealthier, richer nations. Such warfare has been termed "primitive," or otherwise distinguished from "true" warfare, and in the Plains has even been likened to a game, and its economic and historic causation often denied or misunderstood.[26] Plains warfare took on a distinctive form or pattern characterized by small war parties composed of volunteers, sometimes including women, whose leaders organized the force, ordinarily with supernatural sanction. Those who had led successful war parties without loss had little difficulty in organizing new ones; those who were novices or had been unsuccessful often had problems in recruiting members. War parties were organized in order to gain revenge, to steal horses, to loot, and for other purposes. They characteristically set out after the summer bison hunt and following in the wake of the various tribal ceremonies.

War parties were sometimes gone for many months, traveling great distances. Frequently the principal aim of warriors was not the slaughter of the enemy but the counting of coups (literally "blows"), usually used to designate a graded series of honors, varying from tribe to tribe, and including striking an enemy or an enemy's body with a special stick, taking a scalp, cutting loose a picketed horse, seizing an enemy's weapon, and the like. Communications between members of war parties were by smoke signals, and in later years by reflections from mirrors obtained from traders. Plunder taken in a raid belonged to the leader of the expedition, but it was ordinarily distributed among his followers. To retain the loot would have been tantamount to an admission of failing powers and inability to conduct successful ventures in the future. Men bragged of their exploits, and in some tribes validated their claims by counting coup on a pole in front of their peers. Typical Plains conflict was, then, a patterned kind of guerilla warfare, but it would be a mistake to assume that it was invariably of this character. Pitched battles involving several hundred warriors on each side and lasting several days are known.

Religious and Ceremonial Life

As boys approached manhood, they left camp or village for an isolated, lonely place, there to fast, pray, smoke, and among some tribes chop off a finger or otherwise mutilate themselves in order to acquire a vision. It is hardly surprising that in a highly emotional state—faint from hunger, in pain, and desperately thirsty—their prayers were answered and a supernatural being or force came to their aid. The supernaturals who appeared in visions ordinarily gave the vision seeker certain magical songs to sing, imposed various restrictions on his behavior, gave him prayers and incantations, and instructed him to gather a number of articles for a medicine bundle, all of which would help to assure success in various activities and endeavors. In a life that was apt to be brief and fraught with danger, it is obvious that fearful, untried youngsters often gained much emotional security, to say nothing of courage and purpose, from these supernatural experiences. And men continued to seek guidance and help from their guardians at critical junctures in their lives.[27]

Visions varied, of course; some were powerful, as demonstrated by the success their possessors had in war, the chase, curing, and other pursuits. The important point is that an unvalidated vision was worthless; the man who claimed to have certain vision-granted powers and abilities but who could not demonstrate them was considered a liar or worse. This meant that successful men were the ones who had visions, perhaps, in fact, after they had achieved success; and poor, unsuccessful people considered themselves that way because their power was either weak or lacking. In a way, the vison complex served as an explanatory device and justification for the differences in ability and achievement of people.

Among the nomadic, hunting tribes, such as the Comanches and Blackfeet, with their more amorphous, flexible social structure, vision experiences were highly individualistic, and the most desirable were associated with protection from enemies and the acquisition of horses. Among the horticultural tribes, on the other hand, vision experiences were more standardized, stereotyped, and restricted; often kin groups had rights to visions. Among the Omahas, for example, in order to enter the Buffalo Doctor's Society, which was restricted to persons of certain families and wealth, it was necessary to have a certain kind of vision.[28] There were various means for obtaining certain kinds of visions, or what might be described as family or corporate visions, including sending the supplicant to the particular spot where others had received the appropriate vision.

Among a number of Plains tribes, "power" could be transferred, including the ritual, songs, and paraphernalia that went with it. The transfer was usually by purchase, but it might be by gift. In the former case, it meant that successful and wealthy people could acquire supernatural assistance without a vision, and in the latter, that a man could transfer power to a spouse or child as a kind of insurance in the case of his death. Not surprisingly, some medicine bundles and the ritual associated with them took on extraordinary social significance in the sense that they came to benefit the entire band or tribe rather than the individual. Thus, the Cheyennes had four sacred medicine arrows, the Kiowas the sacred *taime*, and there were many others. The most extensive development of tribal medicine bundles was among the Pawnees.

Virtually all of the nomadic tribes held some version of the Sun Dance, and many of the village tribes held comparable tribal religious rituals. The Sun Dance was most elaborated and apparently originated with, or was first synthesized by, the Arapaho and Cheyenne tribes after they had acquired horses, and it spread widely from this source.[29] In minor details the Sun Dance was quite varied, but in its essentials it was quite similar everywhere. It was an annual event, held in the summer when members of a tribe could congregate. Among some, such as the Kiowas, attendance was compulsory. It was held ostensibly in response to a vow an individual had made while in a desperate or critical situation. Socially considered, it was an affirmation of tribal unity, represented by sacred symbols and through the performance of tribal rituals.

The Sun Dance lasted four or more days and was generally initiated by the accumulation of bison tongues, used for feasting before and during the ceremony. The ritual killing of a bison with a single arrow was also a preliminary feature, the hide being hung on the center pole of the Sun Dance lodge. The center pole was a forked tree that was scouted out as though it were an enemy, around which might then be held a sham battle, after which it was ceremonially felled by a specially qualified person or persons. The pole, on which had been placed various offerings, was erected in the center of the dance lodge. The various warrior and women's societies took turns dancing, or persons who had pledged to do so, danced. Dancers were often required to abstain from food, drink, and rest during the dance, so it was an ordeal not lightly undertaken. The most widely known feature of the Sun Dance is the self-torture that characterized the dances of some tribes. Wooden skewers were thrust through the skin of the breast or back, and thongs were attached to these and to the center pole, or to a heavy object. Dancers, straining against these bonds, attempted to tear themselves free.

In sum, the Sun Dance was a spectacular tribal religious observance, marking the high point in the year, at which time there was also much feasting, playing of games, and general socializing of people who had long been separated. Religiously, it was believed to ensure the continued welfare and success of the tribe, and the continued fecundity of their all-important resource, the bison.

NOTES

[1] More has probably been written about the Plains Indians than any other native Americans, and there is room here to list only a fraction of these works. Wissler (1941) and Lowie (1963) have written books dealing with the area as a whole. For social organization, see Eggan (1937) and, particularly, Eggan (1966).

[2] The boundaries of the Plains, particularly its eastern limits, are variously drawn by geographers; they are loosely drawn here. See Webb (1931, 3–9).

[3] The pioneering study of this fascinating animal was made by Hornaday (1887). The most comprehensive study of the bison is by Roe (1951). See also Garretson (1938).

[4] Garretson (1938, 58).

[5] Wedel (1961; 1964); Mulloy (1952); Wendorf and Hester (1962); Willey (1966, 311–29).

[6] Lehmer (1954, 139–40); Wedel (1961, 168, 285–86).

[7] Wedel (1942; 1959, 211–377, 571–89; 1961,104–7, 286–87).

[8] For a diametrically opposed viewpoint and the traditional one, see Kroeber (1939, 76).

[9] Sapir (1916) apparently originated the notion that there were no prehorse bison hunters in the Plains. This view was enshrined as holy writ by many ethnologists and was stoutly defended as late as 1948 (Kroeber, 1948, 823; also see 1939, 76–77). The proponents of this view ignored the well-known eyewitness accounts by members of the Coronado expedition, but it took the added weight of archeological data to finally give it the burial it deserved (Ewers, 1955, 336–38; Wedel, 1961, 297 ff.; Eggan, 1952, 39–40).

[10] McAllister and Newcomb (1970, 1–2).

[11] Strong (1932; 1935); Champe (1946; 1949); Wedel (1959); Gunnerson (1960; 1968).

[12] Ewers (1955, 299–300, 338).

[13] Wedel (1961, 108–11).

[14] Ibid., pp. 117–20).

[15] Dobie (1952); Denhardt (1947); Simpson (1961).

[16] Haines (1938a, b) was the first to point out that the De Soto and Coronado expeditions could not have been the source of Plains Indian horses, and he suggested that the Santa Fe vicinity must have been. For diffusion of horses into the Plains, see Ewers (1955, 3–15); Newcomb (1961, 85–90).

[17] See Thomas (1935, 4, 114, 124, 125) for data on this aspect of Jicarilla history; see also Tunnell and Newcomb (1969, 146–49) for a summary of Lipan dispersal, and McAllister and Newcomb (1970) for a review of Kiowa-Apache history.

[18] Harper (1953a, b, c); Tunnell and Newcomb (1969, 151–53).

[19] Ewers (1955, 7–8).

[20] The older view espoused by Wissler (1914) was that the acquisition of horses by the Plains nomads served "as an intensifier of original Plains traits," but that the most characteristic traits were present before the advent of horses, and that, in essence, the addition of horses had no revolutionary cultural consequences. Kroeber (1939, 76–77) challenged this point of view, and though wrong in his denial of the existence of well-established and flourishing pedestrian bison hunters in the Plains, his insistence that Plains cultures were markedly different after the adoption of horses was well taken. As Ewers (1955, 338–39) has pointed out: "The use of horses not only enriched the material culture of the tribes who acquired them but it altered their habits of daily life, served to develop new manual and motor skills, changed their concepts of their physical environment and the social relationships of individuals. It appears to me that the influence of the horse permeated and modified to a greater or lesser degree every major aspect of Plains Indian life."

[21] See Oliver (1962) for a study of the relationship between the ecological situation and the social organization of Plains tribes.

[22] Eggan (1952); Oliver (1962).

[23] Ewers (1958, 99–100).

[24] Oliver (1962, 71–76).

[25] Eggan (1937, 93ff.; 1966, 58).

[26] Newcomb (1950; 1960) for the distinctions between the psychological motivation of individuals and the causality of tribal and national conflict. See Mishkin (1940) for a study of the economic factors in Plains warfare. Lowie (1963) contains the most recent statement defending the noneconomic interpretation of Plains warfare.

[27] The original study of the Plains vision quest was made by Benedict (1922); also see her broader study for all of North America (1923). A recent study by Albers and Parker (1971) makes a convincing case for the integration of the vision quest into the varied social systems and the ecological bases on which they rested, as well as their reinforcement by the vision complex.

[28] Fortune (1932, 72–75).

[29] Spier (1921).

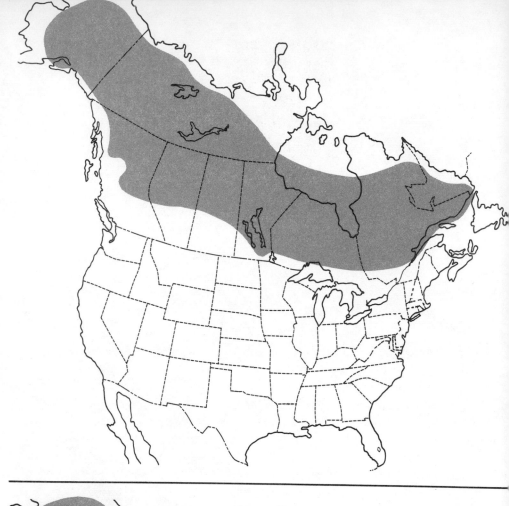

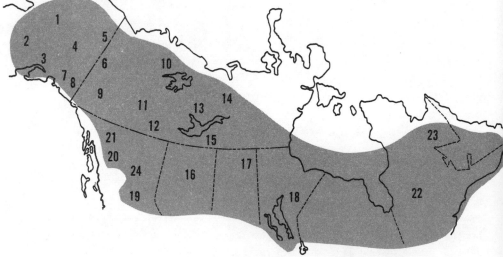

1. Koyukon	6. Han	11. Mountain	16. Beaver	21. Tahltan
2. Ingalik	7. Ahtena	12. Kaska	17. Chipewyan	22. Montagnais
3. Tanaina	8. Nabesna	13. Dogrib	18. Cree	23. Naskapi
4. Tanana	9. Tutchone	14. Yellowknife	19. Carrier	24. Sekani
5. Kutchin	10. Hare	15. Slave	20. Tsetsaut	

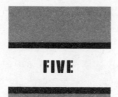

FIVE

SUBARCTIC HUNTERS AND FISHERMEN

South of the treeless, desolate Arctic tundra, fringing the continent's northern rim, lies a vast coniferous forest. Sweeping in a wide belt from central Alaska and the Canadian Rockies eastward around Hudson Bay to Labrador and Newfoundland, it is a land of piercingly cold and excruciatingly long winters, punctuated by short, intense summers. A rugged, wild country of mountains, streams, and innumerable lakes, it includes vast stretches of muskeg—a spongy swampland that is all but impassable in summer. Spruce is the predominant tree of the northern forest, but interspersed in it are balsam fir, birch, willow, poplar, alder, and other deciduous trees. Before firearms were introduced, immense herds of caribou frequented its tundra border; woodland caribou ranged its forests; and musk oxen, cold-adapted relics of the ice age, were far more widely distributed than they are today. But moose still feed along the shores of its lakes and streams, and elk, white-tailed deer, and bear also are common. A wealth of smaller mammals, from beavers and martens to porcupines and rabbits, flourish there, and the glacial lakes and rivers are well stocked with grayling, whitefish, trout, and other fish. By early summer many waterfowl and other birds have arrived from the south to nest, a variety of berries begin to ripen, and swarms of mosquitoes, black flies, and other biting insects make life miserable for man and beast.

The major game animal of the Subarctic is the barren ground caribou (*Rangifer tarandus*), a close relative of the semidomesticated reindeer of Scandinavia and Greenland. Originally distributed from Maine and eastern Canada to Alaska, with a population that must have numbered in the millions, overhunting and other causes have reduced their numbers to less than 500,000. Standing 4 to 5 feet at the shoulders and weighing up to 700 pounds, they and reindeer are the only members of the deer family in which both sexes bear antlers. Their large, splayed hoofs are excellent adaptations for an animal frequently on ice and snow, and in bogs or water. They vary in color from a dark brown to buff and almost white; with a dense undercoat protected by long stiff guard hairs, and a winter deposit of fat that gives them a chunky silhouette, they are well suited for life in the far north.

Caribou are peaceful, leaderless, herd animals, sometimes traveling 400 to 500 miles in annual migrations that generally follow well-worn routes. As with the bison of the Plains, head-long stampedes sometimes lead to mass drownings and other catastrophes. In the spring months caribou migrate north to the open tundra where they spend the brief summer feeding on various grasses, sedges, and horsetails, as well as on birch and willow. The young are born during the spring migration and within a few hours of birth are able to keep up with their mothers. The caribou move back to the forested parts of their range in July, but in September there is a second northward surge to the tundra for the rut, after which most herds move back south. In the winter they paw through the snow and ice for lichens (reindeer moss) and browse on willow and aspen.

Sparsely scattered throughout this austere, remote, inhospitable land were (and in many places still are) hunters and fishermen, their ways of life varying slightly from group to group according to the differing resources available to them and as they were influenced by neighboring peoples. They are among North America's most poorly known people, partly because of their remoteness, partly because their cultures were decimated long ago, and probably because their Eskimo neighbors have attracted much more interest and attention. Surprisingly, their cultures were, in the main, markedly distinct from the Eskimos to the north, although they hunted some of the same animals and shared many of the same environmental problems.

Mammoth Hudson Bay, ballooning southward from the Arctic, almost divides the Subarctic in two, and it served as a linguistic boundary. To the south and east were Algonquian-speaking peoples; to the west and northwest, speakers of languages of the Athapascan branch of the Nadéné family.[1] The Athapascans of the western Subarctic were divided into a large number of small, rather formless groups; because of considerable shifting about, consolidation, and dispersal in historic times, their original numbers, distribution, and relationships are obscure. The principal Athapascan groups, less influenced by outside sources than others, include the Koyukons of the lower Yukon; the Tananas, upstream from them around the junction of the Yukon and the Tanana River; the

Kutchins, on an upper tributary of the Yukon ranging eastward to the lower Mackenzie River; and the Hans and the Tutchones, in the upper drainage of the Yukon. In the lower Mackenzie River drainage were the Hares, to their south the Mountains, and south of Great Bear Lake the Dogribs. The Yellowknives were located to the north of Great Slave Lake, the Slaves to the south. The Beavers inhabited the Peace River country west of Lake Athabaska, and the Sekanis ranged the country to their west. The Chipewyan peoples, the most southeasterly of the Athapascans, ranged the country east and south of Lake Athabaska east to Hudson Bay.

The Athapascans who were on the periphery of the Subarctic were often heavily influenced by their neighbors. Thus, the Ingaliks of the lower Yukon River of southwestern Alaska, whose name is Eskimo, were considerably influenced by them. To their south, in the vicinity of Cook Inlet on Alaska's southern coast, the Tanainas were influenced by both Eskimo and Northwest Coast cultures. The Ahtenas, on the Copper River in southcentral Alaska, were also strongly influenced by Northwest Coast culture, the more inland Nabesnas, somewhat less. Similarly, the Tahltans, Tsetsauts, and related peoples of northwestern British Columbia were considerably influenced by Northwest Coast peoples, particularly by the Tsimshians. To their south the Carriers and Chilcotins were influenced by Plateau tribes, and one group, the Nicolas, had moved onto the plateau. Similarly, the Athapascan Sarsis had moved onto the Plains, and through close contact with the Blackfeet tribes had become thoroughgoing Plains Indians.[2]

There were relatively few groups of Algonquian-speaking peoples in the eastern Subarctic. The Naskapis wandered the immense, inhospitable interior of the Labrador peninsula, and the closely related Montagnais to their southwest occupied equally formidable land between James Bay and the St. Lawrence. The Crees inhabited a tremendous stretch of country on the southern side of Hudson Bay, from Lake Winnipeg and the Churchill River in the west, eastward into Ontario. Mostly north of the Great Lakes were the Ojibwa-Ottawa peoples, who are often set apart in a "Northern Great Lakes" or "North Central Algonkian" culture area, as has been noted. Actually, there was no sharp cultural boundary setting apart the Subarctic Algonquian hunters and fishermen from the more southerly horticultural tribes of the Northeast Woodlands.

The Beothuks of Newfoundland also were probably Algonquian speakers, but they were wiped out before their linguistic affiliations could be surely worked out. What little is known about them aligns them with other Subarctic peoples. They were hunters and fishermen who lived in bark wigwams, used a distinctively-shaped birchbark canoe, cooked in birch-bark vessels, and harpooned seals with a harpoon similar to an archaic Eskimo form. Divided into small bands and apparently never numerous, European fishermen and Micmac enemies killed them at every opportunity, with the result that the Beothuks had been virtually exterminated before the opening of the nineteenth century. The Beothuks smeared their bodies and clothing with red ocher, and, consequently, John Cabot in 1497 referred to them as "Red Indians," the misleading term that has been so widely applied to America's natives ever since.[3]

PREHISTORY

The prehistory of the Subarctic is not well known, and its western and eastern segments seem to have had somewhat differing pasts. In a general way the prehistory of the Algonquian speakers of the eastern Subarctic was one with that of the other Algonquians of the eastern woodlands.[4] As such, they were ancient residents of the area, probably tracing their descent to Archaic peoples of the east. The Athapascans of the western Subarctic, on the other hand, had a different biological, linguistic, and cultural heritage. Physically, as has been observed,[5] they have been set apart as the Deneid variety of Indian, representing one of the last waves of migrants from Siberia. Athapascan languages have a fairly wide distribution in western North America, the Haidas and Tlingits of the Northwest Coast speaking languages related to Athapascan, with a few other scattered Athapascan speakers in southern Oregon and northern California. But the bulk of Athapascan-speaking peoples were east of the Rockies, in the western Subarctic, but also scattered southward through the Plains into the Southwest. How long Athapascan Apaches were in the Plains is not clear; they invaded the Southwest in very recent times, apparently only a few years before the Spaniards rode into the same region from the opposite direction.

The archeological forerunners of the Subarctic Athapascans have been labeled the Denetasiro tradition,[6] and its known geographic distribution extends from the interior of Canada's Northwest Territories to the southwest Yukon, but it may have been much more extensive. It apparently was a local development and adaptation to the interior Subarctic conditions, appearing there sometime after 2000 B.C. It seems to have developed from the earlier Northwest Microblade tradition, known from roughly the same region, whose beginnings may date as early as 6500 B.C.[7] The appearance of the Northwest Microblade tradition may mark the arrival of the Athapascans in the Subarctic, but this is speculative; and even if it does not, it is apparent that the Athapascan-speaking peoples had ancient roots in the region. In brief, the hunters and fishermen of the Subarctic were heir to a way of life worked out in that harsh environment many millennia earlier.

HISTORY

Though remote from centers of New World colonization and occupants of a land that had few attractions for Europeans, the peoples of the eastern Subarctic were among the earliest of North America's natives to be contacted and influenced by Europeans. Well before the opening of the sixteenth century, fishermen from many European ports were taking cod and hunting whales off the shores of Newfoundland. Their numbers increased year by year, and they soon possessed an intimate knowledge of the coasts of Labrador, Newfoundland, the Gulf of St. Lawrence, and Nova Scotia. They used the many harbors of the region to salt their catch and repair ships and equipment, and, almost immediately, they began to trade with the natives. Few records were made of this commerce, but that it was substantial is certain.

As early as 1508 seven Indians, presumably Beothuks, including their canoes, arms, and belongings, had been brought back to France,[8] and by the time European governments undertook explorations, the natives were well accustomed to trading furs for European goods. In 1524 Giovannida Verrazzano, sailing under the French flag, cruised the Atlantic coast from the Carolinas to what was probably Nova Scotia. The natives of Nova Scotia, apparently Micmacs or their close relatives, unlike the Indians farther south, had already had contacts with Europeans, with the result that they were wary of them, though interested in trade. Ten years later, in 1534, when Cartier sailed into Chaleur Bay in the Gulf of St. Lawrence in search of the western passage, he too was met by Micmacs. They came in canoes with furs, eager to trade for knives and hatchets. The Micmacs were culturally marginal to the Subarctic (see Chapter 3), but there is no reason to believe their contacts with Europeans were earlier than those of their northern neighbors. By mid-century, French and other ships were arriving specifically to trade, and by the opening of the seventeenth century, the fur trade had become a thriving, bustling business. Those Indians first affected by the fur trade were near the coasts and close to Quebec and Tadoussac, but most, if not all, of the peoples of the eastern Subarctic must have been directly or indirectly involved in the fur trade before the century was over.

In 1670 Charles II gave a charter to Prince Rupert and a number of noblemen associates as the "Governor and Company of Adventurers of England trading into Hudson's Bay." Granted a monopoly in trade and virtually absolute control of the land and its people, they built a trading post on James Bay, and other coastal posts followed. But until Canada was ceded to Great Britain in 1763, the Hudson's Bay Company, though profitable, suffered many reverses at the hands of the French. After 1763 other fur traders came into the region, finally joining forces as the North-West Fur Company. Most of the tribes of the western Subarctic had been drawn into or were heavily affected by the fur trade economy by the end of the eighteenth century, but, surprisingly, some particularly remote peoples were not contacted by the outside world until the last years of the nineteenth century.

The earlier competition between the English and French and, later, between fur traders and fur trading companies had disastrous consequences for the native tribes. They were quickly brought into a dependent relationship with the traders, adopting their vastly superior weapons, tools, and utensils. Their ancient economy based on use was soon converted to an economy based on trade. To acquire their new necessities, they had to secure furs, leading to wholesale slaughter of fur-bearing animals. Tribes left their old lands as the furbearers were extirpated or as they were drawn to trading posts, and a tremendous increase in intertribal strife and warfare resulted. Cultural chaos and disintegration was furthered by traders who debauched the natives with whiskey in their competition for the natives' furs. But probably most destructive were the inadvertently introduced epidemics of measles, influenza, smallpox, and other diseases. In the 1780s, for example, a smallpox epidemic swept Canada. Ninety percent of the Chipewyans were reported to have died, and the Crees, who had been expanding by virtue of their acquisition of firearms from the Hudson's Bay Company, were so devastated by the disease that they were never able to recover even a semblance of their former tribal strength.[9] These were neither isolated nor rare cases; virtually all of the Subarctic peoples were time and again decimated by epidemics, so much so that their survivors represent but a fractional and distorted shadow of what they once were.

CULTURAL SUMMARY

Subsistence and Material Culture

The peoples of the Subarctic were nomadic hunters and fishermen dependent upon a variety of large game animals and fish, and, secondarily, upon small mammals, birds, and various berries and other wild plants. The most sought-after game animal was the barren ground caribou, although a number of groups, because of their location away from the tundra, were forced to subsist partially or entirely on other animals. The Naskapis of Labrador, for example, hunted caribou throughout the year, save for a short period in late spring and early summer when some groups went down to the coast to fish and others remained inland to hunt small game and to fish in lakes and streams. The neighboring Montagnais, who occupied much more wooded country, hunted moose in the wintertime, coming down to the St. Lawrence coast in summer for salmon and eels, and to harpoon seals. They seldom hunted caribou.[10]

Similarly, in the western Subarctic, such tribes as the Chipewyans, Yellowknives, and Dogribs followed the caribou out onto the tundra in summer to hunt them, retreating to more forested country in winter to subsist on a wider variety of game. The Slaves, living at some distance from the barren grounds, did not enter them to hunt caribou; instead, they hunted moose and woodland caribou (which belongs to a different species than the barren ground animal and is not gregarious), and they also depended much more heavily on fish.[11]

The Athapascans who lived along streams in the Pacific drainage were able to take advantage of the several species of salmon that ascended the rivers to spawn, and this relatively reliable and stable food supply, as well as contact with Northwest Coast tribes, led to an elaboration of culture that is somewhat atypical for Subarctic people. The Tanainas[12] around Cook inlet, for example, had access to five kinds of salmon, other fish and shellfish, sea mammals, bear, mountain sheep, mountain goat, caribou, moose, smaller mammals, birds, and many berries and other plant foods; they obviously lived in a tremendously richer habitat than did most of the inland peoples.

Although the animals and plants the widely scattered Subarctic tribes lived on varied considerably, save for those more fortunate tribes in the far northwestern Pacific drainage, most Subarctic peoples were alike in that their subsistence was apt to be precarious during at least part of the year. It may be that in precontact times most Subarctic peoples managed to get through the year without undergoing much, if any, want, but in historic times impoverishment and starvation seem to have increasingly haunted the region.

Caribou were hunted in many ways, and it was common to intercept migrating herds at river crossings and similar places the animals habitually used. Caribou were often impounded by stringing lines between posts leading to corrals or other places into which they could be driven. Caribou were often snared, their many-tined antlers making them particularly vulnerable to this form of hunting. They were also speared while crossing streams or lakes, and were stalked by hunters using bows and arrows. Musk oxen were hunted to some extent on the tundra, and these animals were also often impounded. Moose and woodland caribou were most easily taken in winter in deep snow, hunters on snowshoes being able to track and approach them more closely during this season. Moose were attracted to hunters during their rutting season by rubbing antlers together, and they were sometimes pursued with dogs. Dogs were also utilized by some tribes for hunting bears and other animals; smaller mammals were usually taken by snares, deadfalls, and other traps. In general the people of the Subarctic were—as they had to be—knowledgeable about the habits and nature of the animals they hunted, and they mustered a considerable array of techniques with which to take them.

During the long, fierce winters, preservation of food was no problem, but during the short summers, some surplus game was often at hand, and several methods were used to preserve it. Meat was cut into thin strips and smoked or dried, as were fish; both dried fish and meat were often pounded and mixed with marrow and berries to be preserved as pemmican. Game animals were often cached, particularly in winter, by wrapping the game in a hide and hanging it from a pole, or by depositing it on a specially built platform. Such methods were necessary when a hunter had slain a caribou or other animal and wished to go on for another, but was reluctant to leave his hard-won game for ravenous wolves or wolverines to enjoy.

Subarctic tribes cooked much of their food in birch- or spruce-bark vessels by dropping heated rocks into them. Large chunks of meat were cooked, as among Dogribs and Yellowknives, by digging a hole, lining it with a caribou paunch, filling it with water and meat, then dropping heated rocks into it. Stone-boiling is a surprisingly effective way to cook, but of course not as efficient or quick as cooking in metal utensils, and Subarctic peoples adopted metal utensils as soon as they became available. Meat was also roasted over open fires, and much seems to have been eaten raw or nearly so.

There has been a continuing dispute over the hunting territories of eastern Subarctic peoples, though it now seems to be pretty much resolved.[13] Frank G. Speck discovered in the 1920s that the Montagnais and other neighboring Algonquians possessed what he described as family-owned hunting territories, passed down from father to son. At that time the existence of some form of capitalism among primitive hunters, and the theory that there was an inborn urge to possess and own property, had many social and political implications. But subsequent investigations among the Montagnais and their neighbors have revealed that rights of inheritance did not supersede band interest, that every person had a right to land to trap on, and even that a person, on occasion, had to give up part of his land for another's use. There was no advantage or prestige associated with holding large hunting territories or more land than could be exploited, and land could not be bought or sold. In short, hunting territories amounted to trapping rights in a particular area; and others could fish, gather berries, and otherwise use such land. A man could even kill beavers in another's territory as long as he needed them for food. As Leacock has shown, these hunting territories developed in response to the fur trade economy and were not an aboriginal institution. The Montagnais were not primitive capitalists, and their historically developed hunting territories did not indicate any innate urge to own land.

Among nomadic people, transportation is always a problem, and to those who live in a land of sharp seasonal contrasts, such as the Subarctic, there are special difficulties. The problems of winter transportation were solved by the use of snowshoes and toboggans. Snowshoes were constructed of a frame of birch with a mesh of hide strips *(babiche)*, the familiar tailed snowshoe being the common form. Toboggans, that is, runnerless sleds constructed of strips of birch turned or curled up at the front, were used to haul camp gear, game, and other heavy loads. Among some groups, women pulled the toboggans, but they were also drawn by dogs, the Subarctic Indians using the fanwise hitch of the Eskimos for their teams. Many loads were also carried on the back, these people utilizing the ubiquitous American Indian tumpline over the forehead or head for the efficient weight distribution of back and shoulder loads. Travel was more difficult in the summer months, and many peoples used the streams and lakes to move about. In the southern parts of the Subarctic, where birch grew to a usable size, birchbark canoes were employed, and farther north, canoes of spruce bark took their place. Skin-covered kayaks were not in use in the Subarctic, although a skin coracle, or bull boat, was known to some groups.

Considerable use was made of bark, wood, bone, horn, and antler, and relatively few tools appear to have been made of stone, although metal tools replaced stone counterparts so long ago that definite knowledge is wanting. Partially tanned caribou hide, and sometimes moose hide, was cut into long continuous strips or was braided in ropes or lines known as *babiche*. These lines were used for a wide array of purposes, being fashioned into netting for the fences employed in impounding caribou, for snares, and many other purposes. The basic hunting weapon was the bow and arrows, and spears and clubs were also in use.

There was some variation in the kinds of shelter employed by the peoples of the Subarctic. The majority utilized what amounted to a small, simplified tipi that, in fact, may well have been the ancestral type of the more elaborate Plains dwelling. With a greater diameter to height than the Plains tipi, the conical framework of poles might be covered with caribou or other hides sewn together with sinew or *babiche*, or it might be covered with brush or bark. Such dwellings were appropriate when following the caribou or being otherwise on the move, but some tribes, such as the Slaves, when settling down for extended periods in the winter, erected small gabled log houses, chinked with moss and covered with earth. Among the Carriers, who were influenced by the Northwest Coast Salish, underground houses were employed in winter. The more southerly Crees utilized a dome-shaped wigwam, like that of the neighboring Ojibwas, covered with sheets of birch bark or rushes. Farther north the Crees employed conical tipis covered with caribou hide or pine bark.

The principal materials for clothing in the Subarctic were caribou and moose hide and rabbit skins. Soft-sole moccasins were often sewn to thigh-length leggings, and for winter wear among people like the Slaves,[14] rabbit-skin leggings were worn inside moose-skin leggings and moccasins. Except for tribes influenced by Eskimos, parkas were not worn. The Naskapis, for example, borrowed the tailored shirt of the Eskimos of the Labrador coast, ornamented it with painted geometric designs, and sometimes added a hood. Semitailored skin shirts to which fur sleeves were attached in the eastern Subarctic, were the basic upper covering. Hats, mittens, and robes were added in cold weather. Clothing was ornamented with porcupine quillwork, with beads sewn on in floral designs when they became available, and often with fringes of hide or moose hair. Rabbit skins were an important clothing item among many Subarctic tribes. The skins were cut into strips, then woven or braided together. Sewn together and reinforced with fiber, they made warm blankets. Rabbit skins were also widely used to line mittens and other garments.

Throughout the Subarctic very little seems to have been done to enhance or beautify the body. The hair was often uncut, but bound by a headband to keep it out of the way. Face painting was relatively unimportant, but tattooing was practiced by some. The Chipewyans, Dogribs, Yellowknives, and Crees tattooed their faces and sometimes their foreheads with several parallel lines.

Social Organization

Scattered out by the demands of their hunting and foraging life, and seldom settled in any one place for more than a few weeks, the social organization of the peoples of the Subarctic was, of necessity, simple and undifferentiated. Unfortunately, few details are known about their aboriginal social organization since their cultures were shattered or much altered by the impact of the fur trade and introduced diseases before descriptions were made. Most Subarctic peoples subsequently have been organized in "composite bands,"[15] that is, rather amorphous groups of families in which the rules of marriage, residence, and kinship are vague and blurred. They came about when the remnants of decimated and unrelated families and bands joined forces. As a result, the basic nuclear families sought marriages for their offspring on the basis of expediency, and a newly married couple resided where they wished. But the view that the social organization of the Subarctic is only an expedient response to past catastrophes probably can be pushed too far. Their social organization may always have been relatively amorphous, unstructured, and leaderless.

Throughout the Subarctic the basic social unit and the only one to exist during much of the year was the simple, individual family. This was apparently most often the case of the tribes that did not have access to the barren ground caribou and that depended on the solitary moose and other game best taken by lone hunters. Two or three related families often habitually camped and hunted together and, on occasion, temporarily joined other similar families. These larger groups are termed bands, but it should be emphasized that they were not continuously in existence, and their membership, if it could be called such, was constantly shifting. Any particular family might, for example, camp one season with one band, the next season with another, depending upon a number of factors, not the least of which was mere whim.

Each band ordinarily had a leader of sorts, usually a particularly successful hunter, often a man who combined hunting skills with some special supernatural powers; but nowhere in the region did he have much authority.[16] Such informal control as he was able to exert was based on qualities of personality, persuasiveness, hunting success, and little more. Among the Dogribs and Yellowknives, who seasonally engaged in communal caribou hunts and drives, the office of band chief took on more importance than it did among the Slaves, who did little communal hunting. There was no tribe or other political subdivision larger than the band in the Subarctic, although a number of bands speaking the same or very similar dialects, following the same way of life, and occupying contiguous territory are referred to as tribes.

The division of labor among members of the nuclear family varied from tribe to tribe, but everywhere it was divided rigorously along lines of sex and age. Men did the hunting, and usually built canoes and other tools and equipment. Women erected the shelters, moved them from camp to camp, gathered and hauled the firewood, performed most of the other camp chores, and also often did much of the fishing, berrying, and other gathering chores. As soon as children were able, they grew into the tasks appropriate to their sex.

The Subarctic Athapascans shared a common method of kinship reckoning, said to represent the original and early Athapascan kinship system.[17] Both parallel cousins and cross-cousins were accorded sibling status—that is, they were referred to as older or younger siblings—and maternal and paternal grandparents were merged under a single term. The siblings of parents were distinguished from one another in that the terms for a father's brother were different from those for a mother's brother. This system indicates the importance of and emphasis on the nuclear family; it also reflects the rules of incest, since marriage to cousins, which is to say people designated as siblings, was not ordinarily practiced. Since kinship was not reckoned beyond the grandparental generation, marriage was possible to descendants of the siblings of grandparents.

The levirate was generally practiced by the Athapascans of the Subarctic, a man marrying or assuming responsibility for his dead brother's wife. This custom is reflected in the kinship terminology in that a man referred to his brother's children as son and daughter. The custom of the sororate, in which a woman married her dead husband's brother, is less well established for Subarctic peoples, but apparently it was also practiced. Joking relationships, consisting of sexual joking and more than usual intimacy, existed between potential marriage partners. But the reverse rules of avoidance, particularly for those people a person could not marry, were weakly developed. Thus, a man was not obliged to avoid his sisters, and among the Slaves and other Athapascans, he had some responsibility for their welfare.

Bride service following marriage was common, a man living with and working for his bride's parents for about a year.[18] Uxorilocal residence was, in fact, common and perhaps usual among the northern Athapascans, which is somewhat atypical for band-level societies.[19] It suggests that the need for close cooperation between hunters, easily achieved by fathers and sons hunting together in a well-known territory and often cited as the reason for patrilocal bands, either was not a factor or was met some other way. The Dogribs, Yellowknives, and nearby tribes were known for the peculiar custom of wrestling for wives.[20] Polygyny, other than that produced by the levirate, was not proscribed, though nowhere does it seem to have been common. Where it did occur, it seems to have been most commonly of the sororal type or of marriage to captive women. Prestige accrued to the man able to support multiple wives.

Among the Athapascans of the western Subarctic, birth took place in a special brush shelter erected for the purpose. Throughout the area there were strong feelings about the dangers of women in childbirth and during menstruation. Women were isolated at such times, and there were a variety of taboos relating to their preparing, butchering, or eating meat. Other than isolation at birth, there were few, if any, special rites or ceremonies connected with birth. Women ordinarily named their children, often after something connected with a dream they had had. Infanticide was practiced by at least some of the Subarctic peoples, ordinarily during times of famine. Among the Kutchins, mothers sometimes killed their infant daughters in order to spare them the hard life that was a woman's lot. Throughout the area babies were carried in hide bags, often lined with moss or fur. The cradleboard was little used, even by the Algonquian-speaking tribes. Some tribes, such as the Chipewyans, emulated Eskimo women and carried babies on their backs or inside folds in their clothing.[21]

The education and training of the young was wholly informal and mostly by adult example. Puberty was not felt to be fraught with danger for boys, although at about this stage in life, boys fasted and isolated themselves in order to acquire "power" or "medicine." But the first menses marked the beginning of a time of peril and possible contamination for girls. Her violation of various taboos, it was thought, might affront game animals so that they would no longer allow men to kill them, and hence was a very serious matter. At menstruation girls and women left camp and built isolated brush shelters where they remained during their periods. Taboos varied among different groups, but they usually included a prohibition on fresh meat and some restrictions on drinking water. Women were regarded as so dangerous at this time that they dared not touch their own bodies with their hands, so they were supplied with special scratching sticks. Their gaze was equally potent, so that they often covered their eyes or were required to keep their eyes averted during their periods. Needless to say, touching a man's weapons would destroy their usefulness, and touching a man could deprive him of his strength and whatever supernatural power he might have. In general, restrictions on menstruating Algonquian women were somewhat less onerous than among Athapascans.

Marriage was not celebrated with any ceremony, a young couple simply taking up residence with the bride's parents. Few adults went unmarried for any length of time since a married couple constituted the basic economic unit. Marriages were relatively stable, though divorce, at least so far as men were concerned, merely entailed desertion of the wife. There was considerable sexual freedom before marriage, and, at least among the Indians of the Great Slave Lake area, wife exchange and loaning of wives was known.[22]

In this region where life was hazardous and normally rather brief, perhaps it should be expected that in order for the group to survive, the old, the weak, and the infirm at times might be sacrificed. Thus,

the Chipewyans, Hares, Kutchins, Crees, Montagnais, and probably
other Subarctic peoples killed or abandoned the aged, sometimes at
their own request. Cannibalism was also known in the Subarctic; it
appears to have been practiced only by those who were starving, consuming those who had already perished. The custom was more prevalent
among the Crees and other Algonquian tribes, although among them
considerable stigma attached to people who had eaten their fellows.
Cannibals were apparently apt to become psychotic, and during psychotic episodes they copied the behavior of mythological cannibalistic
giants. There were a number of legends about these windigos, that is,
humans who had been changed into these monsters by their cannibalism.[23]

The northern Athapascans believed that death was caused by sorcery or other non-natural causes, and there was a great deal of apprehension and fear associated with it. When death was felt to be imminent
among the Slaves, Dogribs, and Yellowknives, a person might confess
the wrong-doing of which he had been guilty in the belief that it would
postpone death. Among the Slaves a person near death was believed
to possess prophetic powers, and his guardian spirit hovered nearby,
perhaps making noises. The lodge in which a person had died was
abandoned, and the dead were quickly disposed of. Several methods
of burial were practiced, including placing the dead on scaffolds built
of poles or in trees by the Naskapis, likely associated with the difficulty
of digging graves in frozen soil. But burial in log tombs, as among the
Slaves, was also practiced by the Crees, Montagnais, and, no doubt,
others.[24] Algonquian burial practices differed from those of the Athapascans chiefly in the self-mutilation the Algonquians often employed to
express their grief at the death of a loved one and in the annual feasts
for the dead that they held.[25] The marginal Carriers, who practiced
cremation, had a curious trait, for which the tribe is named, that required widows to carry the charred remains of their husbands on their
backs.[26]

Warfare

Very little is known directly about the precontact relationships between
Subarctic tribes or with outside peoples. After contact the intertribal
situation was so revolutionized that it is almost hopeless to attempt
to project it backward in time. But indirectly it may be surmised that
Subarctic peoples were, by the force of necessity, relatively peaceful.
They were so thinly scattered over such an immense territory and their
surplus food supply was so limited that to bring together large numbers
of warriors for any length of time to engage in battle was obviously

beyond their capabilities. What intergroup strife there was had to be small-scale raiding and feuding, probably motivated mostly by revenge, witchcraft, and possibly trespass. In postcontact times warriors from several bands might, as among the Slaves, join forces for a brief raid on a neighboring enemy. The Crees, who had obtained firearms, expanded rapidly at the expense of the Chipewyans, appropriating large parts of their territory. Some Subarctic peoples, such as the Hares, however, were so peacefully inclined that they never succumbed to the struggles brought on by the fur trade. They ran from strangers and among their neighbors were held in low esteem for their cowardice.

Nowhere in the Subarctic were warriors honored or did warfare become formalized in the sense that there were special ceremonial preparations for battle. Trophies such as scalps were not taken, and no victory dances or the like were performed following successful raids. The bodies of enemy dead were looted, and all but young women captives were killed. Tribes influenced by Northwest Coast tribes and Eskimos wore slat armor, and the Carriers carried oval moose-hide shields, but elsewhere there seems to have been no special equipment for warfare.

Religious and Ceremonial Life

Coherent, organized, codified beliefs about the supernatural world were absent in the Subarctic, as were virtually all group ceremonies and rituals. Like so many other aspects of their culture, supernaturalistic beliefs and practices seem vague and blurred, and if they can be characterized at all, they would have to be termed individualistic, with an emphasis on personal guardian spirits and a deep-seated dread of witchcraft. Among the Naskapis and Montagnais, there was some conception of a great sky god, but so removed was he from everyday affairs that only occasionally did men bother to smoke to him. There seems to have been no widely shared beliefs about an afterlife or much concern about it, although a few tribes, specifically the Chipewyans and Slaves, did believe that the souls of the dead, helped by the spirits of otters and loons, journeyed through the earth and crossed a lake to a place where life was begun again.

Throughout the area the dominant, and to individuals the important, supernatural beings were the guardian spirits individuals acquired during dreams and visions. Young boys were often sent away from camp in hopes that they might "see something" or be visited by a supernatural. But throughout the area the quest for these spirits was remarkably informal and unstructured. Nevertheless, most men seem to have acquired these spirit helpers, although the potency of personal power thus acquired varied widely. Game animals, birds, and natural forces such as lightning and thunder were common guardian spirits, and they ordinarily imposed various food and other taboos on the recipients. Unlike the guardian spirits of Plains Indians, those of the Subarctic were held to be rather confidential, and a person kept their nature to himself. Guardian spirits were trusted to see individuals through times of crisis and to assist in warding off all sorts of attacks by malicious spirits.

In addition to guardian spirits, there seems to have been widespread concern about the souls of game animals. The underlying idea was that animals allowed themselves to be killed, and if humans, through accident or oversight, offended the animals' spirits or souls, they would not appear in their accustomed places or the hunters would not be able to kill them. Thus, men were very careful to avoid antagonizing animals and did what they could to propitiate their souls. Among the Slaves, for example, animals were not believed to have supernatural attributes, but they were regarded as earthly representatives of supernatural animal people who were dangerous. The Slaves felt that moose and beaver meat should not be fed to dogs, and that to do so was a mark of disrespect. If the dogs were given such meat, the Slaves would be unable to kill these animals again.[27] The bones, hair, and other leftover scraps of these animals were carefully cached in trees or thrown into rivers. Other Subarctic peoples, as a consequence of the same kind of beliefs, had a number of other rules and restrictions surrounding the taking and eating of game animals. Frequently, for example, menstruating women had to be kept away from meat or certain portions of game animals, and many hunting customs were directly related to it.

Some men, because of their special gifts and special ability to deal with the supernatural world, became shamans. Their principal function was to determine the cause of illness and to cure disease, but among the Montagnais and Naskapis, some shamans also functioned to determine why game was scarce and to foretell by scapulimancy (interpreting the markings on the charred shoulder bones of animals) where game might be found. Since sickness and death were often attributed to sorcery, shamanistic performances were often aimed at warding off malicious spells. Violation of dietary and other taboos also resulted in illness, and medicine men often were called in to discover its exact nature. Most Subarctic peoples, like the Eskimos, had few or no herbal remedies, and shamans employed massage and suction to relieve aches and pains, as well as much sleight-of-hand in which various objects, such as slivers of bone, were extracted from a patient's body.

Shamans, logically enough, were the ones who, it was believed, could maliciously turn their special powers on other men to bewitch or incapacitate them, or to cause their deaths.

Apparently witchcraft was generally attributed to outsiders and seldom to a member of a person's own band. Among the more dramatic performances were those put on by Naskapis and Montagnais shamans, who, while hidden inside special cylindrical lodges, were able to escape though bound hand and foot with strong caribou thongs.[28] Many of the Crees had borrowed from their Ojibwa neighbors the Grand Medicine Society, a secret religious organization; but even among them the various taboos and various hunting customs intended to attract and mollify the game were much more important.

NOTES

[1] Wissler (1938, 233–36) places the Athapascans of the western Subarctic in a Mackenzie area, the Algonquians of the eastern Subarctic are grouped with the Algonquians of the Eastern Woodlands. For a recent summary of the area, see Helm and Leacock (1971).

[2] Osgood (1936), in a preliminary paper, divides the Northern Athapaskans into two groups: a "Pacific Drainage culture," and an "Arctic Drainage culture." The Pacific Drainage cultures are distinguished by salmon dependence, the complex of traits associated with it, a more sedentary life, unilateral kinship systems, and ceremonial life, including arts and games. The Pacific Drainage cultures correspond roughly to those listed here as influenced by Northwest Coast culture.

[3] Jenness (1934, 265–67). For various studies of Subarctic Crees, see Knight (1968); Mason (1967); Rogers (1963; 1965; 1966; 1967).

[4] Willey (1966, 414).

[5] Neumann (1952).

[6] MacNeish (1964).

[7] Willey (1966, 415).

[8] Sauer (1971, 51, quoting from Julien, 1948, 336).

[9] Jenness (1934, 284, 385).

[10] Ibid., p.271.

[11] For the Slaves, see Honigmann (1946); for the Chipewyans and Yellowknives, Hearne (1795); Birket-Smith (1930). Oswalt (1973) contains a chapter on the Chipewyans, with an extensive bibliography.

[12] Osgood (1937).

[13] For the basic papers dealing with hunting territories, see Speck (1926; 1927); Speck and Eiseley (1939); Hallowell (1949); Cooper (1939); Lips (1947); Eiseley(1947); Leacock (1954);

[14] Mason (1946, 21–22).

[15] Steward (1955, chaps. 7 and 8) was the first to name and describe this type of social organization.

[16] See MacNeish (1956) for northern Athapascan leadership in aboriginal time and under fur trade conditions.

[17] Kroeber (1937).

[18] Mason (1946, 31).

[19] Service (1966, 32ff.).

[20] Honigmann (1946, 86).

[21] Jenness (1934, 388).

[22] Mason (1946, 32).

[23] Jenness (1934, 285).

[24] Ibid., p. 286.

[25] Ibid., p. 86.

[26] Ibid., pp. 363, 368.

[27] Honigmann (1946, 76–77).

[28] Jenness (1934, 273).

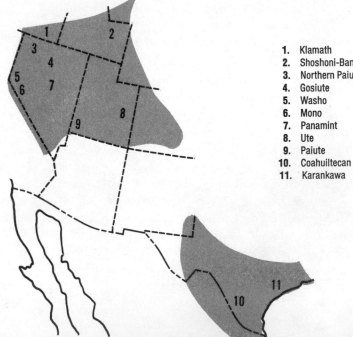

1. Klamath
2. Shoshoni-Bannock
3. Northern Paiute (Paviotso)
4. Gosiute
5. Washo
6. Mono
7. Panamint
8. Ute
9. Paiute
10. Coahuiltecan
11. Karankawa

SIX

DESERT GATHERERS

Among the most inhospitable and forbidding regions of the continent are the deserts and semideserts of western North America. Yet men adapted their lives to the rigors of these arid lands over 8,000 years ago. Though few in numbers, meager in possessions, and simple in social structure, so successful and persistent were they that many scattered Indian groups continued to follow the ancient way of life, little changed, into historic times.

Deserts and near-deserts encompass about 500,000 square miles of stark and varied land in the southwestern United States and northern Mexico. To the north lies the Great Basin, a rugged region of interior drainage, bounded on the west by the Sierra Nevada Mountains of eastern California, which continue northward as the Cascades of Oregon, and on the east by the Wasatch Mountains of Utah. Culturally and in terms of general environmental conditions, part of the Columbia River plateau of Idaho and eastern Oregon belongs with the Great Basin. In this sense the northern boundary of an expanded Great Basin may be thought of as the Blue Mountains of Oregon and the Salmon River and Bitterroot mountains of Idaho. Similarly, the Colorado River plateau of Utah and western Colorado, bounded to the east by the Rocky Mountains, also may be considered part of the Great Basin.

Much of the Great Basin is steppe or semidesert country, but in western Utah and southern Nevada it becomes a true desert, merging into the Mojave Desert of southeastern California. The Mojave, in turn, continues as the Sonoran Desert, extending across southern Arizona into southwestern New Mexico and southward into Baja California and Sonora. East and southeast of the Sierra Madre Occidental lies the Chihuahua Desert, a plateau drained chiefly by the Rio Conchos, a river rising in the Sierra Madre and emptying into the Rio Grande about two hundred miles below El Paso. There are also many ephemeral streams in the region, dry arroyos during most of the year, boiling floods following rains, which disappear into the rocky soil or into lagoons. On its eastern side the Chihuahua Desert merges into the Bolsón de Mapimí, a huge, enclosed, mostly desert drainage basin. To the east lies the low, desolate mountain mass of the Sierra Madre Oriental, which continues on southward to eventually unite with the western mountain mass at the Isthmus of Tehuantepec. On its northeastern side, arroyos and a few rivers, often dry in their upper courses, drain into the Rio Grande. On the Gulf side the San Fernando drains northern Tamaulipas, and the Soto la Marina in the south roughly marks the southern coastal limits of the desert lands.

In a narrow sense much of this tremendous and diverse region does not qualify as a true desert, but in the broad and commonly understood one, use of the term is warranted. Tied together by a dearth of water, precipitation ranges from a yearly average of several inches in its more barren deserts to twenty inches or so in the higher elevations and toward the Gulf coast. But rainfall averages are somewhat misleading since there is apt to be tremendous yearly variation, some localities occasionally receiving far more precipitation than the ten inches that technically classify them as deserts, and regions that usually receive somewhat more rainfall going for months or even years with almost none. In some areas too, as in the lower Rio Grande Valley, which receives between twenty and twenty-five inches of rainfall, precipitation effectivity is much reduced by high evaporation rates, with the result that plant cover, and the environment in general, is little different than in regions receiving much less rainfall. Throughout the arid lands, daytime summer temperatures are extremely hot, with rapid cooling at night. In the Great Basin and at higher elevations, winters are cold; in the more southerly latitudes, however, winters are mild.

The scant precipitation and high evaporation rates at the lower elevations of the desert lands result in xerophytic vegetation adapted to minimal water requirements, such as cactus, agave, greasewood, sagebrush, creosote bush, mesquite, and burroweed. A surprising amount of this vegetation is edible in one form or another, as well as useful in other ways. Many cactus fruits are edible, and other parts also may be consumed, such as the pads of prickly pears once the spines have been removed. There are dozens of species of agaves in western North America, from the familiar century plant, frequently grown in American gardens, to the Mexican maguey, from which pulque, a rather weak beer, is brewed. The rough, spiny, and fibrous leaves of the agaves grow from a central head, or bulb, which is edible after special preparation.

Many of the thorny shrubs of the desert, mesquite for example, produce highly nutritious seeds, and the many grasses and other plants growing along water courses and in damper situations bear small, hard, but edible seeds. There is also a large assortment of other edible roots, bulbs, and berries.

Xerophytic vegetation does not support concentrations of larger game animals, although there is a surprising diversity, and occasionally even abundance, of other animal life. Deer, pronghorn antelope, and jackrabbits were the principal game animals available to the desert peoples, though deer and antelope were absent or sparsely scattered in much of the region, and rabbit populations are markedly cyclic, their numbers swinging from relative abundance to extreme scarcity. There is a diversity of other, smaller animals in the deserts, including insects, snakes and lizards, rats and mice, birds, skunks, javelinas or collared peccaries, and many others, all of which are edible.

The desert lands have relatively few streams and lakes, and many of those that do exist are brackish, or flow into depressions having no outlets, resulting in salt lakes and marshes. The springs, streams, and lakes, from the Snake River in the north to the Colorado and Rio Grande in the south, inexorably attracted human populations. They not only supplied life-sustaining water but also harbored a variety of fish, shellfish, other animals, and aquatic plants; and their valleys supported willows, cottonwoods, and much other vegetation, all of which were valuable assets to desert peoples. At higher elevations, with heavier rainfall, vegetation is also more abundant and, seasonally at least, was attractive to man. In the Great Basin, for example, in the mountainous country between about 6,000 and 8,000 feet, is a zone of juniper and piñon pine forest, piñon nuts being the single most important food in the regions where they occurred.[1] Other plant foods, particularly roots and bulbs, are relatively more abundant in this piñon-juniper belt, as are deer and other game. In the mountains above 8,000 feet, ponderosa pine becomes the predominant tree, and mountain sheep are added to the list of game animals.

Two basically different kinds of native cultures existed in these arid lands of North America: wandering, gathering peoples who subsisted on its wild plants and animals, and sedentary farming peoples who depended primarily on the crops they were able to raise. The realization that these two types of cultural systems had existed side by side for many centuries in the same general environmental region developed rather slowly, perhaps in part because it seemed to vitiate concepts about culture areas; but it is widely accepted today.[2] Kirchhoff's proposals have been followed here, although the term "Desert gatherers" has been substituted for his "Arid American" culture area; and in Chapter

7, "Southwestern farmers" is employed rather than "American Oasis" culture area. Kirchhoff also includes California gatherers (Chapter 9) in his Arid America culture area. Although following a wild food economy, their environment was more bountiful and their cultures were in many ways distinctive, so they have been given separate treatment here.[3]

The farming peoples of the desert lands were much more restricted geographically than the gatherers since they were limited to places where they could irrigate their crops or where natural runoff provided enough water for them. Agriculture spread northward at a relatively early date, and by historic times, farming or part-farming peoples occupied virtually all of the desert lands that could be farmed with their techniques. Many of the part-farmers, as Kirchhoff calls them, were once gatherers who had learned from their neighbors how to raise crops. These part-farmers also are discussed in Chapter 7.

The food gatherers of the Great Basin are better known than the other gathering peoples of the desert regions, partly because ethnographers have been more active north of the international border and partly because many of the gathering cultures in the southern portions of the region changed greatly or were destroyed by Spanish-Mexican civilization long before they could be adequately described. The result has been that the Great Basin often has been set off as a distinct culture area, but the other nonfarming, gathering cultures of the arid lands were left in limbo or attached as "marginal" members to other culture areas. This has had some curious results, such as aligning the gathering peoples of the south Texas brush country with the farming and hunting cultures of the eastern United States, and their relatives south of the border with the high civilizations of Mesoamerica.[4] There is a growing tendency, however, to group the nonfarming peoples of northeastern Mexico and southern Texas in a separate culture area variously termed Northeast Mexico, South Texas, or Western Gulf, the latter designation being used here.[5] Since the emphasis here is on Indians north of the Rio Grande, the gathering peoples of Baja California and the other scattered gatherers of northern Mexico have been minimized in favor of those of the Great Basin and the Western Gulf.

Most of the peoples of the Great Basin spoke Numic languages (superseding "Plateau Shoshonean"), of the Uaztecan family of languages.[6] The Numic-speaking peoples are composed of three language groups, each of which has two subdivisions. The Western Numic languages, Mono and Paviotso, were spoken in southern Oregon, western Nevada, and eastern California, by the Monos, Owens Valley Paiutes, Paviotsos, and Northern Bannocks. The Central Numic languages, Panamint (or Koso) and Shoshoni, were spoken throughout central and eastern Nevada, northwestern Utah, southern Idaho, and western Wyoming. Panamint was spoken by the Panamint Shoshonis of Death Valley, dialects of Shoshoni by the Western Shoshonis of central Nevada; the Gosiutes of the Utah-Nevada boundary region; Northwestern Shoshonis of the Snake River plain in southeastern Idaho; Northern and Lemhi Shoshonis in northeastern Idaho and western Wyoming; Eastern or Wind River Shoshonis in central Wyoming; and the Comanches of the Plains. The Southern Numic languages, Kawaiisu and Ute, were spoken from eastern California into Colorado. Kawaiisu was spoken by the peoples of the Mojave Desert; various Ute dialects were spoken by the Chemehuevis of the lower Colorado River, a number of Southern Paiute bands above them on the Colorado, the Southern Utes of southern Colorado and northern New Mexico, the Northern Utes of western Colorado, and a number of bands in central and eastern Utah.

The only non-Numic-speaking Indians of the Great Basin were the Washos of western Nevada and the marginal Pit River Indians (including the Achomawis and Atsugewis) of northeastern California, who spoke Hokan languages of the Hokaltecan family of languages. Many other desert peoples, including gatherers and part-farmers, also spoke Utaztecan languages. These included the Pimas and Papagos of southern Arizona and Sonora, and a number of northern Mexican tribes such as the Acaxees, Cahitas, Conchos, Coras, Huichols, Jumanos, Mayos, Pima Bajos, Opatas, Tarahumaras, Tepehuans, Tepecanos, and Yaquis. Hokaltecan languages were also spoken in this vast region. The Havasupais, Maricopas, Mohaves, Walapais, Yavapais, and Yumas of the southwestern United States spoke Hokan languages of the Hokaltecan group, as did the Seris and other peoples of northwestern Mexico.

To the southeast, in the Western Gulf culture area, Coahuiltecan languages of the Hokaltecan group were spoken by the many Coahuiltecan bands, the Tamaulipecans, and probably the Karankawas of coastal Texas. The distribution of Hokaltecan-speaking peoples in essentially two blocks, one on the western side of the continent, the other on the Gulf side, with Utaztecans and late-arriving Athapascan speakers between them, suggests that Hokaltecans may well have been the early residents of the region, separated by subsequent invasions of Utaztecans. However, other explanations for such distribution are possible.[7]

PREHISTORY

One of the more intriguing aspects of the gathering cultures of the desert lands is that they were, in a sense, living fossils, little changed from the archeological Desert culture, which, as we have seen in Chapter

1, came into existence, apparently in the Great Basin, by about 9000 B.C. It was characterized by subsistence based primarily on collecting wild plant foods and, especially, seeds of various kinds, but with extensive use of all available resources. Caves and rock shelters were inhabited, and the cultural complex includes milling stones and hand stones for grinding seeds and other wild foods, crude stone chopping and scraping tools, wooden digging sticks, clubs, atlatls, fire drills, basketry, nets, matting, fur cloth, and sandals. Stemmed and notched flint dart points used with the atlatl gave way to smaller arrow points when the bow was introduced somewhere around A.D. 800, and milling stones were replaced by mortars and pestles. The spread of horticulture from the south by about 4000 B.C. established a new way of living in parts of the desert country, and the isolation of the far-flung gatherers from one another and the local adaptations and divergencies that appeared served further to distinguish them regionally. But generally speaking, the Desert culture was remarkably homogeneous and stable, changing little through time.

The reasons some cultural traditions are stable and others are not may be many and complex, but in the desert lands of North America, at least some of the reasons for the static nature of its gathering cultures are fairly obvious. It is apparent, for example, that once a relatively satisfactory means of existence had been worked out, the possibility that another, different one would be developed was remote. They were committed, one might say, to such a marginal and precarious subsistence base that they had no opportunity to hazard the experiment of some other untried way of life. Nor was their environment one that was attractive to outsiders who might have brought the seeds of change with them. The spread of farming people, or the development of farming cultures, in favored parts of the desert lands might seem to be an exception. But such was not the case; farming was practiced where it was profitable, but it did not represent an alternative way of life over much of the desert country.

HISTORY

Large parts of arid North America were explored by Europeans within a century after the Spanish conquest, although most of these contacts do not seem to have been particularly meaningful in terms of their effect on native cultures. Cabeza de Vaca, the treasurer of the Narváez expedition, after being shipwrecked on the Texas coast either on or in the vicinity of Galveston Island, with three other survivors spent eight years (1528–36) as a captive, trader, and healer, mostly among desert gatherers of south Texas and northern Mexico. Partly because of the interest stirred up by Cabeza de Vaca and his companions, Coronado marched northward into New Mexico and then into the Plains with his army a few years later. But the brunt of his conquering force fell on the Pueblo farmers of the Southwest and the natives of the Plains, not on the gathering peoples of the deserts.

Other expeditions soon probed northward, and by the closing years of the sixteenth century, the Spaniards had pushed their mining and other activities well to the north and into the lands of the desert gatherers. The need for laborers in the mines led to the enslavement of large numbers of the indigenous population, and the establishment of presidios and missions in the northern borderlands also contributed to the breakdown, dispersal, and disappearance of the native cultures. The missions were often quite successful in attracting the gathering peoples of northern Mexico, since they offered, or appeared to offer, easy subsistence to these frequently hard-pressed wanderers. But the attraction was often a fatal one as the missions were focal points for the introduction of European diseases, and time and again missions were virtually depopulated by such epidemics.[8]

In the more remote Great Basin, close contact with Europeans was long deferred, the Spanish friars Escalante and Dominguez penetrating the area late in the eighteenth century. More important and earlier than direct contact was the spread of horses to the region. Affected most were the Indians inhabiting the eastern margins of the Great Basin, particularly those who roamed the mountain parks lying between the main mass of the Rockies on the west and the Front Range on the east.[9] Here there was pasturage for horses; and in the north, north of the Great Salt Lake, and in eastern Idaho and western Wyoming were extensive grasslands that supported large herds of bison. Many natives abandoned their ancient gathering way of life to become mounted bison hunters. Utes, who had inhabited the upper reaches of the Rio Grande in what is now south-central Colorado, appeared in the Taos region of northeastern New Mexico soon after 1680. Quickly becoming horse Indians, they appear to have been the major suppliers of horses for other Great Basin peoples farther north. Comanches, in company with Utes, appeared in New Mexico early in the eighteenth century, marking the arrival from the headwaters of the Arkansas of a Numic-speaking people who were to become the most formidable and numerous of the southern Plains Indians. Farther north, the Shoshonis of eastern Idaho and western Wyoming also managed to acquire horses and turned to hunting bison, retreating seasonally into the basin and plateau country to gather camas roots and to fish for salmon. Some of the Northern Paiutes of eastern Oregon also joined the Shoshonis in this migratory, varied life to become the Bannocks of more recent times.

Since pasturage for horses was impossible in the drier parts of the Great Basin, most of its natives were little affected by Western civilization until Americans penetrated the region in the early years of the nineteenth century, following the Louisiana Purchase. The first official American expedition to cross a portion of the Great Basin was that of Lewis and Clark. They employed the *voyageur* Charbonneau as an interpreter in order to command the services of his sixteen-year-old wife, Sacajawea, a Shoshoni girl who had been captured by the Mandans several years earlier. Giving birth to a child on the journey and serving as a valuable guide, she became one of the best, most fondly remembered of Indian women. Unfortunately, these cordial and now romanticized beginnings between Americans and the Indians of the Great Basin were not harbingers of the reality to come. Americans who soon crossed and ultimately settled this land saw only lowly "Digger Indians," scarcely different from beasts. They took the better land, destroyed or demoralized its natives, and ultimately placed the wretched and often debauched survivors on reservations.

CULTURAL SUMMARY

Subsistence and Material Culture

To survive successfully on the wild food resources of the desert lands of North America, men had to be willing to consume a relatively higher proportion of the edible plants and animals than is the case in most areas of the world. They could not afford to overlook any resource that might nourish them, with the result that their knowledge of the nature and uses of the animals and plants available to them was intimate and extensive. An amazing variety of foods was consumed and is convincing evidence of the omnivorous potentialities of the human organism. Plant foods provided the bulk of the subsistence, but animals of all kinds, from insects and lizards to the larger but scarce game animals, were also hunted. The only animals not eaten by the Numic peoples of the Great Basin, for example, were coyotes, apparently because these animals were important mythologically. Dogs were not eaten unless starvation was driving people to desperation; cannibalism, though practiced by Coahuiltecans, and perhaps other desert peoples at least sporadically, was not engaged in because of hunger pangs.

The peoples of the Great Basin utilized almost a hundred different kinds of plants, those having small, hard seeds being the most important.[10] Of these, piñon nuts were the single most important plant resource. Antelopes and rabbits were their most important game, but, quantitatively, all other animal foods taken together may have been more significant. These included rats, mice, gophers, lizards, snakes, locusts, ants, ant eggs, and the larvae of a small fly. Such large numbers of these larvae accumulated at times that they were carried up on the beaches of the saline lakes of the area, where they could be collected, often in such numbers that they were stored for winter usage. The Northern Paiutes of Mono Lake, California, even came to be known as "kutsavi eaters" after this insect, so important a part did it play in their livelihood. In addition, Northern Paiutes consumed acorns, piñon and other nuts, various small grass seeds, cress, sunflowers, burroweed, sego lily bulbs, bulrush rhyzomes, berries of many kinds, and a number of roots.

In the Western Gulf a varied subsistence, with basic reliance on plant foods, duplicated that of the gatherers of the Great Basin, although the plants and animals available to them were somewhat different.[11] In this region the fleshy bulbs, or heads, of the various agaves—maguey, lechuguilla, and sotol—were probably the most important of the wild plant foods. Their fleshy leaves, flower stems, and flowers were also used to some extent as food. Many seeds were also consumed, mesquite beans being of substantial significance in many places. Fruit of various cacti were also eaten, the most common being the fruit, or tuna, of prickly pears. As in the Great Basin, few living creatures were overlooked or rejected as possible food. While the details of Coahuiltecan dietary habits are not known, the list of animals consumed includes spiders, ant eggs, worms, lizards, snakes, earth, rotton wood, and deer dung. They probably also engaged in the "second harvest," the custom of removing seeds and the like from human feces, grinding them up, and roasting and eating them. It was also practiced by some of the desert gatherers of Baja California.

A considerable proportion of the plant foods were ground into a flour or paste with milling stones, and the habit of grinding otherwise inedible materials into a consumable form should probably be regarded as a significant part of a successful adaptation to the desert environment. Typically, as in the Great Basin, seeds were parched with live coals in flat baskets, the contents being kept in motion during the process in order to avoid burning the containers. The parched seeds were ground into a flour, then cooked as a kind of mush, or gruel, in baskets with the aid of heated rocks. The gatherers of the Western Gulf extended the milling and grinding habit to include animal bones; surplus meat throughout the desert region was dried, then pulverized and stored in woven bags.

Agave bulbs were everywhere in the arid west prepared in a similar manner by baking or roasting in earth ovens. A roaring fire was built, sometimes in a depression, and rocks were thrown into the fire. After the rocks were sufficiently hot, the ashes were scraped away and the agaves placed on the rocks. The rocks and agaves were covered with dirt and left for several days, by which time they were thoroughly cooked. After the agaves had cooled, the outer leaves were removed, and the hearts were beaten into thin sheets and allowed to dry. Agaves were either eaten in this form or ground into flour and then converted into a gruel, or baked in the ashes. The flour could be preserved for considerable periods of time.[12] In many places rabbits and antelopes were periodically plentiful enough so that organized communal hunts were profitable. The antelope hunts of the Nevada Shoshonis are particularly intriguing because of the reports of shamans who were able to charm the animals once they were driven into brush corrals so that they would gather and remain quietly until they could be killed. That the shamans took advantage of the antelope's well-known habit of curiosity about strange objects to attract and mesmerize the animals seems likely, though their exact techniques for doing so are unknown. Communal rabbit hunts were held in late fall or early winter by driving the animals into nets, coarsely woven from the long fibers of the milkweed plant. Nets were several feet wide and often several hundred yards long, and were something on the order of family heirlooms, being passed down from generation to generation, each owner carefully repairing and adding to his inheritance. The nets were strung from bushes or from sharp sticks jammed into the ground, ordinarily in a semicircle. At each of the ends, surplus nets were left until the drive was under way, at which time they were strung out to flare away from the semicircle. As the rabbits were driven within the enclosure, these wings were drawn together so that the rabbits were completely enclosed, to be dispatched with sticks and bows and arrows at leisure.[13] Coahuiltecans also hunted deer and rabbits communally, mostly by using "surround" and "fire surround" techniques.

Some of the gatherers on the northern borders of the Western Gulf and of eastern Idaho and Wyoming were able to hunt bison occasionally. And throughout the desert lands, gatherers made use of a miscellany of foods that happened to come their way. Those who were fortunate enough to be near streams made considerable use of fish. Salmon annually ascended the Snake and Lemhi rivers of Idaho to spawn, and permanent Shoshoni villages were located along their banks at favored places. Throughout the desert country, the aquatic life of rivers, from minnows to trout, catfish to garfish, and including turtles, frogs, and many kinds of waterfowl, were taken at every opportunity. "Mormon crickets," or grasshoppers, were a plague to the Mormon pioneers, but they were a welcome windfall to the Great Basin gatherers, who captured them in shallow trenches with the aid of fire, and parched them much as they did various seeds. The parched locusts might be consumed in this form or, like so many other foods, might be ground and pulverized, to be eaten as a gruel or baked as an unleavened kind of bread.

The diversity of foods the desert gatherers utilized and their scattered and sparse occurrence meant that small groups often roamed large regions in search of sustenance. Their movements tended to follow seasonal patterns, gathering seeds or fruits as they matured. In regions like the Great Basin, this meant moving from the basins into the mountains and back again to take advantage of the varying dates of maturation at different altitudes. But seasonal cycles do not follow a regular, predictable rhythm. In the deserts, rains come or do not come to local areas unpredictably; seeds that are plentiful in an area one year are absent the next, and in the Great Basin, for example, piñon pines produce good crops of nuts about once every three or four years. The same was true of the animals, from grasshoppers to rabbits, in that their populations are emphatically cyclic, swinging from scarcity to abundance in a cycle of half a dozen or so years.

Most foods are more easily stored in desert environments than in wetter regions, and the gatherers of the deserts of North America stored most kinds of foods when they had a surplus. In the Great Basin, grass seeds, piñon nuts, and the like were stored in skin bags, and underground chambers were dug for storage purposes. Among the Coahuiltecans, prickly pear fruit was dried in order to be stored. Generally, techniques for preservation of meat and fish were poor.

Throughout the desert country, dwellings were, of necessity, temporary and ordinarily flimsy. The most substantial dwellings, termed "wickiups," were usually conical, sometimes domed shelters, constructed on a framework of willow, juniper, or other saplings or poles, and covered with brush, bark, or a matting of tule or grass. Mat coverings were rolled up and transported to the next camp; the other kinds of shelters were simply abandoned when a move was made to a new camp. Fires were built in the center of these dwellings, and a hole at the apex provided escape for smoke. Cave and rock shelters were utilized as dwellings where available; and depending upon the season and weather, a variety of arbors, windbreaks, and the like might be constructed in lieu of or in addition to wickiups. The Northern Paiutes and other peoples of the Great Basin built sweat houses, which served both for sweat bathing and as meeting places for the men.

Tools and other equipment were limited to what could be conveniently carried from camp to camp and were as complicated as needed to dig roots and gather berries, which is to say that possessions were few and simple. Men employed bows and arrows, spears, and throwing sticks, but they seem not to have been particularly good archers, partly because their bows were of indifferent quality and partly because the big game that required considerable hunting skill and good equipment were absent. Although pottery was sporadically made by various desert gatherers, most containers were of basketry, and the desert peoples were generally quite accomplished in this art. A large variety of plant fibers, from willow withes to bear grass and agave fibers, was used to make an assortment of bowls, trays, mats, bags, sandals, nets, and the like. Vegetable dyes, mainly running to black and tan hues, were employed to decorate basketry with geometric designs. Conical carrying baskets, holding approximately a bushel, were in widespread use. Basketry jugs were made watertight by a coating of pitch; large basketry bowls were woven for stone-boiling and were also sealed with pitch.

The desert gatherers frequently went naked or nearly so. Women often wore only a brief apron of fur or fiber, and men a breechcloth. Fiber sandals rather than moccasins were worn over much of the region. Among Coahuiltecans there was considerable emphasis on tattooing of the body; and shells, seeds, bones, and other ornaments were draped or hung from arms, legs, ears, noses, and lips. Woven rabbit-skin robes, also used as bedding, were the chief protection against cold weather. They were manufactured by skinning rabbits so that their pelts made long strips, which, when dried, curled on themselves, or were twisted, to form ropes. The robes were woven by warping the joined-together fur ropes over pegs or sticks driven into the ground, then twining the ropes tightly together with fiber weft. Worn-out strips of fur could be replaced and new strips added, so that it might be said that they never wore out. Northern Paiute women wore small, round basketry hats.

Social Organization

In the more inhospitable, dryer, and forbidding parts of the desert west, such small groups of people were so scattered that social organization was very simple. Steward has labeled it "a family level of sociocultural integration," since, among these gatherers, virtually all of the activities in the domain of special institutions in more complex societies were functions of the family.[14] Among the Nevada Shoshonis, for example, individual families might camp alone for several years at a time, seldom seeing other humans. Such families were composed of a man, his wife or wives, children, and usually one or two older, or other close relatives. This basic socioeconomic unit has come to be known as a "kin clique."[15] The absence of specific territorial ranges of such groups has been interpreted as a necessary response to the unpredictability of the food supply. Families had to move to places where food was available; they could not follow regular, well-worked-out seasonal routines, remaining within established ranges. In a very real sense, survival depended on the absence of proprietary rights in the available natural resources or in claims to the land.[16]

Collective hunts brought these Shoshonean families together occasionally, as when word was passed that there was a congregation of rabbits in a certain vicinity. At such times an experienced man, termed "rabbit boss," took charge of the hunt, directing the men, women, and children in where to set the nets, instructing the drivers, and overseeing the division of the spoils. In the late fall, too, families moved to the regions where they had heard that the piñon nut crop was good. But gathering piñon nuts was not a communal activity; individual families worked a particular area by themselves, although a number of other families were close by. When the harvest was good, the nuts were stored in underground pits, which might see the family through the winter. During such seasons twenty or thirty families might be camped in the same neighborhood and within visiting distance of one another. When communal hunts or good harvests brought a number of families together, there was a good deal of socializing, with dances and many gambling and other games. By spring, hunger had usually forced kin cliques to scatter to pursue their foraging livelihood.

In the better endowed parts of the desert lands, the struggle for subsistence was somewhat easier and more predictable, and related groups of families often occupied a fairly definite territory and constituted rather amorphous bands. The Coahuiltecans, for example, were subdivided into dozens of ill-defined bands, each composed of a number of patrilineally related families. The component families foraged by themselves during the greater part of the year, joining together when the fruit of the prickly pear was ripe, when it was time to harvest mesquite beans, and for communal hunts. Particularly outstanding or able men served as head men, but their authority was limited since disaffected families could shift their band allegiance at will.

Among the gatherers of the Great Basin, marriage ties linked families together, but the demands of their foraging life kept them from developing more cohesive, and larger kin-based groupings. There were no unilinear kin groups. A young couple after marriage might for a time live with the family of either one, but there was generally a period of matrilocal residence. This was partly a result of bride service and partly because maternal grandmothers served as midwives and helped in the care of babies. Kin on both sides of a person's family were regarded as equally important; that is, descent was reckoned bilaterally. Cross-cousin marriage (to a mother's brother's or a father's sister's child) or pseudo-cross-cousin marriage (to a mother's brother's or a father's sister's stepchild) was customary among some groups, but marriage to any "blood" relative was prohibited among others. The preferred kind of marriage, though often impossible to realize, was for a boy and girl of one family to marry a girl and boy of another family. Steward[17] asserts that this intensified cross-cousin marriage. Such an arrangement served as a double bond between families, and there was an equal gain and loss to both. Sororal polygyny prevailed among the Shoshoneans, as did the sororate. In a complementary fashion there was a form of polyandry in that until a young man found a suitable wife, he might function as a husband of his older brother's spouse. And if a woman's husband should die, his family, if at all possible, replaced the dead husband with one of his brothers, a custom known as the levirate.

Divorce was easy and apparently frequent, though the economic necessity of having a spouse meant that individuals, if at all possible, maintained a married state. Division of labor was according to sex and age, women doing much of the gathering, food preparation, child care, camp chores, and weaving. Men were the hunters, and though the distribution of activity seems lopsided, hunting in such unproductive country was arduous, time-consuming, and doubly important since besides food, animals supplied skins for clothing and other purposes. As soon as children were able, they participated in the subsistence activities of their sex, and at a relatively young age undertook the adult roles.

Among the Coahuiltecans, men sought wives from other bands, men giving presents of meat, hides, or other valuables to the parents of the intended bride. If the man was soon invited to a feast given by the girl's family, his proposal had found favor, and the girl came to live with him without further ceremony. Divorce seems to have been rare among couples who had children, but, in any case, it was achieved simply by separation. Polygyny was not common, and apparently both the levirate and sororate were practiced. As among other gatherers of the desert, women did much of the gathering, cooking, and hauling of wood, water, and the gear when camp was moved; men were the hunters.

Warfare

Many of the desert gatherers were peaceful to a degree seldom attained by other types of cultures. Numic speakers in more arid portions of the Great Basin, for example, lacked territories to defend, had no groupings larger than the family to which they might have given allegiance in war, and could not take time from the food quest to indulge in long campaigns. Outsiders did not covet their land, nor did warfare make heroes or confer honors on valiant warriors. In short, there was no necessity for and minimal ability to be warlike. Such strife as existed was more in the nature of sporadic feuding. It came about as a result of suspected witchcraft and disputes over women. Since, like many peoples of the Subarctic, death was often attributed to witchcraft practiced by shamans whose powers had turned in evil directions, and the living had to avenge the death of a kinsman, feuds might erupt spontaneously. But witchcraft was ordinarily attributed to unrelated shamans, not to relatives, so that it must often have been difficult or impossible to locate supposedly guilty parties and do away with them.

The Coahuiltecans who ranged within given territories and were organized in somewhat more structured bands seem to have had considerably more strife than the gatherers of the Great Basin. Competition over natural resources seems to have been a source of friction, but fights over women also were important. Band exogamy led to a chain of relatives in other bands who normally could be expected to be friendly and cooperative. But it also meant that young men whose offers of marriage to girls in other bands were spurned, sometimes took up arms to redress personal grievances. Feuds thus hatched at least occasionally led to female infanticide, a band being unwilling to lend future strength to their enemies by supplying them with wives. Coahuiltecan warfare consisted of nighttime hit-and-run raids, pitched battles being avoided. Surprise attacks were thwarted by hiding camps in dense thickets and by digging trenches around encampments, from whose safety defenders could shoot arrows at attackers. Warfare was normally a summertime activity, a season in which disputes over rich harvesting grounds were more apt to develop, and a time when men could afford a few days away from subsistence activities. Feuds or petty wars could be initiated or terminated by emissaries, such persons entering enemy camps to challenge them by performing a war dance, or suggesting peace by shooting arrows in the air, and the like. Coahuiltecans celebrated victorious attacks on their enemies with scalp dances, scalps being placed on poles around which men and women danced. Captives were also, at least occasionally, roasted and eaten.

Throughout the desert lands the entry of Europeans very quickly distorted the essentially peaceful aboriginal condition of many of these people. But even though some of the gatherers quickly became predatory raiders, and strife and dissension increased immeasurably, some remained peaceful until the end, avoiding conflict simply by running away.

Religious and Ceremonial Life

Most and probably all of the desert gatherers lacked a coherent, organized body of beliefs about the supernatural world. Some, such as the Southern Paiutes, at least in their mythology, credited a supernatural wolf as the creator of heaven and earth; coyote, wolf's brother, was only somewhat less powerful.[18] But nowhere was there a hierarchy of deities of any particularly well-formulated theological concepts. Instead, the world was peopled or might be peopled with many different kinds of supernaturally powerful creatures and forces, their importance varying from family to family and person to person.

Guardian spirits, or supernatural helpers, were not actively sought by fasting, isolation, or ordeals, as was common in so many parts of North America, although dreams and visionary experiences were welcomed. Through dreams, men, and among the Coahuiltecans women too, might acquire power and guardian spirits. They appeared in the form of animals, plants, and various kinds of natural phenomena such as clouds. The power conferred on a person might be strong, weak, or limited in its uses. Those who received strong curing powers, validated in practice, became shamans. Their performances, which included sucking evil out of a patient's body, singing, dancing, and laying-on-of-hands, often attracted considerable audiences and were the closest things the desert gatherers had to group religious gatherings. Cabeza de Vaca and his companions were coerced into becoming curers among the Coahuiltecans, using the laying-on-of-hands technique, and the efficacy of their cures was remarkable.[19]

Shamans gained prestige through their cures, but also were feared because of their ability to manipulate supernatural forces, particularly to turn their powers to witchcraft. Often the power that came to a person was purely personal, bringing him success in the hunt, luck in gambling, and the like; but often the powers were socially beneficial too, as among the antelope shaman of the Shoshoneans, who were regarded as crucial to the success of communal antelope hunts.

There was little group religious activity in the more barren parts of the arid lands, reflecting the lack of collective activities of all sorts. The Circle Dance of some of the Shoshoneans, for example, was thought to promote fertility and general welfare, but was secondary to its secular aspects. Few, if any, of the other limited group activities had even as much in the way of religious overtones. Among Coahuiltecans, group ceremonial activity was more common, and much of it had religious purposes. When Coahuiltecans could congregate, all-night dances and feasts were held as a means of thanksgiving, to celebrate victories over enemies, to entertain neighboring bands, and to celebrate other events. Besides feasting and dancing, many ceremonies involved the ingestion of peyote. This small, spineless cactus when eaten green, dried, or as an infusion, has the property of seeming to heighten perceptions and of inducing vivid hallucinations. The cactus itself and quite possibly some of its ceremonial usages were borrowed from Coahuiltecans or other gathering people of northern Mexico by reservation Indians of the United States toward the close of the last century. It came to them as a peaceful intertribal religious cult, and so great has been its appeal that it is the dominant religious cult of present-day Indians of the United States.[20] Other plants, notably the mescal bean, which is the hard, red seed of the Texas mountain laurel *(Sophora secundiflora),* also have similar properties when consumed and were probably used by Coahuiltecans and other gathering peoples in a similar way. Mescal beans are found in archeological sites in the area once inhabited by the forerunners of the Coahuiltecans, and a mescal bean cult was known to historic Tonkawas, Caddos, Wichitas, and other tribes outside the range of the shrub. Presumably it spread to them from the less well-known Coahuiltecans who lived within its natural range.[21]

Prehistoric rock art sites, at which rock surfaces have been painted or incised, are concentrated in the arid lands of western North America. Exposed rock surfaces are more common and conditions for preservation are much better in such environments. Whether the frequency of rock art in the desert lands should be attributed to the environment or to a shared heritage derived from the ancient Desert culture is problematical. In any case, the tradition of rock painting and engraving was pursued and elaborated in some parts of the area (the Colorado plateau, parts of Baja California, and the lower Pecos River region of Texas, to mention the most prominent). It is likely that much of it was associated with religious and ceremonial activities, though it seems to have fallen into neglect among many of the historic peoples. In the lower Pecos River region of Texas, for example, an ancient and long-pursued pictographic style has been interpreted as being associated with the mescal bean cult and shamanistic societies.[22]

NOTES

[1] Steward (1955, 104).

[2] Goddard (1913) established the Southwest culture area, limited to prehistoric and historic cultures of New Mexico and Arizona. Kroeber (1928) extended the boundaries of the area tremendously, and Beals (1943) proposed to join the Southwest and Northern Mexico into a very much enlarged Greater Southwest. Kirchhoff (1954) gave the classification its modern form.

[3] Kirchhoff (1954).

[4] Kroeber (1939, 70–74, 119–26); Wissler (1938, 224–27) lumps the Great Basin with the Plains.

[5] Driver (1961, 22–23); Kirchhoff (1954, 543–44); Newcomb (1956b).

[6] "Numa" was used first by Powell (Fowler and Fowler, 1971), but was superseded by Krober's (1907) "Plateau Shoshonean." The classification proposed by Lamb (1958; 1964) and Miller (1966) is followed here.

[7] Newcomb (1961, 32–33); Taylor (1961); Hopkins (1965).

[8] See, for example, Weddle (1968, 3–28).

[9] See Hyde (1959, chap. 3).

[10] The standard monograph for the Shoshoneans of the Great Basin, and extensively used here, is Steward's *Basin-Plateau Aboriginal Sociopolitical Groups* (1938). Much of this information has been condensed in his *Theory of Culture Change* (1955), particularly chaps. 6, 7, and 8. See also Euler (1966); Forbes (1967); Fowler (1966); Harris (1940); Kelly (1932; 1964); Lowie (1909; 1924); Malouf (1966); Murphy and Murphy (1960); Opler (1940); Riddell (1960).

[11] Newcomb (1961), particularly chaps. 2 and 3, is drawn on for material on the Western Gulf.

[12] Newcomb (1961, 115–16); Kelly (1964, 44–45).

[13] Interesting descriptions of rabbit drives and other subsistence activities written by a Mormon pioneer, Major Howard Egan, may be found in Egan (1917); excerpts drawn from Egan were made widely available by Coon (1948).

[14] Steward (1955, 109).

[15] Malouf (1966, 4); Fowler (1966, 61–62). Service (1971, 83–88) has challenged Steward's ecological explanation of the fragmented kinship-based groups in the Great Basin, insisting that the Great Basin Shoshoneans aboriginally had patrilocal bands. Fowler (1966) has shed a good deal of light on the dispute. It seems to me that the relatively important economic role of women in the Great Basin, coupled with the need for flexibility in social groupings, may account for the seeming anomaly of the maternal emphasis of some groups.

[16] Steward (1955, 108).

[17] Steward (1938, 160).

[18] Kelly (1964, 133–34).

[19] Newcomb (1961).

[20] See La Barre (1960) for a summary article concerning the peyote cult. La Barre (1969) contains the 1960 article as well as the definitive study of the cult.

[21] Howard (1957); Troike (1962).

[22] Newcomb and Kirkland (1967, 65–80).

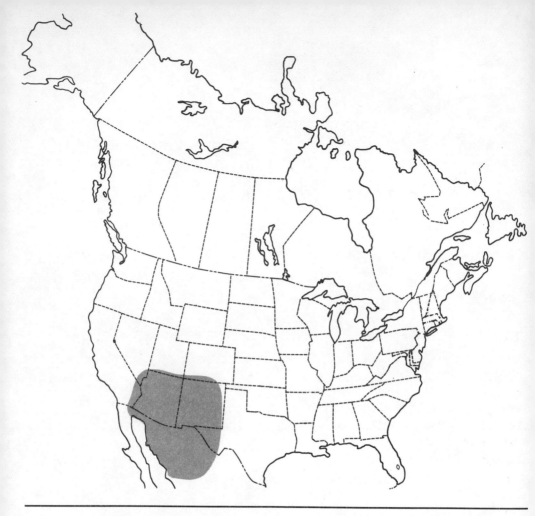

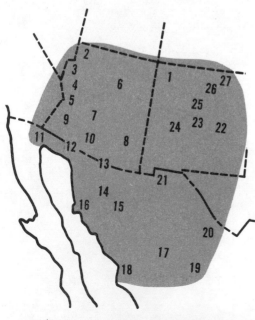

1. Navajo	**15.** Opata
2. Havasupai	**16.** Seri
3. Walapai	**17.** Tarahumar
4. Mohave	**18.** Cahita
5. Halchidhoma	**19.** Concho
6. Hopi	**20.** Jumano
7. Yavapai	**21.** Suma
8. Western Apache	**22.** Tano
9. Yuma	**23.** Eastern Keresan
10. Maricopa	**24.** Western Keresan
11. Cocopa	**25.** Tewa
12. Papago	**26.** Tiwa
13. Pima	**27.** Jicarilla
14. Pima Bajo	

SEVEN

SOUTHWESTERN FARMERS

To many Americans the words "Southwest" and "Indian," if not quite synonymous, are invariably associated with one another. There are good reasons for this association. The Southwest is one of the few areas north of Mesoamerica where abundant and spectacular ruins serve as constant reminders of the ancient peoples who once possessed this land. Descendants of these ancients have managed to survive in many parts of the Southwest. Best known are the colorful Pueblo tribes, scattered out from the Rio Grande Valley in New Mexico to Arizona, doggedly clinging to a way of life old in the time of Columbus. This is also the land of the Navajos, relatively recent newcomers to the Southwest and largest tribe in the United States, whose giant main reservation takes in about 25,000 square miles (an area slightly smaller than the states of New Hampshire, Vermont, and Massachusetts combined). These and the other Indian peoples of the Southwest inevitably make the association of Southwest and Indian a close and very real one.

Geographically the Southwest may be taken to include Arizona, New Mexico, southern Utah, southern Colorado, extreme west Texas, and bordering areas of northern Mexico. As part of what has been described as desert country (Chapter 6), the chief feature of this starkly beautiful land of mountains, mesas, and deserts is its aridity. It is set apart from the rest of the desert country because it was here that farming people became established. Ultimately three different though related groups of cultures came to inhabit this land. The peoples designated as "part-farmers" by Kirchhoff[1] and here termed "farmer-gatherers," combined farming and gathering in a variety of ways, and some are culturally quite similar to the Desert gatherers discussed in Chapter

6. The second group are the sedentary, town-living, intensive farmers, known as the Pueblos. The third group are the Athapascan-speaking Apaches and Navajos.

The farmer-gatherers were composed of a number of linguistically and, to some extent, culturally varied tribes. Similar to the Desert gatherers in many respects were the Yuman-speaking peoples of the Hokan linguistic stock, inhabiting northwestern Arizona and often known as Upland Yumans. Best known of them, because of their location on the valley floor of the Grand Canyon, are the Havasupais, closely related to and apparently a band or offshoot of the neighboring Walapais.[2] The Walapais, located to the south of Grand Canyon, were divided into seven subtribes, or bands. The third tribe of Upland Yumans were the Yavapais, composed of three subdivisions, occupying lands to the south of the other two. All three tribes farmed where they could, and the Havasupais, considerably influenced by the Puebloan Hopis, were able to irrigate their crops from Cataract Creek in the beautiful and inaccessible canyon in which they lived. But after their crops were harvested in the fall, they climbed out of the canyon to forage for half the year in the old gathering tradition. The Walapais lacked places where they could raise crops and led an essentially hunting and gathering life, as did the Yavapais, who in historic times developed close ties and many cultural similarities to the Athapascan-speaking Carlos and Tonto Apaches.

Inhabiting the lower Colorado River downstream from the Grand Canyon, as well as part of the Gila River valley, was a second group of Yuman-speaking tribes, often designated as River Yumans. They were farming peoples relying on the annual flooding of the Colorado and Gila for moisture, and all were quite similar to one another in speech and culture. Most northerly were the Mohaves, downstream from whom were the Halchidhomas and Yumas. These three tribes plus the Maricopas, who occupied the middle reaches of the Gila River, presumably moving there in relatively recent times, constituted a single linguistic grouping. Farther down the Colorado was a second group of River Yumans: the Kohuanas, Halyikwamais, and Cocopas.

Maize, tepary (but not kidney) beans, pumpkins, squash, sunflowers, gourds, and tobacco were the principal crops of the river Yumans. There was considerable supplementary gathering by women of mesquite beans, screw beans, and other seeds, and men obtained several varieties of fish from the Colorado and Gila, but did relatively little hunting. Material culture was rather simple, or perhaps it would be more accurate to say that there was a general disinterest in all but unadorned and necessary utilitarian objects. In other respects the culture was characterized by an emphasis on dreaming and dream experiences as the focus and basis of religion, and the existence of patrilineal clans that had few functions other than denying marriage of clansmen, the important social and economic unit being the nuclear family. No formal tribal council or other similar governmental structure existed, but there seems to have been a deep-seated feeling of tribal cohesiveness. Internal conflict over land rights seems to have arisen quite often, and ritualized and relatively nonlethal warfare was an important and emphasized part of life.

In the desert of southern Arizona and adjacent Sonora were other farmer-gatherers, the Pimas and Papagos, who spoke a Utaztecan language. The distinctions separating the two tribes were primarily environmental, the Pimas practicing irrigation agriculture in the Gila and Salt river valleys, and the Papagos, who lived away from these streams along the Mexican border, relying much more heavily on hunting and gathering. The sedentary, village-living Pimas raised corn, beans, squash, and some cotton in their irrigated gardens, obtained fish from the rivers, engaged in some hunting, and also did considerable gathering of wild plants.

The Papagos, on the other hand, could not be sedentary and had to move with the seasons and to or with the rainfall. In summer they lived near the gardens they had planted in floodplains, often constructing crude reservoirs at strategic places to impound the summer rains. After the harvest they moved into the mountains near springs and other water sources, remaining throughout the winter to hunt. Both groups built thatch and earth-covered, flat-topped, round houses, and also open-sided arbors for use during the extremely hot months. Few clothes were necessary or were worn by these desert peoples, and material culture was, on the whole, rather simple. Both tribes are well known for their superb basketry, and they also manufactured pottery and wove cotton cloth. Pima villages were governed by head men and a council of adult males, dominated by the older men. The various village chiefs elected a tribal chief, so that the Pimas formed a cohesive tribe, at least relative to the Papagos whose village units were autonomous.[3]

Other Utaztecan-speaking, culturally similar relatives of the Pimas and Papagos were widely scattered in northern Mexico. These included the Pima Bajos or Nevome, the Mexican Papagos, and the Opatas in central Sonora, and the Tepecanos and Tepehuans of the northern Sierra Madre. The Cahita-speaking Yaqui and Mayo tribes were floodplain agriculturalists in the lower river valleys of Sonora. The Yaquis, who have persisted culturally, were dispersed after revolting against Spanish and Mexican authority, some fleeing to Arizona, where they occupy six villages.[4] In the Sierra Madre of Chihuahua are the Tarahumaras who speak a Utaztecan language closely related to the Cahita languages, and they are also similar to the Cahita speakers culturally.[5] In the southern Sierra Madre were the Coras and Huichols, both Utaztecans, who were, in terms of their rather simple agricultural base, like the other farmer-gatherers, but who, in the elaboration of other segments of culture, evince affinities with the high civilizations of central Mexico. In the vicinity of the junction of the Rio Grande and Rio Conchos, near present Presidio, Texas, were the Jumanos, who practiced floodplain agriculture, and south of them on the Conchos River were the related Conchos, both apparently Utaztecan speakers.[6]

Scattered out in the sixteenth century from the upper Rio Grande Valley of New Mexico to the Hopis of northeastern Arizona and the Zunis of western New Mexico were some ninety Pueblo villages.[7] Pueblo culture is one of the most distinctive and advanced of those north of the Valley of Mexico, and despite tremendous pressures exerted on them by Spaniards and Americans, much of the aboriginal culture has been maintained. The Pueblos are subdivided into western and eastern or Rio Grande divisions, based on a number of cultural distinctions. The western group is composed of the Utaztecan-speaking Hopis; the Tanoan-speaking Hanos, who sought refuge among the Hopis from Spanish oppression; the Zunis, whose language has no known affiliation to any other; and the Keresan-speaking Acomas and Lagunas of western New Mexico, who are in some respects transitional between the two groups. The Eastern or Rio Grande Pueblos are composed of the Keresan-speaking Pueblos of Santa Ana, San Felipe, Santo Domingo, Cochiti, and Sia. The remaining Rio Grande Pueblos are speakers of Tanoan, which is divided into three mutually unintelligible languages (Tewa, Towa, Tiwa). Tewa-speaking are the Pueblos of Tesuque, Pojoaque, Nambé, San Ildefonso, Santa Clara, and San Juan, plus the village of Hano among the Hopi, already mentioned. Towa-speaking are the Pueblos of Jemez; Pecos Pueblo was probably a member of this group. Tiwa-speaking are the Pueblos of Taos, Picurís, Sandia, Isleta, and the extinct Piro Pueblo in the vicinity of Las Cruces.[8]

The third group of Southwestern Indians, the Athapascan-speaking Apaches and Navajos, were recent immigrants, arriving in the region probably from the southern Plains during the first quarter of the sixteenth century.[9] They quickly infiltrated almost all parts of the Southwest, and if they were fairly homogeneous culturally when they arrived, they soon diverged as they were variously influenced by the indigenous tribes among whom they settled or alternatively raided. Culturally they may be divided into five groups, the first of which is the Western Apaches (composed of the White Mountain, Cibecue, Southern, and Northern Tonto, each of which is subdivided into a number of bands), who occupied east-central Arizona and became farming people. Linguistically and culturally, they are closely allied to the second group of Southern Athapascans, the Navajos, whose homeland is generally regarded as north-central New Mexico, though they soon spread out to occupy much of the old Anasazi territory. The third group of Southern Athapascans, the Chiricahua Apaches, occupied the Chiricahua Mountains of southeastern Arizona, and ranged into Mexico and New Mexico. The Mescalero Apaches, linguistically close to the Chiricahuas, roamed to their east in New Mexico and, at times, well into Texas. They had much in common culturally with Plains tribes, particularly the Lipan Apaches. The bison-hunting Lipans and Kiowa-Apaches of the southern Plains, plus the Jicarillas, are linguistically a unit as they probably were culturally before Comanche invaders scattered them.

PREHISTORY

As we have seen, the Desert tradition had appeared at least as early as 7000 B.C. in the Great Basin region. Before 5000 B.C., this foraging kind of life had also appeared in the Southwest as the Cochise culture, and it was, in large part, ancestral to the later and somewhat divergent cultural traditions of the region.[10] The grinding stones and chopping tools found in Cochise sites indicate that, like other Desert cultures, primary dependence was on plant foods. Caves, when available, were used as habitation sites, but camp sites in the open have also been found. Little more can be said about the early Cochise, except that domesticated plants were added to its economy at a surprisingly early date. Presumably spreading from the south along the rugged uplands of the Sierra Madre, the earliest remains of corn in the Southwest have been found in sites at altitudes over 6,000 feet. At Bat Cave and at Tularosa and Cordova caves in west-central New Mexico, and at Point of Pines in east-central Arizona, a primitive form of corn, probably adapted to high altitudes, was being planted, as indicated by radiocarbon dating, as early as 3000 B.C. Probably squash or pumpkins (*Curcubita*) and gourds were introduced at the same time as corn, but the other basic member of the Indian trinity of crop plants, kidney beans, was not grown until about 1000 B.C.[11]

For upwards of two millennia, domesticated plants had little impact on the life of these gathering peoples in that, so far as archeology reveals, they continued their wandering, foraging existence in the same simple social groups. But after 1000 B.C., a new and more productive variety of corn was introduced, and the transition from a collecting economy to a producing one was made. Permanent or semipermanent villages usually located along ridges near cultivable land appeared. The people lived in semisubterranean pit houses covered with beams, brush, and earth, which were entered through lateral passageways. Large, sunken ceremonial buildings were usually associated with each village. About 100 B.C., manufacture of a polished brownware pottery was begun, another item presumably diffused from Mexico.

With the addition of pottery, which makes identification and relationships of cultural groups and knowledge of their alteration through time much surer, the Mogollon culture is defined as having its beginnings. It was a stable, upland, somewhat backwoods culture that changed relatively little through the centuries. In comparison to the other prehistoric cultures of the Southwest, perhaps because land for cultivation was limited, hunting and gathering played a larger part in subsistence. In its early years there was considerable heterogeneity in Mogollon culture, but as time passed it became more homogeneous. After A.D. 1100, it became less distinctive and was ultimately absorbed by the more northerly and expanding Anasazi. The Zunis are said to be Mogollon descendants.[12]

In the period between 100 B.C. and A.D. 400, while the Mogollon culture was taking shape, similar developments were occurring elsewhere in the Southwest. In the low, hot desert country of central and southern Arizona and Sonora, along the Gila, Salt, and other rivers, another distinctive culture had its beginnings. Known as the Hohokam, after a Pima word for those who had preceded them, it also originated in the Cochise culture. But its subsequent development was quite different from that of the Mogollon. Instead of dry-land farming, the Hohokam became irrigation farmers. Their first extensive irrigation canals were dug during the initial Pioneer Period (100 B.C.–A.D. 500), and they were greatly extended in subsequent periods. From diversion dams on the Salt and Gila rivers, canals up to thirty feet wide and ten feet deep carried water to fields up to thirty miles away. Considering that they had only crude tools and no domestic animals to help them, the magnitude of their accomplishments is considerable. They suggest a well-organized population of considerable size.[13]

Hohokam dwellings varied through time. In the early periods they were large, multifamily, wattle and daub, jacal-type structures; in later periods they were smaller, apparently used by single families. The Hohokam practiced cremation by burning bodies in pits, sometimes subsequently moving the bones and ashes to other places of interment. The Hohokam culture has more obvious affiliations with Mesoamerican civilizations than others in the Southwest, as demonstrated by the presence of ball courts, truncated pyramids, ornaments such as pyrites inlaid on slate mirrors, pottery figurines, and copper bells probably imported from Mexico, among other things.

About A.D. 1200, Hohokam culture entered what is known as the Classic Period, a time of change in parts of the area in architectural and art styles. It was brought about by what seems to have been a peaceful invasion of the Salado, an Anasazi group. The Salado people manufactured distinctive black, red, and white polychrome pottery, buried their dead rather than cremated them, and built single- and multiple-room adobe and caliche buildings in walled compounds. The ruins at Casa Grande and Los Muertos in the lower Salt and Gila rivers are imposing testimony to their massive architectural habits; their walled compounds also suggest that warfare had come to the traditionally peaceful lands of the Hohokams. At the same time, the Hohokam people continued to maintain their irrigation systems, built ball courts, and pursued their old ceramic traditions. Whether warfare was responsible is unknown, but sometime after A.D. 1400, the Saladoans and perhaps many of the Hohokams left the area for parts unknown. When the Spaniards entered the region in the sixteenth century, they encountered Pimas and Papagos, no doubt descendants of the Hohokams; but their culture was hardly suggestive of the great desert agriculturalists their forefathers had once been.

In the Colorado River valley of western Arizona, below the Grand Canyon, another distinct but related cultural tradition took shape at an early date. Known as the Patayan (a Yuman term for "ancient ones"), or Hakataya (the Yuman word for the Colorado River),[14] it grew out of a variant of the ancient Desert culture known as the Amargosa. The earliest Patayans may have been related to, or perhaps drew upon, the same sources as the Hohokams of the Pioneer Period for their cultural stimulus. In any case, the Patayans were a farming people who relied on the floodwaters of streams, primarily the Colorado, for their crops, but did considerable hunting and gathering as well. They lived in impermanent brush huts; made distinctive pottery, though often showing affinity to or influence from other Southwestern pottery traditions; cremated their dead; and obtained shells from the Gulf of California that they made into ornaments and traded widely in the Southwest. This ancient tradition, apparently little changed through the years, persisted into historic times, the Yuman tribes being its modern representatives.

In the Four Corners area of the Southwest, where the states of Colorado, Utah, Arizona, and New Mexico come together, in the drainage of the San Juan and Little Colorado, another cultural tradition, known as the Anasazi after the Navajo term for "ancient ones," had its beginnings. Though it began somewhat later than the Mogollon or Hohokam and was, in part, derived from the Mogollon, it surpassed them in the area it encompassed, in architectural development, and in other ways, and eventually, in part at least, absorbed them. The Anasazi, as the other prehistoric traditions in the Southwest, grew out of a Desert culture background. The first stage in the Anasazi sequence is known as Basketmaker (A.D. 300–500) after the abundant and skillfully made basketry that characterized it. But the new trait that set the Basketmakers apart was the cultivation of corn and squash. It allowed these people to settle more or less permanently in domed dwellings constructed of horizontally laid logs chinked with mud. Surplus food and other objects were stored in stone slab-lined chambers erected above ground. The chief weapon was the atlatl, and considerable hunting and gathering were still done. The rabbit-fur robe and sandals, and much of their material culture reflected their Desert culture origins.

In the following Modified Basketmaker Period (A.D. 500–700), agriculture became more important to subsistence with the introduction of new, more productive varieties of corn as well as protein-rich kidney beans. The appearance of clusters of circular pit houses indicates an increase in population and a more sedentary way of life. The pit houses, probably derived from the Mogollon culture, were partially underground, slab-lined, wooden-roofed, and entered through the roof or by an antechamber. Many of these pit houses were built in the immense caves or under the great overhanging cliffs that are common in the region. The bow and arrows were introduced during this period, as were pottery, crude clay figurines, and turquoise jewelry. By the end of the Modified Basketmaker Period, all the ingredients were present for a great elaboration and diversification of the culture.

During the Developmental Pueblo Period (A.D. 700–1050), cotton and loom weaving diffused from the south, and cotton textiles supplanted rabbit-fur robes. Turkeys were widely kept as domestic animals, and pottery underwent marked development. Population increased substantially, and there was considerable areal expansion, but no basically revolutionary traits were introduced. The most obvious new feature was that aboveground houses constructed of stone with mud mortar, or of closely set posts plastered with mud, became popular at the expense of pit houses. But special pit houses survived to become the sacred ceremonial chambers, or kivas, which came to play an important role in religious and ceremonial life. By the end of the period, considerable towns (or pueblos to use the Spanish term) had appeared, often with the houses built contiguously around plazas or courts, or in semicircular or L-shaped complexes.

During the Great Period (A.D. 1050–1300), Anasazi culture reached its zenith. Great multiple-storied buildings with hundreds of adjoining rooms were built on mesas, against massive sheltering canyon walls, and in other places. Anasazi settlements spread across the Colorado plateau, some of the more notable being Mesa Verde in southwestern Colorado and Pueblo Bonito in Chaco Canyon in northwestern New Mexico. Their settlements also spread southward into the Mogollon area, or the local people there adopted much of the Anasazi culture;

and Anasazi influence was felt widely throughout the Southwest. Tools and utensils were many and varied, from attractive painted pottery, to colorful cotton textiles, turquoise, coral and other jewelry, feather robes, and dozens of other objects, reflecting a life that was rich and colorful, and especially one that was triumphant in a hard land of adversity.

But in the latter part of the thirteenth century and continuing into the next century, there was a sudden abandonment of many of the recently flourishing northern Pueblo towns, and a retreat to the Rio Grande Valley and to the south and east generally. By the time the Spaniards entered the Southwest, the Pueblos remained only along the Rio Grande Valley and in the isolated Zuni, Hopi, and Acoma villages to the west. The reasons for the sudden contraction of the Pueblo area are not entirely clear. Enemy raids, epidemics, social breakdown, a shortened growing season, and prolonged and severe droughts, accompanied by deep arroyo cutting, which discouraged or precluded flood-plain farming and perhaps irrigation, have been offered as explanations. Most experts are now agreed that environmental changes, specifically droughts, were basic to the contraction.[15]

HISTORY

Two decades after the conquest of Mexico, tales of great cities and a rich land to be plundered drew Spaniards northward to the Southwest. Marcos de Niza, a Franciscan friar, at the head of a small party guided by Estevánico, the Negro survivor of the Narváez expedition and companion of Cabeza de Vaca, first penetrated the region in 1539. Estevánico, with Indian companions, had preceded Fray Marcos; but in a Zuni pueblo, Estevánico was killed. De Niza dared not continue, and he returned to Mexico to spread glowing tales of the Zuni town he had glimpsed. The Viceroy of Mexico authorized the expedition of Francisco Vasquez de Coronado, and in 1540 his massive and formidable force descended on the Pueblos. Coronado established his headquarters in the pueblo of Tiguex, near modern Bernalillo, New Mexico, and from it explored the other Rio Grande pueblos and the western pueblos, and led the expedition into the Plains. The Pueblos were at first friendly, but the Spaniards' increasing demands for provisions and other things during their two-year stay led ultimately to an attempt to expel them. Coronado countered by executing several hundred residents of Tiguex. It established a pattern of events to come, of Spanish exploitation, atrocity, and ultimate native rebellion.

Coronado's reports cooled interest in these northern lands for a time, for neither gold nor cities of fabulous wealth had been discovered. But in the last decades of the century, the Spaniards returned. Francisco

Chamuscado visited the Rio Grande pueblos in 1581, leaving behind two friars who appear to have been killed soon after the expedition departed. In the following year Antonio de Espejo, with a small expedition, visited the Pueblo country searching for the friars, but with equal, if not greater, interest in mines and possible locations for settlements. Several unauthorized expeditions subsequently penetrated the Southwest, and in 1598 Don Juan de Oñate rode into the Pueblo country at the head of some four hundred soldiers, priests, and settlers, to begin the official colonization of New Mexico.[16]

In the tradition of his predecessors, Oñate quickly established military supremacy, brutally punishing those natives who dared to resist his ambitious program to convert and "civilize" them. Chapels, churches, and missions were rapidly constructed (with Indian labor) in the Pueblo villages; Father Alonzo de Benavides reported in 1630 that 90 chapels had been built and 60,000 Pueblos converted. The Indians were coerced into attending Mass, though they had little opportunity to learn or understand anything other than the externals of Christianity, and the missionaries did everything they could to suppress and destroy Indian beliefs and practices. While the missionary program was earning the enmity of the natives, settlers and soldiers were competing with the missionaries for the labor and the products of the labor of the natives, primarily through the *encomienda* system. In this system the governor assigned to his soldier-citizens the services of a number of Indians, most of whom labored on special parcels of land for the *encomenderos*. Friction between the clerical and civil arms of Spanish authority, essentially over the exploitation of the Indians, hampered development of the colony and fostered the revolt of the oppressed natives.

Following a number of minor and abortive uprisings, which taught the Indians that they would have to unite if they were to be successful, in August of 1680 the scattered Pueblos joined forces under the leadership of a Tewa medicine man, Popé, and drove the Spaniards from New Mexico. In this rebellion, 21 out of a total of 33 missionaries and about 380 settlers out of approximately 2,500 colonists were killed, the survivors retreating to El Paso.[17] Attempts were soon made to reconquer the Pueblos, but it was a dozen years before Don Diego de Vargas was able to recapture the bulk of the lost lands. Unaccustomed to unified action, the Pueblos had soon after the rebellion fallen to squabbling among themselves. The raids of Apaches and other nomads were becoming a serious problem, and many Pueblo leaders recognized the need for peace with the Spaniards. But the relationship between the two peoples was never quite the same again. The Western Pueblos were but partially subdued, the missionary movement was never again as coercive, the *encomienda* system was never reinstituted, and the settlers and Pueblos found common cause in defending themselves against the costly raids of the Apaches.

The Pueblo Revolt speeded up the spread of horses and other livestock from Santa Fe and the Rio Grande Valley, and considerable numbers of Pueblo Indians also fled their old homes to join the Navajos and other "wild" tribes. Navajos and Apaches had raided the Pueblos and Spanish settlements for many years before the rebellion, but the most extensive adoption of Pueblo arts, crafts, religious concepts, and other things, as well as the actual assimilation of numbers of Pueblo Indians, took place in the years immediately following it. It was a period of growth and expansion for the Navajos, who, from their homeland in north-central New Mexico, spread throughout much of the old Anasazi territory.

During the eighteenth century, Spanish attention was diverted from the Pueblos by a medley of other problems, and the Pueblos accommodated themselves to the presence of Spaniards while managing to preserve their ancient traditions. With the decline of Spanish power in the New World, control of the distant frontiers weakened, and the situation was little changed when in 1821 New Mexico became part of the Republic of Mexico. In the early years of the nineteenth century, mountain men and other Americans began to appear in the Southwest. An active commerce via the Santa Fe Trail soon grew up with the United States, and during the Mexican War the United States occupied New Mexico. In 1847 the Pueblo Indians actively joined in a revolt against the new intruders, but it was bloodily quelled. However, at least in the beginning, the Pueblos were better off under the Americans than under the Spaniards or Mexicans. Their land was not taken from them, they were not forced to work for the Americans, and they had a much more powerful ally in their struggle with Navajo and Apache raiders.

For many years the Americans were unable to satisfactorily solve the Navajo and Apache problem, and it was not until 1863 that Colonel Christopher "Kit" Carson was able to subdue the Navajos and some of the Apaches. A majority of the Mescaleros were brought into Bosque Redondo on the Pecos River, about 180 miles southeast of Santa Fe, in 1863, and in the next year a systematic campaign was begun to defeat the Navajos. By destroying their crops and appropriating their sheep and other livestock, the Americans starved most of the Navajos into submission; they surrendered at Fort Defiance in western New Mexico, then made the long walk to Bosque Redondo and Fort Sumner. In 1868 the Navajos signed a treaty that provided them with a reservation in their old homeland, and they were able to leave the hated Bosque Redondo. But without flocks, seed, or tools at first, and frequently at the mercy of corrupt officials, they did not become self-supporting again for many years.

The pacification of the Chiricahua and Western Apaches was long in coming, and the Chiricahuas, in particular, are remembered for the stubborn and skillful stand they made against the overwhelmingly superior forces of the United States. But finally, the famous Chiricahua leader, Geronimo, surrendered in 1886, and thenceforth all Indians of the Southwest were under the authority and control of the United States.

PUEBLO CULTURAL SUMMARY

Subsistence and Material Culture

The Pueblos were skillful and resourceful farmers who depended on their crops for the bulk of their food. Beans, squash, gourds, tobacco, and cotton were raised besides corn, the mainstay. The Eastern Pueblos in the Rio Grande watershed were irrigation farmers, leading precious water from the Rio Grande or one of its tributaries to their fields in a series of sometimes quite extensive ditches. The Western Pueblos depended on the scant rainfall that, fortunately, is concentrated in the summer growing season; they located their small plots in places where the runoff would supply enough moisture to raise a crop. This system was obviously much more chancy than irrigation farming, particularly since the growing season was brief in the high altitudes of their rugged country. Success depended on an intimate knowledge of local conditions and terrain, small garden patches in a number of different places to spread the risk of failure, and special planting techniques for their drought-resistant strains of corn.

Men of the Eastern Pueblos did the bulk of the farm work, leveling and preparing the land, working on the irrigation ditches, as well as planting, weeding, and harvesting the crops. Women assisted the men at planting time and during the harvest. The tools used in farming were remarkably simple—wooden digging sticks and hoes—success depending upon the diligent application of practical knowledge rather than on a complicated technology.

Hunting was also an important subsistence activity of the men, the chief game being deer, antelope, rabbits, and bison in the pueblos nearest the Plains (Taos, Picuris, Pecos). Special hunting societies existed among some Pueblos whose members joined together in communal hunts for deer and antelope, and virtually all Pueblos conducted communal rabbit drives. Large flocks of turkeys were kept in most pueblos in the early days for meat and feathers. Women did the gathering of wild plant foods, harvesting piñon nuts, cactus, various berries, mesquite beans, and other seeds and roots. Surplus crops were carefully husbanded against future crop failures by storage in granaries within the pueblos. In a general sense the Pueblos had worked out a very productive and successful mode of subsistence in a difficult environment, and the Rio Grande Pueblos, through the development of irrigation, may well have been on the threshold of another breakthrough to an even more productive economy when the Spanish entered the Southwest.[18]

As their Spanish name suggests, the Pueblos were a town-living people. Their stone and adobe dwellings were built in compact clusters, often several stories high, with each upper level set back from the one below in a series of terraced tiers. Movable ladders were used to reach the upper levels, and before being influenced by Europeans, the lower story had no doors but was entered through a roof hatch, as were rooms on the upper tiers. Rooms were usually small since timber for spanning large rooms was not easily available. Before chimneys were introduced by Spaniards, fireplaces were generally located in a shallow pit or box in the center of the room, smoke finding its way out through the roof hatch. Except for all but the hardest labor, women did much of the building of the pueblos. Furnishings in the rooms were sparse, being limited to a bench along the walls, a suspended pole over which blankets and various garments could be thrown, and the grinding slabs of metates on which the women ground the household corn.

The ground plan of pueblos is quite varied since rooms were often added as the need arose, with the result that few conform to a symmetrical or regular plan. Most pueblos have at least one kiva, the underground or partially underground ceremonial chamber, meeting place, and workshop of the men. The largest surviving pueblo is that of Zuni, inhabited by 2,500 people, and the Western Pueblos can also claim the oldest, continuously inhabited towns in the United States in Acoma and the Hopi's Old Oraibi, both dating to the early years of the twelfth century.

The tools and utensils of the Pueblos were essentially quite simple, but the care with which many objects were made and the esthetic traditions they express have given them a deservedly high reputation. Pueblo women wove good basketry, but it was overshadowed by their pottery, which originally was watertight and fire resistant, manufactured by the coiling process and often polished and painted. The women were the potters, but men the weavers, using a narrow waist loom to manufacture cotton cloth before the Spaniards introduced the upright loom.

Among the Rio Grande Pueblos closest to the Plains, skins were extensively used for clothing, and among the Western Pueblos, cotton clothing largely took its place. Men wore a breechcloth, a tunic or skirt of cotton or skin, a kilt or knee-length trousers, leggings of cotton or skin tied at the knees, and moccasins or yucca-fiber sandals; in cold weather a rabbit-fur robe might be added. In hot weather men might doff all but a breechcloth, and little children often wore nothing at all. Women wore a knee-length dress, which was essentially a blanket worn over the right shoulder, passed under the left, and secured with a belt at the waist. They also wore leggings and moccasins or sandals, and for festive occasions donned bulky leggings consisting of an entire deerskin wrapped around each leg.

Considerable care was devoted to appearance, particularly the hair. Men wore their hair in bangs, trimmed evenly across the forehead and cut horizontally at the sides above the shoulders, with the hair at the back of the head gathered into a knot and tied. Married women parted their hair in the middle and wrapped or braided it on either side behind the ears. Among unmarried Hopi girls, and apparently widespread among other Pueblos in early times, was a custom of dressing the hair in two large whorls over the ears, said to represent squash blossoms, which were symbols of fertility. The Pueblos also painted the face and body with red ocher and other pigments, and made extensive use of turquoise, other stones, shells, seeds, and the like for necklaces, earrings, and other ornaments.

Social Organization

To build and maintain a fairly complicated and extensive irrigation system requires a centralized and well-developed social and governmental organization. As a result there are a number of differences that distinguish the Rio Grande Pueblos who practiced irrigation from the Western Pueblos who did not. But all Pueblos were similar in that each was an autonomous, rather tightly-knit unit, governed by religious leaders; and a strong emphasis was placed on the subordination of the individual to the welfare of the group. Among the Western Pueblos (Hopi, Hano, Zuni, Acoma, and Laguna), society was characterized by matrilineal exogamous clans, matrilocal residence, and ownership by women of houses, gardens, and crops; the Katchina cult was an important religious and social grouping. Among the Rio Grande Pueblos, matrilineal clans were absent, bilateral extended family groups taking their place, and a dual or moiety division was of considerable importance. The moieties were patrilineal, with the Squash People or the Summer People being in charge of the ceremonial activity in summer, the Turquoise or Winter People being responsible for the winter's ceremonies. Men were the owners of land and houses, and the Katchina cult was weak, or as among the Tiwa Pueblos, absent.

The government of the Pueblos was theocratic, religious leaders having ultimate authority and making the basic decisions about Pueblo life, although they delegated the day-to-day running of the Pueblos to secular officials. In each pueblo a supreme priest was the village chief. The position was for life, but his powers were not absolute since war chiefs and councils of priests could discipline him or even remove him from office for malfeasance or incompetence. The heads of the various religious societies generally formed a town council. The Tewa and Tiwa Pueblos had dual chieftainships, each chief ruling half the year, and there were a number of other variations among the Pueblos in how priestly leaders were appointed, in the nature and number of their assistants, and the like. All, however, were similar in that they were expected to be somewhat withdrawn from ordinary affairs, they could not take part in quarrels or internal strife, and they were treated with considerable deference and respect as was due a person who was deeply involved in spiritual matters. The term *cacique* (picked up from the Arawaks of the Caribbean by the Spaniards) is used by the Rio Grande Pueblos and non-Indians for these village chiefs.

As Bunzel[20] has pointed out, the Pueblos were so preoccupied with their round of ceremonial activities dealing with rain, seasons, and the agricultural cycle that the passage of individuals from one stage of life to another was seldom marked by elaborate ceremonies. Expectant mothers were attended by their feminine kin, and for several weeks after birth, as among the Hopis, they were considered to be ritually unclean and so were restricted in their activities. In the first weeks of life, infants were shown to the sun by a relative or a person designated by the mother and, at the same time, given a name. Other names might be bestowed in infancy or as the child entered various ceremonial activities. The years of childhood were not marked ceremonially, young girls and, among some Pueblos, older men spending considerable time caring for the children. They were fond of children and seldom punished them physically, though in some Pueblos, particularly among the Rio Grande group, masked bogeymen carrying whips were used to frighten disobedient children.[21]

Between the ages of about six and ten, boys received preliminary initiation into a kiva group or moiety. Induction usually involved various ordeals, and often included whipping by masked katchinas. As the boys matured, they were again brought into the kivas, and perhaps whipped; ultimately the katchinas removed their masks, and the various other esoteric secrets were revealed to the boys; the boys were threatened with severe punishment should they ever reveal the secrets.

Marriage was not marked by an outward display of courtship, nor was there any emphasis on a marriage ceremony. Gifts were exchanged between the families of the bride and groom, and marriage was ordinarily within the confines of the pueblo. The Pueblos were monogamists, and chastity before and after marriage seems to have been regarded as a virtue. Divorce was easy and apparently frequent among childless couples. In the Western, matrilineally oriented Pueblos, women might divorce husbands by the simple expedient of placing their possessions outside her door, and husbands might terminate an unsatisfactory marriage by the act of moving back to their mother's home.

Old age was not a time of retirement; aged people continued to function insofar as they were able in their old roles. As with the other crises of life, death was not accorded elaborate ceremonial. Burial was prompt after death, partly, no doubt, because the Pueblos shared with other Southwestern peoples a dread and fear of the ghosts of the dead. A surviving spouse underwent a brief period of fasting and purification.

Warfare

The Pueblos, specifically the Zunis, were once stereotyped as being an unaggressive, noncompetitive, docile people with personalities characterized as "Apollonian."[19] The Apollonian characterization has been found to be a serious distortion and simplification of Pueblo personality, and the peaceable nature of Pueblo culture is amply controverted by the historic facts. A prevailing personality type, if one could be shown to exist, would not, it might be added, determine whether or not a particular people became embroiled in warfare. In any case, there have been many aggressive, assertive, contentious Pueblo Indians, and warfare has been a continuing fact of life for them throughout the historic period. If the defensive sites picked for some of their prehistoric towns, such as Mesa Verde, are any indication, warfare was an old, established custom. Societies of warriors existed in every pueblo, and among Tanoan Pueblos there was also a female counterpart, a scalp association that greeted returning warriors and held wild victory dances. Conflicts between closely related but politically autonomous villages were chiefly over charges of witchcraft and, perhaps occasionally, over arable land; but they were relatively nonlethal and small-scale, and were more in the nature of feuding than full-blown warfare. The nature of the conflict with the invading Athapascan nomads is difficult to judge, but it seems likely that Puebloan peoples from time immemorial had had to defend themselves against hungry and aggressive nomads. Nevertheless, the Pueblos, in comparison to many North American Indians, were not oriented toward warfare. Their chief struggle was with the natural elements, and they bent their energies practically and religiously toward a satisfactory accommodation with them.

The Pueblos were preoccupied with religion; it permeated virtually every aspect of life and was so intertwined with every activity that its nature and meaning may well be distorted by separating its discussion from the other segments of Pueblo culture. In an overt sense, dramatic, complex, and meticulously performed ceremonies took up a large part of their time and energy. Often of nine days' duration, they followed one after another in a continuous annual cycle. Most of them began in the kivas where priests instructed and led the members of the religious societies, and they usually included ritual purification, fasting, and the preparation of feathered prayer sticks. Subsequently, there were often public performances that blended in various ways songs, poetry, dancing, and mythology. In some of them, masked dancers impersonated katchinas. Models of the katchinas were whittled out of wood and appropriately painted and attired for the instruction of children. These have become popular items in the tourist trade, but they are in no way sacred objects, as some would believe.

The beliefs behind religious practices were much the same throughout the Pueblo world. Basic to them was a conviction that daily activities were controlled by supernatural gods and forces and that men must please, appease, conciliate, and accommodate themselves to the needs and desires of the supernatural world in order to lead successful lives. The important concerns of the Pueblos—rainfall and weather in general, fertility, health, success in hunting and gathering, victory over enemies, and social harmony—were singled out for special and separate religious treatment. The supernatural world of the Pueblos was peopled with large numbers of deities and ancestral spirits, and these supernaturals were influenced to act in the behalf of mankind by cajolery and flattery rather than by a humble or subservient attitude. There was something of a mechanistic attitude about religious observances, the feeling being that if the ceremonies were performed exactly as tradition had prescribed, the supernaturals would be constrained to bring rain, health, or the other kinds of assistance the people were attempting to get. It followed that mistakes in ritual or innovations or errors in costuming participants in ceremonials could have serious consequences. The Western Pueblos, as one would expect, emphasized weather control in their religious life much more than did the Rio Grande Pueblos, who were more concerned with social control and social harmony.

All Pueblos shared a similar origin myth in which men emerged from an underworld, coming through an opening or hatch into this world. This opening is represented in some kivas by a stone-lined pit or hole in the floor, and is generally referred to by its Hopi name, *sipapu*. All Pueblos appear to have believed in an original creator or twin creators who were female, and men and animals lived with them and were immortal before their emergence into the world. The Pueblos believed in a life after death, but there was no concept of heaven or hell in a Christian sense.

SOUTHERN ATHAPASCAN CULTURAL SUMMARY

Subsistence and Material Culture

When the Athapascans invaded the Southwest, it is likely that they were all quite similar to one another culturally. As wandering hunters and gatherers, some of whom may have had some knowledge of agriculture, they possessed no centralized tribal organizations, but were split up into numerous transitory bands. No doubt there were also a number of ceremonial, religious, and other similarities. There is not space here to sketch the varying cultures of all the Southern Athapascans, but at least an outline of the Navajo way of life seems a must, if for no other reasons than that the farming-herding life they came to follow is a persistent, viable one, and that they are the most numerous of the Indian peoples of the United States.[22]

During the seventeenth and eighteenth centuries, the Navajos—or the Apaches de Navajo as they were known to the Spaniards—came to occupy the scenically magnificent plateau country of the Four Corners region. There, in close contact with various indigenous tribes, particularly the Pueblos, the Navajos began to adopt the traits and practices that, often reworked and always fitted into their own special scheme of things, were to result in the emergence of the distinctive Navajo culture. After the Pueblo Revolt of 1680, many Pueblo Indians sought refuge with the Navajos, to be absorbed by them. In the process, the Pueblos taught them farming, stock-raising, and weaving; and they influenced many aspects of their social, religious, and ceremonial life. Much was also adopted from the Spaniards and later the Americans.

The Navajos came to subsist on the agricultural produce of small, scattered garden patches, located in places where there was enough moisture or runoff to produce a crop. Their basic crops were corn, beans, and squash, to which were added wheat, oats, and fruit trees obtained from the Spaniards. The Navajos also acquired sheep and goats, as well as cattle and horses, and soon became a semipastoral people, moving seasonally with their flocks in search of pasturage. In terms of ecological destruction, sheep may well have been the worst, most insidious acquisition the Navajos made; their ever-increasing flocks stripped large areas of the ground cover, which was never very luxuriant. Erosion followed, and today large areas of the reservation are barren and unproductive. Even though the main Navajo reservation contains about sixteen million acres, it is estimated that it can support only about one-third of the present tribal population.

The early dwelling of the Navajos was the forked-stick hogan, built on a foundation of three poles, usually of cedar, and interlaced at their forked tips. Other poles and saplings were laid against the foundation poles and then covered over with mud and dirt. These have been largely supplanted by hogans built on a circular ground plan, with horizontally laid logs, upper courses being successively reduced in diameter so that they have domed roofs. The roof is covered with packed earth, and an opening is left in the center for smoke to escape. A doorway, always facing east, is covered with a blanket, and the structure is typically windowless. Brush corrals and arbors or ramadas are generally constructed near the hogans, and small forked-stick hogans without smoke holes are used for sweat houses. Hogans are sparsely furnished; the family sleeps on the floor around the fire; and possessions are stored in boxes or hung from the roof or walls. Most families have several hogans used seasonally as they move back and forth with their flocks.

Little is known about the aboriginal dress of the Navajos, and since the eighteenth century it has been derived from Pueblo and American models. During the eighteenth century, Navajo women favored a Mother Hubbard style of dress in which two woolen blankets were sewed together, with openings left for head and arms. In the nineteenth century, following their stay at Bosque Redondo and exposure to American styles, they adopted the full skirt and the colorful velveteen blouses that continue to find favor among them, as does the inevitable Pendleton blanket. The men have moved during this period from buckskins to denims and bright shirts, and both sexes have been lavish in their use of silver jewelry. The Navajos learned how to work with silver in the nineteenth century, probably learning from Mexicans; and soon after the Bosque Redondo experience, they had developed silver-working into a distinctive and flourishing craft. Weaving was learned from the Pueblos, using their simple upright loom, although among the Navajos women became the weavers. Raising the craft to a great art, most Navajo blankets for many years have been manufactured for sale rather than use; only a few smaller ones are used domestically as horse blankets.

Social Organization

The basic unit of Navajo society, beyond the nuclear family, is an extended family composed of parents, married daughters and their husbands, and children, all living close together in a cluster of hogans.

This group of relatives forms a cooperative unit in farming, herding, house-building, and the like, and with one or more other related extended families comprises an "outfit" numbering between fifty and two hundred people. Outfits occupy and have jurisdiction over a specific territory and are also cooperative economic entities as well as joint sponsors of ceremonies. Each outfit recognizes an informal leader, who comes from a prominent family or is an outstanding person. Several outfits occupying contiguous territories are termed "communities" and may elect a head man.

Such communities or local groups are similar to the earlier Navajo bands.[23] Like other Southern Athapascans, the Navajos were politically undeveloped in their early years, lacking any governing organization above the local bands. By the mid-nineteenth century, bands had developed the office of *natani*, a peace chief who served for life and, on occasion, may have had authority over several bands. Bands also had war chiefs.[24] Despite the lack of formal structure, the Navajos very definitely considered themselves a people, the *Dinneh*, separate and distinct from other men. In order to deal effectively with the United States, a tribal organization was necessary, and in the 1920s a General Council was established. Now called the Navajo Tribal Council and made up of seventy-four elected representatives, it has become increasingly important in running tribal affairs and in dealing with the federal government and the Bureau of Indian Affairs.

Ordinarily, extended families are matrilocal, a newly married couple building a hogan near that of the bride's mother. The matrilocal orientation of the extended family reflects the importance of women in Navajo society. Children grow up chiefly among maternal relatives; women own or control a good deal of property, including much livestock, which is passed on through the maternal line; and women figure prominently in political and religious affairs. By marriage a man does not acquire his wife's property, but rather retains his interest and many economic obligations to his mother's extended family. Like many other matrilineally organized societies, the maternal uncle has many obligations and duties with respect to his nephews and nieces, assuming, for example, the role of disciplinarian. This leaves a child's father free to be a confidant, advisor, and friend to his children, a role that has obvious benefits.

In Navajo kinship reckoning, a mother's sisters are called mother, and the children of a mother's sister (parallel cousins) are called brother and sister. Navajos were and still are, to some extent, polygynous, the sororal type being preferred, and this cousin terminology accords nicely with this custom. Men also might marry a woman and her niece or a stepdaughter, which may be considered an extension of sororal polygyny. Distinctions are made between older and younger siblings, but the important point here is that they are ordinarily members of the same extended family and clan. Cross-cousins, the children of siblings of opposite sex, normally live in different communities and are members of different clans; nonsibling terms are applied to them. Their special relationship is, however, recognized by a joking relationship that involves teasing one another and, occasionally, obscene jesting. In general, maternal relatives are set apart terminologically from their corresponding paternal relatives. The Navajo men, as other Apaches, observe a strong avoidance relationship with a mother-in-law, and though friendly with sisters, they have no physical contact with them and observe other restrictions as well.

The Navajos have sixty large matrilineal clans, mostly named for localities, though they are not now localized, and some are named for alien groups, such as Zuni, Mexican, and Apache. In the early days, too, some clans were particularly close to others, and marriage was restricted between their members. The clans seem to have originated from local groups and from the foreign groups who joined them. The political and religious functions of the clans are now slight, their chief function being that of regulating marriage. Clans are exogamous, marriage within a clan being regarded as incestuous; Navajos also prohibit marriage to a person belonging to the father's clan. It is apparent that such marriage rules, presumably operating during a time of rapid expansion and absorption of outsiders, worked to bring together and to unify disparate and possibly conflicting groups.

Unlike the neighboring Pueblos and perhaps reflecting the much more individualistic orientation of Navajo society, passage of the individual through the various stages of life receives considerable attention, concern, and ceremonial treatment. Birth is not, however, greeted with important ceremonies. Women are usually helped in childbirth by an experienced female relative, and newborn infants are sprinkled with corn pollen before they are bathed. The baby's ears are pierced shortly after birth, and the midwife may gently knead and rub the baby so that he will grow strong and sturdy. When infants are about a month old, they are introduced to the cradleboard in which they will remain for long periods until they can walk. Child-rearing is essentially relaxed and permissive, a child growing up among a group of largely indulgent relatives. By the time he is six or so, he begins to take part in the daily activities of the family—herding sheep, gathering firewood, and the like.

The Navajos emphasize the transition from childhood to adult status with an elaborate series of ceremonies. When a girl first menstruates, a ceremony lasting four nights is held during which she undergoes dietary and other restrictions. Her body is kneaded every day by an older woman to make her like Changing Woman, the beautiful and most popular of the Navajo supernaturals. She races toward the rising sun each morning, grinds corn, and has her hair ceremonially washed; an all-night "sing" concludes the ceremony. Boys' puberty rites are somewhat simpler.

Marriages are arranged by a boy's father with the girl's family and generally by consulting with her maternal uncle, the chief concerns being to establish or to better the family connections. If a match is agreed upon, a gift, usually livestock, is made to the girl's family. A simple wedding ceremony is held in the hogan of the girl's parents, the couple ceremonially eating corn mush from a wedding basket, after which a feast is held by the couple's relatives. If a couple does not get along, divorce is by simple separation. A wife puts her husband's belongings outside the hogan; a husband divesting himself of an unwanted spouse returns to his mother's hogan.

As with other Southern Athapascans, the Navajos were terrified of the ghosts of the dead, believing that all people are partly evil and that this part after death becomes a wicked ghost who may return to harm people, even those whom in life he loved best. As a result, burial after death is rapid and, if possible, a non-Navajo is employed for the task. If death occurs in a hogan, the body is removed through a hole in its north side, and the hogan abandoned and often burned. After burial, preferably in a distant or remote place, four days of mourning are observed in which survivors purify themselves.

Religious and Ceremonial Life

The Navajos have borrowed many elements of Pueblo ritual and, no doubt, many religious concepts as well, but their religious beliefs and practices are strikingly and basically different. Navajos conceive of the universe as inhabited by two kinds of beings: mortals, or Earth Surface People, and Holy People, who are anthropomorphic supernatural beings. The mysterious Holy People are very powerful, capable of helping or harming Earth People. But they are not omnipotent, at least in the sense that they can be persuaded and cajoled into preserving or restoring harmony in the universe, and in individual men. The idea that individuals must maintain harmony within themselves and with the universe is a basic one, and its achievement is the principal aim of their ritual and ceremonial life.

Preeminent among the Holy People is Changing Woman, the only completely benevolent supernatural. Conceived of as forever young and of breathtaking beauty, she is something of an earth mother. It was she who gave corn to the Navajos and is regarded as the mother of other Holy People. In Navajo belief, Sun is her husband, and their children are the Hero Twins, Monster Slayer, and Child of the Waters. These supernatural beings figure in most ceremonials and are heroes young men should emulate, since they were the slayers of monsters. There are many other Holy People, including personalized natural forces such as Thunder People, animals, and others. The Holy People once lived in a subterranean world, but they finally ascended to the surface, after which Changing Woman was born and the world took on its present form. The Holy People then met, created the Earth Surface People, and showed them how to live. One of the major Navajo ceremonials, known as Blessing Way, is a reenactment of this meeting of the Holy People and the creation of mankind.

To the Navajos the world is constantly dangerous and hazardous, not only because the Holy People may bring misfortune and disaster, but also because men may be attacked by ghosts and witches. All kinds of illness are attributed to these forces, and in order to effect cures and to restore harmony, diviners are called on to discover the cause. Several methods of divination were employed in the early days, but in recent years "hand tremblers" have been the chief diviners. These shamanistic specialists employ corn pollen and prayer, and while in a trancelike state, their hand trembles. The way it trembles indicates what chant is necessary in order to cure a patient. There are over fifty kinds of chants, each of which may have variations. The chants, conducted by shamans who are usually referred to as singers, are normally long, intricate ceremonies consisting of songs, prayers, ritual actions, and the making of highly symbolic sand paintings. Chants must be performed exactly as prescribed by tradition, mistakes destroy the efficacy of the ritual and may bring more sickness and evil.

It is expensive to hold a chant, and the relatives of the ill person usually help to defray the costs. Although the ceremony is held for an individual, its benefits extend to his family and, in a lesser sense, to society in general. Many of the chants have become occasions for large social gatherings. It is believed that, if performed correctly, the chants force or compel the Holy People to remove the sickness, thus restoring the harmony between the individual and the supernatural world.

[1] Kirchhoff (1954).

[2] Kroeber (1939, 41). The rich variety of still viable Indian cultures has drawn numerous ethnographers to the Southwest to make its peoples among the most thoroughly studied of North American Indians. The literature is voluminous, and only some of the basic works can be cited here. See Forde (1931); Spier (1933; 1936); and Forbes (1965) for the basic ethnography of the Yumans.

[3] For a fuller description of the Pimas and Papagos, see Russell (1908); Underhill (1939; 1946); Castetter and Bell (1942; 1951); Hackenberg (1962).

[4] Spicer (1940; 1954).

[5] Bennett and Zingg (1935); Pennington (1963).

[6] Sauer (1934); Newcomb (1961, chap. 9).

[7] Dozier (1970, 125); see Dozier (1964) for a review of the voluminous Pueblo literature. A basic bibliography includes Aberle (1948); Bahti (1968); Bunzel (1932); Crane (1928); Dozier (1966); Eggan (1950); Fox (1967); Lange (1959); Leighton and Adair (1966); Parsons (1939); Stevenson (1904); Titiev (1944); Thompson and Joseph (1944); White (1932; 1935; 1942; 1962; 1964).

[8] Swanton (1952, 336). See also Parsons (1925; 1929); Harrington (1910); Trager (1942); Ortiz (1969).

[9] Forbes (1960); Vogt (1961, 285); Newcomb (1961, 103–9); Gunnerson and Gunnerson (1971).

[10] For summaries of Southwestern prehistory, see Willey (1966, chap.4); Haury (1962); Jennings (1956; 1968).

[11] Mangelsdorf and Smith (1949); Martin et al. (1952); Woodbury (1961).

[12] Wheat (1955); Martin et al. (1952).

[13] Woodbury (1961).

[14] Colton (1945); Schroeder (1957).

[15] Dozier (1970, 39–40); Hack (1942); Martin et al. (1967).

[16] Winship (1896); Hammond and Rey (1929).

[17] Dozier (1970, 59).

[18] Dozier (1970, 131–33); see also Wittfogel and Goldfrank (1943).

[19] Benedict (1934); Li An-che (1937); Goldfrank (1945); Ellis (1951); Farb (1968, 89–92); and Dozier (1970, 78–82) contain summaries of the controversy.

[20] Bunzel (1932, 540).

[21] Parsons (1939, 203–4); Goldfrank (1945); Dozier (1970, 179–81).

[22] The literature on the Navajo is voluminous. For general works, see Kluckhohn and Leighton (1946); Underhill (1956).

[23] McCombe, Vogt, and Kluckhohn (1951).

[24] Vogt (1961, 306).

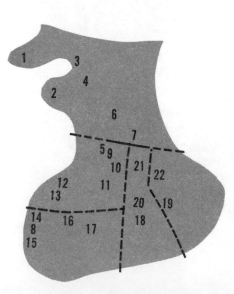

1. Lillooet
2. Thompson
3. Shuswap
4. Nicola
5. Okanagan
6. Lakes
7. Kutenai
8. Tenino
9. Sanpoil
10. Colville
11. Spokane
12. Columbia
13. Klikitat
14. Wishram
15. Molala
16. Umatilla
17. Cayuse
18. Nez Perce
19. Flathead
20. Coeur D'Alene
21. Kalispel
22. Pend D'Oreille

EIGHT

PLATEAU FISHERMEN-GATHERERS

Hemmed in by the Rockies to the east and the Cascades and the Coast Range to the west, merging in the south with the semideserts of the Great Basin, and fading on the north and northeast into the vast coniferous forests of the subarctic, is the Columbia-Fraser Plateau. It is a region of marked natural diversity, with sagebrush and juniper flats, verdant meadows and prairies, volcanic wastelands, precipitous canyons, and heavily forested mountains. The Rocky Mountains serve to protect the Plateau from the fierce winter blizzards that sweep down the Plains, with the result that the climate is milder, particularly in protected valleys, than its latitude and altitude might seem to indicate. The prevailing westerly winds drop much of their moisture over the mountains before reaching the Plateau country, and though rainfall amounts are as varied as its spectacular topography, much of the warm, arid southern section receives less than ten inches of moisture annually, while in the cooler, more humid north it exceeds twenty-five inches.

Particularly important to the human utilization of the region are its two great river systems, the Columbia and the Fraser, whose fish provided an abundant, reliable, and rather easily secured food supply, and which also served as avenues of communication among Plateau tribes and with the Northwest Coast. The diverse vegetation of the Plateau was also a very important food source for its aboriginal inhabitants. Many berries, fruits, and seeds were available and utilized, but far and away the most important plant resources were roots and tubers. There was considerable game in this country too, but it did not provide the stable, dependable subsistence that other wild foods did. Buffalo were once sporadically plentiful on its plains, and elk, moose, prong-horn antelope, mule deer, white-tailed deer, bighorn sheep, mountain goats, black bears, grizzly bears, beavers, wolves, coyotes, jackrabbits, and many lesser mammals inhabited the Plateau, though they were not universally available.

The Indian peoples who inhabited the Columbia-Fraser Plateau have posed something of a problem for anthropologists since they have been characterized as lacking a distinctive cultural stamp of their own, many tribes being heavily influenced by the cultural patterns of nearby regions.[1] Thus, such tribes as the Lillooets and Klikitats may be described as provincial outliers or up-country cousins of the Northwest Coast tribes to the west. Similarly, the Kutenais and Flatheads, whose territory originally extended to the eastern slopes of the Rockies, were heavily influenced by Plains tribes, as were tribes like the Nez Perces and Cayuses, who acquired horses and became marginal participants in the equestrian Plains culture of the eighteenth and nineteenth centuries. Nevertheless, a considerable portion of the Plateau peoples evince few or no connections with other areas, and though their life-styles may not be impressively distinctive, or at least not have any particularly unique or bizarre emphases, there is considerable justification for setting them apart in their own cultural province. Within a larger framework, they may be regarded as a somewhat different version of the many aboriginal peoples of western North America who depended on wild foods for their sustenance.

Two language families dominated the Plateau. The southern half of the region was almost solidly held by speakers of the Penutian family of languages. On the Columbia in the vicinity of The Dalles were the Wishrams, who had moved upriver in relatively recent times. They and the closely related Cathlamets and Clackamas, collectively known as the Upper Chinook, were speakers of Chinook-Tsimshian, and are, at best, figured as marginal Plateau tribes. Other Penutian speakers belonged to the Klamath-Sahaptin division. The Wallawallas, Yakimas, Umatillas, Palouses, Wanapams, and Nez Perces all spoke related dialects of Sahaptin and were almost identical culturally. The Cayuses, Teninos, and the Northwest Coast marginal Molalas also spoke languages of the Klamath-Sahaptin division of Penutian.

The northern portion of the Plateau, including the drainage of the Fraser River and the upper Columbia was dominated by Salishan-speaking tribes. On the upper Fraser were the Shuswaps, downstream from them the Thompson Indians, and to their west the Lillooets. On the upper Columbia were the closely related Kalispels (or Pend d'Oreilles, "ear drops" to the French for the shells they wore in their ears), Spokans, and Flatheads; the linguistic and cultural differences between these peoples were minor. Other Salishan-speaking peoples included the Coeur d'Alenes ("awl hearts," or "pointed hearts," in French), and the Okanagan group of peoples, distinguished by only slight dialectic differences, and including the Okanagans, Sanpoils, Colvilles, and Lakes. The Athapascan-speaking Nicolas had moved onto the Plateau from their subarctic homeland, and in the upper reaches of the Columbia were the Kutenais, who spoke a distinctive language belonging to the Algonquian-Ritwan family. Some of the Kutenais, as has been noted, lived east of the Rockies, but the Blackfeet drove them west of the mountains after they acquired guns sometime after 1755.[2]

PREHISTORY

Archeologically, as ethnographically, there are good reasons for setting apart the Columbia-Fraser Plateau as a separate cultural province. There were, it is true, many mutual influences and interconnections between the Plateau, the Northwest Coast, the Great Basin, and the Plains, but the Plateau cannot be described or understood merely as a marginal or transitional area.[3] The beginnings of human habitation of the Plateau go back, it will be recalled (Chapter 1), at least as far as the Old Cordilleran culture, the remains of which are best known from the lower levels of archeological sites in the Dalles-Deschutes region of the Columbia River Valley and in the Fraser River canyon several hundred miles to the north. Located on the border between the Plateau and the Northwest Coast, where the Columbia and the Fraser break through the Cascades and the Coast Range, these were attractive places for hunters and fishermen. The rapids of The Dalles and the Fraser Canyon were excellent places to take salmon bound for spawning beds higher up.

The characteristic tool of the Old Cordilleran culture was a bi-pointed, leaf-shaped flint Cascade point. Other flint artifacts, bone and antler tools representing harpoon, atlatl, and other tool fragments, as well as animal and fish remains, indicate that the Old Cordilleran people followed a generalized hunting and fishing livelihood. The first occupancy of these sites apparently dates before 7000 B.C. and perhaps as early as 9000 B.C., so that these people were likely contemporaries of the Paleo-Indian big game hunters of the Plains.

Other scattered evidence of the Old Cordilleran culture has been recovered from the McNary Reservoir, upriver from The Dalles, and in a cave on the lower Snake River. But other early sites on the Plateau seem to have other associations. The Bitterroot culture of the Idaho Rockies, at least in projectile point types, is probably related to the Desert culture.[4] The Lind Coulee site of eastern Washington represents a people associated with the big game hunters of the Plains, as do the lanceolate projectile points of the middle zone of Stratum C, in Wilson Butte Cave, located in the south-central part of Idaho, a few miles north of the Snake River.[5] Incidentally, a lower level in this cave, Wilson Butte I, contained three stone artifacts that might possibly be developmental forerunners of the fluted point tradition. Two radiocarbon dates for this level of 12,500–13,000 B.C. suggest that man may have been in this region at a very early time, though Haynes has thrown considerable doubt on their accuracy.[6]

The archeological record for the four or five thousand years after the Old Cordilleran occupancy of the Plateau is not yet very clear. Presumably there were no very revolutionary changes in ways of living, though new peoples and influences probably entered the region, and there must have been a continuing adaptation to local conditions. Sometime during the span of 1500–1000 B.C., however, there was a very substantial influx of new traits—ground and polished stone mauls, tubular stone pipes, stone atlatl weights, circular stone net sinkers, stone pestles, and distinctive stone carvings. These traits are generally described as having a "boreal" origin, or as characterizing a Northern Forest culture, which ultimately may have had a northern Asiatic origin, associated with a circumpolar Mesolithic cultural tradition. This cultural complex combined to some degree with traits derived from the ancient Old Cordilleran culture and, no doubt, from other old cultural complexes of the region to develop into what is known as the Northwest Riverine tradition.[7] It appears to have been essentially similar and ancestral to the cultures of the historic Plateau tribes, though at least one of the region's prehistorians believes that the specific Plateau cultural pattern did not crystallize until A.D. 1200–1300.[8]

HISTORY

The Columbia-Fraser Plateau, tucked away in a remote corner of the West, escaped exploration by white men until 1805 when the Lewis and Clark expedition crossed the Plateau and descended the Columbia to the Pacific. But well before Lewis and Clark reached the Plateau, some of its native cultures had been affected by European civilization, for early in the eighteenth century horses had reached the region. Spreading northward through the Great Basin country, horses flourished on the native grasses of the prairies of the middle and upper Columbia River basin. Many of the Sahaptin-speaking tribes of the region quickly adopted horses. Some of them had traditionally made excursions to the buffalo plains to hunt, and once equipped with horses they made longer and longer expeditions to them, sometimes staying away from their homeland for several years at a time. The Kutenais and Flatheads on the eastern margins of the Plateau early became horse-using, bison nomads, and their already marginal Plateau culture was skewed even more toward that of the Plains tribes.

It may seem inappropriate that peoples who were salmon and root eaters should take so avidly to horses. But parts of the Plateau have good grass, water, and protected valleys and are, in short, ideal for horses, though in the early days the economic usefulness of horses may have been minimal. The ancient variety of spotted horse, known today as the Appaloosa, was redeveloped in the region. Its name is derived by way of the Palouse River from the Palouse Indians. Lewis and Clark found Appaloosas among the Nez Perces in 1805, and this tribe became the preeminent horse breeders among the North American Indians. They gelded their poorer stallions, a rare custom among Indians, and they seem to have sold off much of their inferior stock. The result of their selective breeding was that they succeeded in raising some of the finest horses in the west.[9] The name of another tribe of inveterate horse dealers, the Cayuses, has become synonymous with Indian pony, or western horse.

The well-publicized reports of the Lewis and Clark expedition spurred American trappers to push westward across the Rockies into the rich beaver lands of the Columbia River basin. But for a number of years they faced difficult problems. John Jacob Astor's American Fur Company had established a trading post at the mouth of the Columbia in an attempt to monopolize the fur trade of the Columbia drainage, but with the outbreak of the War of 1812, Astor sold his company to the British North-West Company. As a result, the British, with the aid of the many Plateau tribes with whom they traded, were able to bar Americans from the region. After the war, the Americans continued to have difficulties as Plains tribes, particularly the Blackfeet and their allies, who did not want traders supplying their Nez Perce and other enemies with weapons or goods, barred easy access to the Plateau. But by 1824 American trappers had breeched the Indian barrier of the Missouri River region by ascending the Platte River and crossing the Rockies through the South Pass of Wyoming. For many years afterward there was intense competition between the American fur traders and the Hudson's Bay Company, which had absorbed the North-West Company in 1821.[10]

Many of the Plateau tribes were quickly involved in the fur trade economy, becoming dependent upon the trader's goods, often moving from their old homes to be near trading posts or to find better hunting grounds. Conflicts between tribes were inevitably heightened as they jockeyed with one another for the benefits of this new kind of existence and as they were drawn into the various competitive orbits of the traders. Epidemic diseases, as everywhere in North America, accompanied the British and American traders, and many tribes were soon decimated. Oddly, the Indians themselves were inadvertently responsible for bringing missionaries to their land, which encouraged a rush of emigration to the Oregon country and, in turn, was of considerable importance in settling the boundary between the United States and Canada at the 49th parallel.

Catholic Iroquois of Canada had been members of fur trading brigades before 1820, and they had done some missionary work among the Nez Perces. Canadian fur traders in the 1820s sent several Nez Perce boys, as well as children of other tribes, east to attend a mission school. When these young men returned, they sparked an interest in the tribal leaders who seem to have felt that if they could get teachers or missionaries—and it is unlikely that they made any distinction between the two—they might be able to learn the secrets and acquire the spiritual helpers, and consequently the power and know-how, of the white men. Whatever their precise motivation, in 1831 the Nez Perces sent a delegation across the Plains to St. Louis with returning fur traders, and put their request to General William Clark. News of the Indian appeal excited the Christian community in the eastern United States, and within a few years a number of missionaries had established themselves in the plateau country.

Reverend Jason Lee, a Methodist, settled in the Williamette Valley in 1834 to minister to the fragmented Chinookan tribes, and he was soon followed by Dr. Marcus Whitman, his wife Narcissa, and the Reverend Henry H. Spalding and his wife, who were all Presbyterians, to establish missions among the Nez Perces and Cayuses. The Jesuit, Father Pierre Jean De Smet, built missions for the Flatheads and related peoples, and other missionaries followed. Settlers followed in their wake, and by 1840 there were upwards of 10,000 settlers in the Oregon Territory, mostly in the Willamette Valley. When the boundary issue was settled in 1846, the tide of emigration became a flood, and the Indians and their lands were soon under violent assault.

The first of the Indian wars was apparently sparked by a measles epidemic among the Cayuses, but the influx of settlers and competition among the missionaries seem to have been the underlying motivating forces. In any case, the Cayuses killed the Whitmans and ten other whites at their mission near modern Walla Walla, Washington. Other missions were threatened; the Spaldings abandoned their mission among the Nez Perces, and the Catholic mission for the Flatheads was terminated. These initial conflicts were more or less resolved, but they were really merely the opening round of the struggles yet to come. People continued to fill up the country, and in 1853 Washington Territory was created and Isaac I. Stevens became its governor. Eager to provide land for settlers and a safe route for the transcontinental railroad, he quickly entered into negotiations with the Indians of the Puget Sound area, as well as with the inland tribes. By arm-twisting, chicanery, fraud, and the other techniques employed to divest the Indians of their land, Stevens soon had a number of legal-looking treaties; he also had Indian "insurrection." The coastal tribes were quickly defeated and herded onto small reservations. It took a little longer to crush the Plateau Indians; by 1858 most of them had been broken, their chiefs hanged or shot, their lands taken from them and opened to white settlement. But it took until 1880 to quell the last of the violence.

The most chillingly poignant defeat and near extermination of any of the Plateau peoples was that of Chief Joseph's band of Nez Perces. The various Nez Perce bands had been provided with a large reservation in 1855, but within five years whites discovered gold on it. Government agents soon bribed and coerced some Nez Perce head men into signing a new treaty agreeing to another, but substantially smaller reservation for all the Nez Perces. Though the chiefs argued that the treaty could not be binding on them, the government held to the contrary. Chief Joseph's band refused to leave their homeland in northeastern Oregon, but in 1877 the government threatened force to make them comply. Sorrowfully, angrily, with little left but despair and fighting hearts, they agreed to move. But white neighbors, anticipating their departure, stole several hundred Nez Perce horses. Some young warriors, now driven to the fury of desperation, slaughtered eighteen settlers. The Nez Perces had never before killed white men; now no choice existed.

Troops quickly attacked Joseph's Nez Perces, but they were repulsed. And the Nez Perces, joined by others who had similarly refused to bow to government demands, began their celebrated retreat. They were pursued through Idaho, into western Montana and Yellowstone Park, and were finally surrounded just short of Canada in the vicinity of the Bear Paw Mountains, where Joseph surrendered. Their retreat had covered over 1,000 miles and consumed four months' time, and it was one of the most incredible fighting retreats any people has ever made. Time after time they had defeated, slipped away from, or confused various armies of regular and volunteer troops, though inferior in numbers and much less mobile since women, children, the aged, infirm, and wounded were with them. Chief Joseph appears not to have been directly responsible for the brilliant strategy displayed during the flight. But ironically, his now famous surrender speech and other public utterances leave no doubt but that it was he and not his conquerors who understood justice, honor, and the obligations of civilized men.

CULTURAL SUMMARY

Subsistence and Material Culture

Salmon not only made annual spawning runs up the major rivers of the Pacific Northwest in tremendous numbers, but they succeeded (before there were artificial barriers) in ascending the rivers for hundreds of miles, far up the Columbia, Fraser, and their tributaries. The result was that the native population of the Plateau was concentrated along the major rivers and streams, particularly in places where the fishing was good. The arrival of the salmon was avidly awaited after a winter of dried fish and roots, the time of arrival depending upon the particular river location and the species. The salmon season usually began in May and lasted throughout much of the summer.

Salmon and other fish were taken with spears, nets, weirs, traps, and hook and line. Spear fishing was often an individual activity, but it was most successful where artificial channels had been jointly created and platforms erected over them. On these, men took turns in spearing the upward-bound fish. More fish were taken with traps and weirs, often placed near the mouths of smaller rivers. These ordinarily consisted of a fence, or weir, through which the fish could pass, then a second impenetrable barrier that led the fish into traps. Besides salmon, steelhead trout (sea-run rainbows), sturgeon, and, in places, eels were important.

Often great quantities of salmon were taken, and the salmon season was a time of sustained labor for the men who caught the fish and the women who split open, cleaned, and dried or smoked the surplus on racks, then pounded and stored them in cache pits. Dried salmon "pemmican" was, incidentally, one of the Plateau's important articles of trade. When the salmon run was not productive, there was widespread hardship.

The significance of plant foods varied considerably among Plateau tribes, but generally they were of substantial importance. Among the Nez Perce, for example, plant foods were a major and reliable resource and were of more importance than game animals.[11] Most valued and plentiful were camas bulbs (Quamasia), of which there are several species. Members of the lily family, they grow lushly in many of the damp valleys along the foot of the Rockies, carpeting them in spring with a sea of blue flowers. The main camas harvest came after the flowers and leaves had dried down. The gathering of the bulbs, in fact all plant foods, was women's work. Camas bulbs might be eaten raw but were ordinarily cooked in earth ovens. This was accomplished by digging circular pits some three feet deep and up to ten feet in diameter, building fires under rocks thrown into the pit, then, when the fire had burned down, covering the rocks with a layer of earth and grass on which up to thirty bushels of cleaned bulbs were piled. Grass several inches thick was added, and water was poured on until steam began to rise. Then several inches of dirt sealed the oven. The bulbs were allowed to cook from twelve hours to several days, after which they could be eaten, or further processed for storage.

In many parts of the Plateau, cous, kouse, or cowish (*Lomatium cous*), an herb with an edible carrotlike root, rivaled camas bulbs in importance. Harvested in early spring when anything fresh was apt to be welcome, cous was eaten raw or cooked, and tasted something like parsnips. When cooked, the root was scraped clean, then pounded in a mortar. It could then be cooked as a gruel or formed into bricks and partially baked over a fire. The dried bricks were said to taste something like stale biscuits, hence the name "biscuit root" applied to this food by whites.[12] Many other roots, a wide assortment of berries, nuts, and other plant foods were also utilized by Plateau peoples.

Many kinds of game animals were found in the varied Plateau country, but they were generally not abundant enough, or they could not be depended on for a reliable subsistence. In the early days, bison were present in eastern Idaho, especially on the Snake River Plain, but also in the Lemhi, Lost River, and Salmon River valleys; and Plateau tribes made expeditions to hunt them. Other game were deer, elk, moose, antelope, mountain goats, bears, and many smaller animals. Most of the larger game animals were pursued by parties of hunters under particularly qualified leaders, and they were often accompanied by women who served as camp cooks and beaters. Elk and deer were often driven over cliffs, and various "surround" and other hunt techniques were also employed.

Typically, Plateau peoples lived in small semipermanent villages along the streams and rivers where they harvested fish. Among the Salish-speaking groups of the middle Columbia, for example, three to perhaps five families, each living in their own home, constituted the typical hamlet community. At particularly good fishing stations, however, there might be many more houses and a population of perhaps 400 during the fishing season.[13] A number of different kinds of houses were used by Plateau peoples. The most widespread and probably the most ancient was a semi-subterranean, circular earth lodge, entered through the roof by a ladder. The roof aperture also served as the smoke hole. The circular pit had a diameter of about forty feet and was dug to a depth of four or five feet; a conical roof was built over it, by laying cross-members from one or more central posts to the perimeter. Covered with mats and earth, such houses might hold several families, and were warm, fairly easily constructed dwellings. A number of Plateau tribes utilized mat lodges, often using this type of dwelling when visiting the camas prairies, berry-picking, and the like. But others built only mat structures. The Coeur d'Alenes and neighboring Salish-speaking tribes, for example, before they hunted bison and used tipis, erected a conical framework of poles that they covered with tule mats. In winter they doubled and tripled the mats, and sometimes built the lodge in slight depressions, throwing the excavated soil on the mats. When congregated in the summer months, these tribes erected lines of communal mat lean-tos, and if the weather was cold, the lean-tos were erected facing one another, with a fire between, thus creating a more-or-less double lean-to lodge.[14]

The tools and weapons of the Plateau peoples were, on the whole, rather simple and meager. They made no pottery, but were skilled in weaving baskets, including watertight baskets used for stone-boiling food, carrying bags, mats, and other items. The geometric decoration of baskets among the Salish-speaking peoples was by the curious technique known as imbrication. But in general the Plateau peoples were not artistically inclined. The chief hunting weapon of men was the bow and arrows, and the bow of the Nez Perce came to be eagerly sought by other tribes for its excellence. It was a compound bow made from the horn of mountain sheep and about three feet long. A section of the horn was straightened by steaming and stretching, then backed with deer sinew. When completed it was handsome and powerful, and superior to the sinew-backed cedar and yew bows of most Plateau tribes. Before the advent of horses, transportation was by rather well made dugout canoes, and by bark canoes in the northerly parts of the Plateau.

Clothing was surprisingly skimpy considering the nature of Plateau climate. In summer men wore only a breechcloth, women an apron front and back, woven of bark. In colder weather bark or fur robes or blankets were thrown over the body. By the nineteenth century most Plateau tribes had been considerably influenced by Plains clothing styles, and the older bark and plant fiber clothing had been largely replaced with buckskin. Hair was worn in a number of styles, faces were painted for festive and ceremonial occasions, and men plucked out whatever scant facial hair they possessed. The Plateau was not an area where head deformation was widely practiced, though the Coeur d'Alenes and Nez Perces, among others, at least on occasion copied Northwest Coast peoples in artifically deforming their children's heads. The Flathead tribe, contrary to what one might expect, acquired their name from the contrast their natural head shapes had with those of the somewhat pointed forms that were popular among the Northwest Coast peoples. The Nez Perces ("pierced noses" in French, usually Americanized to "nez purse") borrowed the custom from coastal peoples, of piercing the nose for small shell decorations, although even when French trappers gave them their designation in 1812, the custom was not universal and was soon altogether abandoned.

Social Organization

Throughout the Plateau the village settlements were the basic social and political units. They had grown up at the better fishing stations, and they controlled these and often the nearby camas meadows or berry patches as well. But there was a general absence of proprietary feelings about various resources, and there was much intervillage utilization of more distant resources. The villages themselves were permanent entities, though their constituent families could move in and out at will. The villages were politically autonomous, each one having its own head man. These men, whose authority was more advisory than authoritarian, were usually selected formally or informally on the basis of personality and achievement, although among a few tribes the position tended to become hereditary. They functioned mainly to preserve the peace and to settle disputes. Among some tribes the village political structure included subchiefs and councils of all adults.

The independent nature of every settlement meant that there was no tribal political unit as such; instead there was a larger or smaller number of settlements glued weakly together by their similarity in language, culture, and kinship ties. Neighboring villages frequently met for social and ceremonial activities, but each maintained its own essential independence. Perhaps it is even misleading to distinguish the Nez Perces from the Umatillas, Palouses, and other closely related peoples, since they intermarried freely and had no concept of tribe until it was imposed by their conquerors. The same kinds of comments can be made about the Kalispel, Spokan, and Flathead "tribes," and, no doubt, other Plateau peoples.

Households were composed of a nuclear family or several such related families. Descent was reckoned bilaterally, though the paternal line was emphasized; a man who married a girl from another settlement usually brought her to live in his own village. That descent was counted on both sides reflects the importance of women in subsistence activities, and though women were barred from some activities, such as fishing because of supernatural beliefs, most activities were open to them, from their vocal and substantial participation in regulating village affairs to their becoming shamans.

Throughout the Plateau region, puberty was set apart as a particularly significant stage in a person's life, whereas other transitional phases were generally little noted socially or ceremonially. Women approaching childbirth were isolated in menstrual lodges where old, experienced women served as midwives. Infants spent several months in bark carriers, then were transferred to cradleboards, at which time such tribes as the Coeur d'Alenes instituted their head-deforming practices. The training of children was informal and unstructured until about the age of puberty, when they were given rigorous preparation for adult life. At puberty girls were isolated, often for several months, during which time older female relatives gave them instructions about proper conduct. Their hair was generally done up in a special way, and they were provided with body scratchers and combs. They were required to bathe in cold water and take sweat baths frequently, with the purpose of making their bodies strong. There was emphasis on correct behavior so that they would have good fortune in later life. It was at this time that they might also seek guardian spirits. Boys' training at puberty was longer and more rigorous than that of girls, and was climaxed by the mandatory vision quest. During this period boys and girls might be scarified and tattooed.

Marriages were most frequently arranged by a man's family, but at least occasionally a girl's family might take the initiative, as among the Coeur d'Alenes. There was little emphasis, it would seem, on the exchange of presents or on the payment of a bride price among Plateau peoples, and little public celebration of marriages. Marriages seem to have been rather stable and ordinarily monogamous, although among the Salish-speaking Flathead peoples, polygyny has been noted. Marriage to a brother's widow (levirate) was obligatory for men among the Salish tribes, but widows might choose not to take this step.

Simple burial soon after death was widespread; the corpse was sewed or tied in mats or robes in a flexed position. Widows and widowers cut their hair shorter than normal, and there were usually some restrictions placed on mourning widows.

Warfare

Throughout the Plateau there was a strong tradition of peaceful coexistence and an emphasis on solving disputes without bloodshed. This is not to say that its peoples were entirely without strife in precontact times, for there was sporadic, small-scale raiding between some groups. After acquiring horses, conflicts became much more frequent and widespread. The Nez Perces and their Sahaptin relatives had an ancient enmity for the Shoshonean-speaking peoples of the Great Basin, who lived in the mountains and arid lands of western Idaho and southeastern Oregon. But, oddly too, the Sahaptins also met peaceably with Shoshonis in the summer to trade. Many Plateau tribes journeyed down the Columbia to the Dalles to trade for coastal products, and their intercourse with Northwest Coast tribes generally seems to have been peaceful. The tribes on the eastern margins of the Plateau, the Salishan Flatheads and related peoples, as well as the Kutenais to their north, apparently had few conflicts with Plains peoples until historic times. In the north, Shuswaps and the Thompson Indians engaged in some raiding activities, but warfare was not emphasized anywhere on the Plateau.

In keeping with the village-oriented, unstructured nature of Plateau society, there was little group religious activity and few widely shared, well-organized beliefs about the supernatural world. To most Plateau peoples the world was filled with a great number of animistic spirits and supernatural forces, which could harm or help people, and to which they appealed directly. Throughout the region there was a marked emphasis on the acquisition of guardian spirits, though there were many minor differences in the nature of the quest and in other details. The guardian spirit quest was open to both sexes, though it was not mandatory for women, and some particularly powerful guardian spirits might linger after the death of their "host" to be appealed to by his close relatives. Among the Nez Perces, who seem to have been fairly typical for the region, both boys and girls, after a lengthy course of instruction from an elderly person who had a particularly powerful guardian spirit, left their village or camp to find a lonely, isolated spot for their vigil. Unarmed, without food or water, the emotionally tense youth awaited the appearance of the animal or force that was to be his helper throughout life. Considering the psychological preparation, the lonely situation, and the effects of his fast, it is easily understood why most individuals were able to acquire spiritual helpers. Some did so very rapidly, others had to wait several days, straining every fiber of their being to be receptive to the thunderclap, the ghostly grizzly bear deep in the night, the little bird, or the other apparitions that might come to them. Surprisingly, a few unfortunates never were able to acquire guardian spirits, or spirits who were very powerful. Nor were individuals limited to one guardian spirit; they might have as many as six. It was, incidentally, highly unlikely that these supernatural helpers were invented by the youthful seekers, since to do so was to bring down the vengeance of the supernatural beings and forces.

Those who had been successful in their guardian quest did not return to their homes to broadcast the good news. Instead, they waited until winter, when, during the Spirit Dance, all those who had acquired a guardian spirit during the preceding year made the fact public. The winter Spirit Dance lasted several days, during which there was feasting, visiting, and other social festivities, climaxed by exciting and stirring dances. In their emotional frenzy, dancers might fall down unconscious. When revived they sang their songs, given to them by their spirit helpers, in which they hinted at or obliquely divulged the guardian spirit they had obtained. Often, experienced shamans had to interpret for the fascinated onlookers what the song signified.

Men and women who had acquired strong or special powers might become shamans, but they do not seem to have been particularly numerous. Shamans or people especially qualified because of the nature of their guardian spirits played an essential role in all important activities. The taking of salmon, for example, was under the supervision of a salmon chief, frequently a shaman, whose guardian spirit was the salmon. This man had complete control of the communal aspects of salmon fishing, setting the time for constructing weirs and traps, overseeing the work on them, conducting the First Salmon Ceremony, supervising the distribution of the catch, seeing that women did not come too close to fishing sites, and the like. In the minds of the people, his most important function was his ability to ensure an adequate supply of salmon. If the fish were few, it was necessary that he communicate with his guardian spirit, determine why the salmon had not come, and pray for forgiveness should, for example, some individual have offended the salmon by breaking a taboo.

Other important activities, such as hunting and warfare, were also undertaken and directed by men who were skilled practically and equipped religiously to succeed. Thus, for example, during a communal hunt for elk, a man who had an elk for a guardian spirit supervised hunt preparations—which usually involved sweat bathing, sexual continence on the part of participants, and the like—and subsequently supervised the hunt and the distribution of the catch. Shamans of both sexes cured illness, which, among the Plateau tribes, was thought to be caused by witchcraft and loss of the soul.

NOTES

[1] Kroeber (1939, 55–56).

[2] There is no single work that deals with the Plateau culture area as a whole. For trait and tribal distributions, see Ray (1939; 1942); Berreman (1937); Jenness (1934) for the Canadian tribes. For the Nez Perces, see Spinden (1908); Haines (1955); McWhorter (1940;1952); Josephy (1965); Howard and McGrath (1941). For Salishan tribes, Teit (1898; 1900; 1906; 1909; 1930); Ray (1932); Turney-High (1937); Ewers (1948); Johnson (1969). For the Kutenais, Chamberlain (1892); Turney-High (1941). For the Wishrams, Spier and Sapir (1930). For the Klamath, Spier (1930).

[3] Ray (1939); Osbourne (1957); Shiner (1961); Willey (1966); Butler (1968).

[4] Swanson (1962a).

[5] Gruhn (1961, 127); Daugherty (1956).

[6] Gruhn (1961; 1965); Haynes (1969). Also see Willey (1971, 28); Crabtree (1969).

[7] Swanson (1962b); Daugherty (1962); Willey (1966, 402).

[8] Swanson (1962b, 81–84).

[9] Haines (1963; 1955); but see Josephy (1965, 648).

[10] Sources on the history of the Northwest are rich. See, for example, Thwaites (1904–5); Irving (1961); Chittenden (1902); De Voto (1947; 1953); Drury (1936); Johnson (1969).

[11] Spinden (1908, 200).

[12] Ibid., p.203.

[13] Ray (1932).

[14] Teit (1930, 58–59).

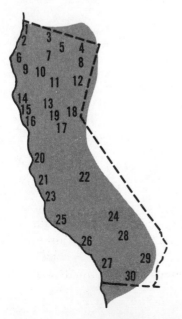

1.	Tolowa	**16.**	Coast Miwok
2.	Yurok	**17.**	Miwok
3.	Karok	**18.**	Maidu
4.	Modoc	**19.**	Nisenan
5.	Shasta	**20.**	Costanoan
6.	Wiyot	**21.**	Esselen
7.	Wintu	**22.**	Yokuts
8.	Achomawi	**23.**	Salinan
9.	Yuki	**24.**	Tubatulabal
10.	Wintun	**25.**	Chumash
11.	Yana	**26.**	Gabrielino
12.	Atsugewi	**27.**	Luiseno
13.	Patwin	**28.**	Serrano
14.	Pomo	**29.**	Cahuilla
15.	Wappo	**30.**	Cupeno

NINE

CALIFORNIA GATHERERS

Embracing most of the state of California from the western slopes of the massive Sierra Nevada to the Pacific Ocean, and from the desert country of southern California to the vicinity of Mt. Shasta in the north, was the land of linguistically diverse but culturally similar wild food gathering peoples. The region is dominated by the huge interior valley of California, drained by the San Joaquin River system in the south and the Sacramento River and its tributaries in the north, both flowing ultimately into San Francisco Bay. The interior valley is cut off from the ocean by the coast ranges, a series of rather low but rugged mountains. Arid with few watercourses in the south, north of Monterey Bay rainfall becomes much heavier, and the coast ranges are heavily clad with pine, cedar, fir, and redwood.

On the eastern side of the interior valley, rolling foothills lead gradually to the crest of the Sierra. With its steep fault escarpment to the east, there are few passes through it into the valley, and to the north access is similarly poor, as the coast ranges and the Sierra converge in the rough, wild country of northern California. On the south the Tehachapi range juts westward from the Sierras to block off the interior valley from the coastal plains and the interior deserts of southern California. With respect to North America east of the Rockies, it is an isolated land, and in comparison to the arid lands of the Great Basin and the deserts of the Southwest, those who gained it likely found it a primeval Shangri-la.

With its narrow coastal plain, warm interior valleys, and mountain systems stretching for almost a thousand miles along the Pacific, California is a diverse region with varied natural resources. Its native peoples, depending upon their particular locale, differed in the animals and plants they were able to utilize. A variety of oak trees grow throughout much of California, some species flourishing on the dry coastal plain and coast ranges of the south, others on the interior savannahs and foothills, and still others interspersed among the redwoods and more heavily forested country of the north. Only along the coast and in the higher mountains do they fail to thrive. Techniques had long since been developed by prehistoric Californians for leaching the bitter tannin from their acorns, which provided a common subsistence base for much of the area. Many other plant foods were important locally, and the region was well endowed with animals, from shellfish, fish, and sea mammals of the coast and rivers to the deer and elk of the interior. With a generally mild climate and a relatively bountiful and dependable supply of wild foods, it was an attractive area for human habitation.

The California Indians spoke a tremendous babel of dialects and languages, indicative of the attractiveness of the region to an assortment of people and suggesting that once they had established themselves, they became isolated from one another, allowing further linguistic divergence to occur. That small groups could sustain themselves for many generations within circumscribed territories and without appreciable outside contact suggests the bountiful nature of the habitat and successful and widespread techniques for exploiting it. At least half a dozen major language families were represented in California, some including a number of distinct languages, a few having no known relations to others. All in all, over one hundred dialects and languages were spoken. Two linguistic families, Penutian and Hokan, dominated California, with Penutian speakers concentrated in the northern and central portions of the state. In the northeastern corner these included the culturally marginal Modocs. In the interior valleys of northern California were such tribal groups as the Wintun and Maidu. To their south in the San Joaquin drainage were the Miwoks and Yokuts, and on the central coast south of San Francisco Bay, the Costanoans. Hokan languages had a more scattered, dispersed, and perhaps marginal distribution, with the Karok, Shasta, and marginal Achomawi-Atsugewi occupying the northern border region, the Yana in the Sacramento River drainage of northern California, the Pomo inhabiting the coast and mountainous country north of San Francisco Bay, the Salinan and Chumash tribes in the Santa Barbara vicinity, and the Yuman tribes in southern California extending into Baja California.

The Athapascan family of the Na-Dene phylum was represented in the northwestern coastal margin of California and southern Oregon by the Tolowa, Hupa, Mattole, and Kato-Wailaki groups. The Ritwan division of the Algonquian language family was spoken by the Yurok and Wiyot, also of northwestern California. To their south were Yukian speakers, including the Yuki and Wappo, unrelated, so far as is known, to other linguistic groups. Speakers of Uto-Aztecan languages dominated the southeastern third of the state, and included within cultural California the Kawaiisu (Tehachapi), Tubatulabal, Luiseño, Cahuilla, Cupeño, Juaneño, Gabrielino, and Serrano.[1]

PREHISTORY

Excluding the possible existence of an ancient pre–projectile point stage culture (and a number of its more prominent, supposed sites are in the area), California does not appear to have been inhabited as early as many other regions of North America. Its relative isolation and the absence or relative absence of the great ice-age, grasslands animals were probably responsible. About 100 miles north of San Francisco at the Borax Lake site, however, fluted projectile points have been found that closely resemble Clovis-Folsom points of the Paleo-Indian big game hunters of the Plains. But their occurrence with artifacts attributed to later times has led to the conclusion that they probably represent marginal survivors of the fluted point tradition.[2] Significantly, no other definitive indications of Paleo-Indian hunters have been discovered in California.

The earliest known archeological complexes in California seem to represent a mixture of traits derived from the Old Cordilleran complex, whose center was to the north, and the Desert culture. Perhaps it would be more accurate to describe these complexes as a Proto-Desert culture because diagnostic seed grinding implements and basketry are absent, and because early manifestations have been discovered in the Great Basin country to the east. The Lake Mojave complex of the southeastern California desert country and the related coastal complexes of San Dieguito, Malaga Cove I, and the early Topanga represent these early cultures. They are characterized by leaf-shaped projectile points in the Old Cordilleran tradition and other chipped stone tools. There is doubt about how early they first appeared; they may have been in existence as early as 8000 B.C., and there is general agreement that they were well under way by 5000 B.C.

Archeologists subdivide the long and interrelated subsequent prehistory of California areally and chronologically. But in a broad sense it may be thought of as an Archaic stage complex of cultures that depended on a generally ample wild food subsistence base. In addition to a chipped stone technology, they became adept at grinding and polishing stone both for seed-grinding implements and for an assortment of ceremonial and ornamental objects. The latter became more plentiful and elaborate as time went on. Once adapted to local conditions, these cultures changed very slowly, with scarcely any basic alteration. In the southern deserts, reliance on seed gathering and small game hunting characterized the Oak Grove and Topanga cultures. In the great interior valley and in more mountainous sections, dependence upon acorns, fish, and small and large game animals, such as deer and elk, became characteristic. In coastal regions a more diverse economy was possible, some groups relying on shellfish, others on sea mammals, and still others on fish.[3]

Population appears to have been scattered and relatively sparse during the Early Period (5000–2000 B.C.). In the Middle Period (2000 B.C.–A.D. 250), occupation sites were more widespread and larger, suggesting a growing and expanding population. By the end of this period the special adaptations to local conditions, such as the hunting of sea mammals by coastal groups, had been completed. During the Late Period (from A.D. 250 to historic times), the bow and arrow was introduced, as it was over much of North America during this interval, and there was a good deal of minor regional and local differentiation, though an overall similarity of cultures presaged the historic situation.[4]

In sum, California appears to have been first populated by migrants filtering through the high passes in the Sierra, escaping into the more amiable California climate from the deserts to the south and east, and expanding southward from the Pacific Northwest. Once in California, the wild food subsistence pattern of these hunters and gatherers was altered to adjust to local conditions; the rich environment provided a stable subsistence base, particularly after the rather complicated technology of acorn utilization was worked out. The diversity of languages that characterized the historic California Indians suggests that local groups became isolated from one another, their restricted territories supplying their needs, and also that immigrants continued to crowd into this attractive region, and once there were unwilling to depart, a hypothesis known as the "fish-trap theory."[5]

HISTORY

In response to rumors that the Portuguese had discovered the mythical Strait of Anian connecting the Atlantic and Pacific oceans, Juan Rodríguez Cabrillo, at the request of the Spanish king, was dispatched in 1542 to explore the Pacific coast northward from Cedros Island, off Baja California. Late in September of that year, he landed at San Diego Bay to find friendly natives, although, as it turned out, they already had heard tales of Spaniards killing Indians in the interior. Sailing north, Cabrillo landed on Santa Catalina Island in early October, where he was again greeted by throngs of friendly Indians. Exploring the Santa Barbara channel, Cabrillo found many people fishing from large dugout canoes. Presumably the seafaring Chumash, they too were friendly, and gladly supplied the Spaniards with fish. On the mainland Cabrillo found many villages of large round houses and the natives occupied with the nut harvest. Fall storms soon hampered Cabrillo's explorations, and he died in winter quarters in the harbor of San Miguel Island. His successor, Bartolome Ferrelo, subsequently appears to have explored the coast as far north as Cape Mendocino before turning back.[6]

A generation later, in 1579, the Englishman Francis Drake anchored north of San Francisco in the small bay that today bears his name. The local natives, apparently Coast Miwoks, greeted the English in a friendly fashion. After Drake had done some local exploring and had formally taken possession of the land for the queen, he set sail across the Pacific. These explorations had little impact on the mother countries, and in Cabrillo's case were scarcely remembered, for when the merchant Sebastían Vizcaíno rediscovered the California coast in 1602, he renamed islands and harbors Cabrillo had already visited. These brief contacts also were apparently inconsequential as far as the natives were concerned, though it is possible that diseases were introduced by the Europeans. In any case, it was not until late in the eighteenth century, when Franciscan missionaries trekked north to establish missions, that close and lasting relationships were established with the California Indians.[7]

In 1769 the aged Junipero Serra, riding muleback and coming by way of the Baja California peninsula, established the first of the California missions at San Diego. In the following year Gaspar de Portola built a presidio at Monterey, and during the next fifty-odd years a string of missions, ultimately totaling twenty-one, with half a dozen presidios and settlements, were established as far north as Sonoma, north of San Francisco. The Spaniards settled principally along the coast, and though they penetrated the interior and their influence was widespread, they never really settled the interior valley. The priests, with the help of soldiers, gathered up the peaceful, and no doubt shocked and bemused local Indians for the missions. There the attempt was made to convert them to Christianity and to replace their ancient ways with those of Hispanic civilization, the ultimate aim being to incorporate the Indian into the colonial Spanish empire. They were clothed, were taught Spanish and the agricultural arts and other skills, and were severely punished when they showed an inclination to revert to their old ways.

In California, as in the missions of northern Mexico and Texas, the mortality among the Indians drawn, coerced, or shanghaied into settling at the missions was awesome. Unaccustomed to the new conditions, concentrated together as they had never been before, often demoralized, and exposed to strange foreign diseases, whole tribes were virtually wiped out. The priests then had to go afield again to recruit more neophytes, with the result that, particularly in southern California, largely detribalized, much acculturated, and mixed Indians came to be concentrated in the vicinity of the Spanish missions, while the "wild" tribes fled to remote interior valleys and to the slopes of the Sierra. Some of the peoples who fled appear to have been considerably influenced by European civilization in that they adopted horses and developed a horse-and-cattle-raiding existence, preying on the Spanish herds and those that had escaped to run wild.[8]

The natives of northern California were long spared the experience of being missionized, though after the Russians built what was intended as a supply base at Fort Ross in 1812, the Spanish attempted to counter them by establishing missions north of San Francisco Bay. But the power of Spain was waning, and after Mexico gained her independence in 1821, the California missions quickly declined. They were secularized in 1833, and though theoretically to be partially controlled by the Mission Indians, in actuality they were taken over by Mexican citizens who had been awarded large land grants by the government. The Mission Indians had become so dependent upon the mission padres, so destroyed and demoralized culturally and psychologically, that they would have been incapable of assuming control of their lands even if no others had coveted them.

At about this time, Yankee traders were becoming active in California, the Russians at Fort Ross sold out in 1841 to John A. Sutter, and Americans were pushing westward across the Oregon Trail to settle the Northwest. In 1846 American settlers in northern California proclaimed their independence from Mexico, and in the same year, following the onset of the Mexican War, Commodore John D. Sloat raised the United States flag at Monterey. A few days before Mexico and the United States signed the treaty of Guadalupe Hidalgo in 1848 ending the war, gold was discovered at Sutter's Mill on the American River.

The news of gold brought a sudden flood of prospectors who virtually inundated the Indian peoples in their path. Prospectors paid no attention to the rights or property of the white people already there and, not surprisingly, they treated the local Indians with even more contempt. In the mining regions of California the natives were all but obliterated. Though the gold rush itself lasted but a few years, the surge of immigration continued unabated. California was a state by 1850, and within twenty years San Francisco was one of the nation's major cities. In the three decades after mid-century, there were a number of what are euphemistically described as wars with the native Indians. Almost entirely one-sided, they were actually cold-blooded massacres of Indians who had few or no warlike traditions to sustain them and no adequate means to defend themselves when they dared to do so.

The American onslaught was so sudden and devastating, particularly in the coastal region, that, unlike other parts of the United States,
no attempts were made to expel native peoples or to place them on
reservations. For the first time in American history, there was no frontier across which the local Indians could be shunted. Those Indians
who survived did so in small, scattered enclaves, often in squatter communities on the outskirts of towns. While small reservations and *ran-
cherias*, often only an acre or so in size, were tardily established, most
Indians continued to shift for themselves as best they could. In southern
California, the Mission Indians, with their partial adoption of Hispanic
civilization, were identified by Americans as Mexicans, and they have
largely disappeared into this minority group. In northern California,
where some of the Indians were better able to resist the white tide,
more substantial reservations were set aside, with the result that a
number of Indian groups have managed to persist more or less well.

At the end of the Spanish period it is estimated that the Indian
population of California amounted to about 100,000 persons. In the
decade following the gold rush, 70,000 Indians perished from starvation
or disease, or were ruthlessly shot down—sometimes for sport. Many
groups were completely exterminated, and the surviving remnants demoralized and poverty-stricken. By the beginning of the twentieth century, about 15,000 California Indians remained. In short, the wanton
genocide practiced by Americans on the North American Indians
reached its macabre depths in California.

Among one of the groups that survived for a time was a harassed
band of Yahi (Yana) in northern California. They managed to hide
out for many years, living more or less as they had in the old days.
The last survivor of this band, Ishi, came down from the slopes of
Mt. Lassen and gave himself up in 1911. His life story has been poignant-
ly set down by Theodora Kroeber.[9] Another lone survivor was a woman
taken off San Nicolas, the most remote of the Santa Barbara islands.
Missionaries had removed most of the island natives to the mainland
missions, but it was not until 1835 that Mexican authorities attempted
to remove the people of San Nicolas. Some years earlier, Aleut sea otter
hunters had been left on the island by a Captain Whitmore of Boston.
The hunters had feuded with and apparently finally killed all the adult
males of the local populace. By 1835 there were only twenty people
left on the island, and when the authorities attempted to remove the
survivors, one young woman, discovering that her baby had been left
behind, dived overboard into the wild sea. She managed to reach shore
but never found her child, and no effort was made to rescue her. She
survived in solitude for eighteen years before finally being rescued and
taken to Santa Barbara. The children's book *Island of the Blue Dolphins*,
by Scott O'Dell, is based on her life.[10]

A gross sameness in cultural essentials typified the many tribes and "tribelets" inhabiting the varied expanse of California, but a tremendous amount of specific and local variation and differentiation also existed. Traceable to differing adjustments to the varied resources of this amiable land, as well as to influences from other culture areas, three or four subcultural divisions are often distinguished: (1) a Northwestern subarea concentrated in the Klamath and Trinity river systems of northern California and southern Oregon, owing much of its distinctiveness to influences from the adjacent Northwest Coast cultures; (2) an Interior Valley, sometimes split into the North Central tribes of the Sacramento Valley and adjacent mountains, and the Central Interior peoples of the San Joaquin Valley, who together constituted the most "typical" of the California peoples; and (3) a Southern subarea, dominated by Numic speakers, concentrated south of the San Joaquin drainage system, and influenced, to some extent, by the nearby Great Basin and Southwest areas. Some would also include the peoples of the lower Colorado River as a fourth subarea, but they are here aligned with the other part-farmers of the Southwest, since they differed from the California peoples in raising crops, being more warlike, and having a more structured tribal organization, among other differences.[11]

Subsistence and Material Culture

The native Californians depended on wild foods for their subsistence, with basic reliance on acorns. In a broad sense, they made rather extensive use of the food sources available to them, much as hunters and gatherers of arid lands are apt to do, but the resources of California were richer and probably more varied. Combined with this bountiful environment and catholic dietary habits were effective techniques for storing surplus foods, so that the California Indians had a relatively bountiful and assured food supply. Why crop-raising failed to spread to California from the Southwest has been a matter of some speculation. One factor was undoubtedly climatic in that corn horticulture was not well suited to the dry summer–wet winter nature of the California seasons. The absence of the need to supplement an already ample wild food subsistence pattern, and the inertia of this ancient habit would also have worked against the spread of farming to the area.

For a region in which subsistence was provided solely by wild foods, California had a relatively dense and sedentary population. Earlier estimates, though high for an area of hunters and gatherers, have been revised upwards, and it is confidently estimated that the native California population lay between 250,000 and 300,000.[12] It has often been claimed that the aboriginal California population was denser than that of any other area north of the Valley of Mexico, not excepting the Southeast and Southwest, where native farming techniques were highly productive and supported considerable populations.[13] The hypothesis should be called into question, however, not for the inaccuracy of the California figures, but for the inadequacy of population studies for these other areas, particularly the Southeast.

Many minor differences distinguished how various native peoples gathered, stored, and prepared acorns, but in general the acorn complex was much the same throughout California. In the fall when the acorns were mature, the women, often assisted by men and boys, shook down the nuts or knocked them down with poles. In preparing the acorns, the women first dried, then hulled them. The hulled nuts were next reduced to a flour by pounding them with a stone pestle in a bottomless basket attached to a rock slab. The acorn meal was then spread out in a shallow, sandy depression, and hot water was poured into the basin in order to leach the bitter tannin from the flour. The dough was subsequently combined with water and cooked by stone-boiling in a tightly woven basket, or occasionally the dough was baked in hot ashes as a kind of bread. Acorn mush and gruel was apparently rather tasteless, but nutritious, with a high fat content.[14]

If one grove of oaks failed to produce a crop of acorns, there usually were others nearby that did have a crop. Tribes located away from a good source of acorns made journeys to gather them, and there also was considerable trade for them. In addition, they were relatively easy to store in basketry granaries. Collecting acorns was a simple procedure that could be accomplished by individuals or groups without complex social or political structures. Acorns were, in short, an ideal food source for wild food subsistence—plentiful, dependable, easily secured, storable, and nutritious.

A tremendous assortment of other plants and animals were utilized by California Indians for food. Like the desert gathers, they made rather complete utilization of the wild foods available to them, although their generally ample food supply did not force them to do so. Along the narrow, cool, and foggy coast, from Estero Bay to the Oregon border, the Costanoan, Esselen, and Salinan groups in the south to the Tolowa and Yurok on the northern border made primary use of shellfish and fish caught in the surf, with acorns and game animals playing a secondary role. These tidelands gatherers possessed only balsas (frail boats or rafts constructed from bundles of tules) and small dugout canoes, and were unable to fully exploit the ocean's resources, seldom venturing far from shore. But to their south to Santa Monica Bay, including the channel islands, mostly beyond the foggy coast of the north and sheltered from the westerly winds, were the truly maritime Chumash and

Gabrielinos. Though they did not hunt sea mammals from boats, they took stranded whales, sea lions, sea otters, and others, as well as fish and shellfish. The similarity of the Chumash plank canoes to those of the Polynesians and the Northwest Coast tribes, incidentally, has raised speculations about the alternative possibilities of trans-Pacific contacts and/or influence from the adjacent Northwest Coast culture area. Besides taking many animals from the sea, they did considerable hunting on land. Even with their orientation toward the sea, and despite the fact that they did not inhabit a region well endowed with oaks, acorns were their most important vegetable food.

Chiefly in the north, centering in the Klamath and Trinity river systems, but also in others where there were annual runs of salmon, considerable reliance was placed on these and other fish. Similarly, groups located near inland lakes modified their basic acorn subsistence pattern to utilize fish and waterfowl, and to consume such plants as bulrushes (tule) or, as among the Modocs, the seed pods of the water lily. In the more northerly parts of California and at higher elevations, root and bulb crops were important articles in the diet. Seeds of the digger pine and manzanita were utilized over a wide area, as were many grass seeds. In the Mojave Desert country of the south, piñon nuts and the seed pods of mesquite were of prime significance to subsistence.

Relatively total utilization of the available wild foods was characteristic of California Indians. In the interior valley, for example, such typical peoples as the Pomos, while depending upon acorns, consumed a tremendous array of other foods. They included grass seeds, roots, bulbs, tubers, clover, and other leaves and stems gathered principally in the spring while they were still tender. They hunted deer, rabbits, and quail, and took smaller animals in traps and snares. Fish, including salmon, trout, perch, suckers, and blackfish, were caught in streams and lakes in a variety of ways. Pomos located on the coast, and others who made the journey, also utilized salt water fish, abalones, clams, and other shellfish, and some sea mammals. In addition, Pomos collected army worms (caterpillars that sometimes infest various trees and shrubs in large numbers), roasting them in hot ashes or boiling them, and sometimes drying them for use in the winter. Other insects consumed included grasshoppers, hornet and yellow jacket grubs, and a number of other insects. They also ate earthworms. Virtually the only edible items they did not eat were reptiles, and even in this case turtles were excepted. In a wider sense, amphibians, dogs, coyotes, grizzly bears, and, to a lesser extent, black bears were generally not eaten by California Indians, primarily for religious reasons. Nor has cannibalism been reported among California tribes. But virtually everything else the human digestive apparatus could cope with seems to have been consumed.

The relatively ample subsistence of most California Indians permit
ted the existence of permanent villages, though many of the villages
were periodically or seasonally deserted for journeys to harvest various
plant foods, to secure seafood, or the like. In the Northwestern subarea
such peoples as the Yurok, Hupa, and Karok utilized square or rectangular redwood plank houses, similar to those of Northwest Coast tribes.
Elsewhere there was considerable variation in house types, from conical,
redwood bark or slab, tipi-like houses of the coastal Pomos, to the more
widespread round or oval pole and sapling dwellings covered with brush,
bark, rush mats, or earth. Houses were scattered in village communities
without plan, and in addition to ordinary dwellings, California Indians
typically built large, round, often semi-subterranean, earth-covered
buildings for social and ceremonial events. Also typical of California
communities were sweat houses, often built partially underground.
Here men took daily sweat baths and visited with their fellows.

The mild California climate did not stimulate interest in clothing,
and many of its natives wore very little except on special occasions.
Then their costumes were elaborate and colorful. Among the Pomos,
for example, children and men normally wore nothing at all, while
women dressed in a two-piece skirt reaching to the knees, and made
of plant fibers or buckskin. Often the "skirt" of California women is
described as composed of two aprons, a narrow one in front, a wider
one behind, which might be stretched around the hips to reach the
one in front. In northern California a basketry cap was a normal part
of feminine attire, and in southern California, women also wore a cap
when needed as a protection against the chafing of pack straps. In
inclement weather, skin or fur blankets or cloaks were thrown around
the body. One-piece moccasins were worn in central and northwestern
California in cold weather and on long journeys. In southern California,
yucca fiber sandals, reflecting influence from the Southwest, were worn.

Acorn subsistence did not necessitate complicated tools and utensils, and the material culture of most California Indians was relatively
simple. The Chumash and other maritime peoples of the southern coast
made use of plank canoes propelled by double-bladed paddles; elsewhere
dugout canoes or balsas were used. Fish were taken with shell hooks,
particularly in the deeper waters off the southern coast, and nets and
traps of various kinds were also widely employed. Harpoons were used
in taking sea lions and other marine mammals. Streams and ponds
were also poisoned in some inland waters to obtain fish. Deer, elk,
and other game were hunted with bow and arrow, the sinew-backed
bow being used in central and northern California, unbacked bows
elsewhere. Apparently stimulated by a Southwestern source, some of
the southern California peoples such as Chemehuevis, Dieguenos, Lui-

seños, and Cahuillas made pottery, and the Chumash manufactured handsome soapstone bowls. But it was in basketry that most California Indians excelled, both in techniques and design. Their basketry compares favorably with any in the world, and among them the Pomos are usually accorded preeminent rank. They employed both coiling and twining techniques, and also wove wickerwork seed beaters, a rare technique in North America. A large variety of baskets was produced, from utilitarian storage baskets, sifters, and bowl forms used in cooking, to coil baskets lavishly decorated with brightly colored feathers and beads, which were used as gifts and in funeral sacrifices. Some of their baskets had as many as sixty stitches to an inch.

Social Organization

Nowhere in California did subsistence patterns or other forces bring into being large, cooperative groups of people; instead there were over one hundred distinct tribes and "tribelets" each independent of others, normally occupying a well-defined territory, and often differing from neighboring peoples dialectically or in other minor ways. In the Northwestern subarea, there was hardly any feeling of village community or unity, with a lack of village councils, head men, and chiefs. Among the Hupas, for example, the basic social unit was a nuclear family of parents and children, plus perhaps another close kinsman or two. This household group lived near several other similar households, related to one another through the male line. These little communities, ranging in size up to perhaps two hundred persons, had no leader, village council, or other governmental structure. They recognized that there were other communities like themselves in language and life-style, but even though their children found spouses in other villages, neither economic nor other necessity drew them together.

In this Northwestern subarea, where influences from the Northwest Coast were strong, relationships between patrilineal kin groups rested largely on and were organized around wealth. It was reckoned primarily in terms of strings of dentalium shells secured in trade from the north. Those who were rich in dentalium shells occupied high social positions; those who were poorer, lower positions. Wealth was largely inherited and it was difficult to enhance status. Unlike the Northwest Coast, destruction of wealth to validate or enhance social position was an utterly alien, unthinkable concept. An elaborate and complex system of fines regulated the behavior between kin groups. The idea was that all misbehavior, accidental or not, from an accidental insult to adultery and murder, had to be recompensed by the payment of money or other wealth by the transgressor. Through a go-between, the affronted party brought suit, and after much haggling, most disputes were resolved.

Among the North Central tribes, clamshell beads replaced dentalium shells, but there was much less emphasis on wealth and the status associated with its possession. Headmen, by right of inheritance, were discernible as village leaders, but they had little real authority. The patrilineally oriented family was the important social unit and the group to which the individual looked for support. To the south among the Central Interior tribes, several villages within a common territory gave allegiance to a chief who was ordinarily the head man of one of the villages. Such diminutive "tribelets" extended from the Yokuts in the north into southern California.

Moieties were also typical of central California, organizing its tribes and "tribelets" into complementary halves. Widespread was the association of one moiety with the land, and other with water, and many animals and plants were associated with one or the other. The moieties were exogamous, a man marrying a woman of the other moiety, and they had a number of reciprocal, mostly ritual functions, particularly in death and mourning customs. The aboriginal social structure of the peoples of the Southern subarea is less well known, since most groups were extensively altered by mission influence. But most groups, like the Cahuillas, were organized into small, localized patrilineages, which also were grouped into moieties. Lineages were led by men who normally inherited the position from their fathers. They were also the ritual and ceremonial leaders of the lineage and were often distinguished from other men by plural wives and larger houses.

There was considerable variation in California in the emphasis placed on the life crises. In general, puberty rituals and those associated with death and mourning received more attention than others. A widespread custom associated with the birth of a child was the couvade, although in this region mothers as well as fathers often observed various taboos and restrictions on activity for a considerable period after the birth of their children. The couvade is generally explained as a mechanism by which a man socially declares himself to be the father of a child, based on the consideration that the paternity of children is not biologically obvious. The extension of couvade restrictions to the mother may call this kind of explanation into question. The rationale of Californians for the custom was that it was a means of protecting and benefiting the child.

Throughout California the rearing of children was casual and informal, with little emphasis placed on naming ceremonies or on the formal instruction of children. Puberty rites for girls were universal and were generally celebrated by dances, some of which, particularly among Northwest subarea peoples, lasted for as many as ten nights. In the northern half of California, a girl during her first menstruation was regarded as unclean and potentially dangerous to others, so she was isolated or concealed, required to avert her eyes from others, to cover herself when going out, and the like. Also widespread among northern Californians was the belief that the behavior of the girl at this time was indicative of her nature throughout adult life, so that it was essential that she be industrious, modest, and exhibit the other traits deemed desirable in women. In the Southern subarea these customs were overshadowed by a concern for the girl's future health, which was assured by denying her cold water, requiring bathing in warm water, and among the Gabrielino and Luiseño, by literally cooking her in an earth oven. Puberty ceremonies were also held for boys, in the north as initiations into the religious Kuksu cults, and in the south as initiations into the jimsonweed or toloache cults.

Marriage everywhere in California was by purchase. In the Northwestern subarea, with its preoccupation with wealth, dowries in the form of shell money and other valuables were closely negotiated, but were as generous as possible since the social ranking of the children depended on the bride price. Elsewhere there was generally an exchange of presents between kin groups when they were linked by the marriage of two of their members, so that use of the term "purchase" may be somewhat misleading. As with many other traits, there was less emphasis on purchase and formal negotiations among the poorer highland peoples than among the richer lowland tribes. Polygyny was permitted, though not common anywhere in California, and usually was restricted to head men. The levirate and sororate were also universal in their distribution.

There was considerable variation in customs associated with death. In the Central area widows cut off or singed off their hair when their spouses died, then smeared their heads and faces with pitch. In the Northwestern subarea a braided necklace was worn in mourning. The dead were disposed of in two ways; in the central and southern areas, most peoples practiced cremation, while simple interment was in vogue in the Northwest subarea and sporadic in other regions. Mourning ceremonies were elaborate in many parts of California, reaching their height in the Southern subarea where they were varied and complex.

Warfare

The California Indians were generally peaceable, though many of them could have afforded, at least seasonally, to support considerable numbers of warriors. One might suppose that in such a Balkanized area, strife, perhaps to gain control of more productive lands, would have been common, perhaps endemic. But such was not the case. Apparently a combination of factors worked against the development of warlike traditions. In the Northwestern subarea, when feuding erupted or intervillage fighting took place, the kin of those who were injured or killed had to be recompensed in dentalium shells and other valuables. This resulted in the winners, militarily speaking, being the losers in terms of wealth. No doubt, this was an effective deterrent to warfare. In other regions, where the tradition of compensation was unknown, the absence of intergroup strife should probably be attributed to social atomism, the absence of any widespread disparity in wealth so that there was no interest in plundering neighbors, and the fact that no prestige attached or accrued to the warrior. Even the most "primitive," mostly noneconomic warfare requires organization—groups of people joining together under leaders to attack or destroy an enemy—so that in this sense the Californians were barely able to involve themselves in warfare. This is not to say that the aboriginal Californians enjoyed a golden utopia of absolute peace. Conflict, but more in the nature of feuding than anything else, was brought on by charges of witchcraft, and there was also, here and there, apparently some strife over territorial rights. When conflict did occur, it was usually brief and few people were killed. Captives were not taken; in some regions scalps were. Victory and scalp dances were known, as were preparatory dances to incite those going to war.

Religious and Ceremonial Life

In California's Northwestern subarea, reflecting the concern with wealth and its ostentatious display, annual ceremonies of renewal served as vehicles for the display of treasures—obsidian blades, woodpecker scalps, white or oddly marked deerskins, and dentalium shells. The religious belief behind the annual renewal rites was that they ensured a continuing food supply and warded off disasters of various kinds. Among the Hupas, for example, two of these ceremonies were held annually in late summer or early fall. Both were linked to particular, sacred localities, and the men who carried out the rituals did so in a rigidly prescribed manner after undergoing ritual purification. The ceremonies lasted ten days, and aside from exhibiting the treasures of important kin groups, they were sacred in the sense that during them a long narrative formula was recited which explained that the ceremony had been originated by supernatural beings who had once inhabited the earth. The recitation of their activities was believed, in magical fashion, to benefit the Hupas. In addition to the annual rites of renewal, the Hupas held first fruits observances when the acorns began to fall and when the salmon began their runs.

Among the peoples of the interior valley, the focus of religious practice was in Kuksu cults. These were secret societies to which most or all men belonged. Initiation rites were involved and sometimes of considerable duration, pubescent boys being housed in the semi-subterranean ceremonial chambers where they received religious and cosmological instruction. The Kuksu ritual itself consisted of a series of dances and dramatizations in which men impersonated various supernatural beings. During it boys underwent formal initiation and, as among the Pomos, were symbolically killed and then brought back to life.

In the southern California desert and coastal country, the Kuksu cults gave way to somewhat different religious beliefs and practices, in that gods and spirits were not impersonated. Here pubescent boys also underwent long and complex initiation rites, during which they drank infusions of dried and crushed roots of the jimsonweed. The narcotic qualities of the plant brought on unconsciousness, and while in this state—which lasted from two to four days and was sometimes fatal—the boys acquired supernatural guardians. As with the Kuksu cults, initiations were the principal ceremonies of these jimsonweed or toloache cults. Also in the south, sand paintings were used as ritual instructional devices in the initiation of boys and girls, and they appear to be related and probably derived from the sand paintings employed in the Southwest. But apart from the ceremonies associated with initiating boys and girls into adulthood, and those associated with death and mourning, there were relatively few collective rituals in southern California. It should be noted that among Gabrielinos, Juaneños, and Luiseños, a deity known as Chungichnish was recognized. He was a wise, powerful god who was said to have introduced the jimsonweed initiation rite and other rituals; he was also a moralistic god in that he punished misconduct, and it is probable that this aspect of his nature, and perhaps the entire complex, was borrowed from concepts introduced by Spanish missionaries.

Throughout California the primary business of shamans was curing disease, and since illness was usually ascribed to some kind of foreign object in the body, their task was to extract it. Diagnosis of the problem by dancing, singing, and smoking was followed by the removal of the offending object by sucking. In some performances shamans went into a trance or trancelike state, in others they did not; but in any case the patient was shown the splinter, piece of bone, or other object, materialized through sleight-of-hand, that had caused his sickness. Illness was also treated by rubbing and blowing on affected parts, and there were many home remedies for cuts, bruises, and the like, which did not require shamanistic treatment.

Over much of the California area, shamans received power in a trance or dream, which might or might not be sought. In the Northwestern subarea, shamanistic power took an odd twist in that the shaman did not obtain clairvoyant or curative abilities from a supernatural spirit or force, but rather was the host for disease objects. He differed from ordinary people in that he learned to tolerate and negate these "pains," which to others might well be fatal. Among the Yuroks, for example, during a dream, a supernatural spirit, usually ancestral, inflicted a "pain" upon a person. An experienced shaman then diagnosed the nature of the individual's pain and, through a course of instruction, taught him how to get along with it. The climax of his training was a doctor's dance, publicly signaling his arrival as a shaman.

Among Northwest and North Central tribes, women as well as men could become shamans, and their curing rites were often elaborate and complex. They also held dramatic shamanistic contests in which shamans were pitted against one another. Among the Hupas and other peoples of the Northwest subarea, becoming a shaman was one of the few ways in which status could be enhanced, since successful cures were costly.

NOTES

[1] The basic, authoritative, and comprehensive work on the California Indians is Kroeber's *Handbook of the Indians of California* (1925). Heizer and Whipple's *The California Indians* (1971) is particularly useful for lay readers and contains a good bibliography. See also Downs' summary (1971).

[2] Harrington (1948); Meighan (1959); Willey (1966, 364).

[3] Meighan (1959).

[4] Heizer (1964); Beardsley (1948).

[5] Heizer (1964, 118).

[6] Wagner (1941); Sauer (1971).

[7] Wagner (1926); Heizer (1947).

[8] Downs (1971, 305).

[9] Kroeber (1961).

[10] O'Dell (1960); also see Hardacre (1971).

[11] Downs (1971).

[12] Cook (1971).

[13] See, for example, Kroeber (1939, 143ff.); Cook (1971).

[14] Heizer and Whipple (1971, 305 n).

1. Eyak	**16.** Klallam
2. Tlingit	**17.** Makah
3. Kaigani	**18.** Quileute
4. Niska	**19.** Quinault
5. Haida	**20.** Chehalis
6. Tsimshian	**21.** Lower Chinook
7. Haisla	**22.** Tillamook
8. Gitksan	**23.** Siletz
9. Bella Bella	**24.** Alsea
10. Bella Coola	**25.** Coos
11. Wikeno	**26.** Rogue River
12. Kwakiutl	**27.** Takelma
13. Nootka	**28.** Kalapuya
14. Comox	**29.** Suislaw
15. Cowichan	

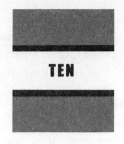

TEN

NORTHWEST COAST FISHERMEN

Scattered along the continent's northwestern coastal rim, isolated by heavily forested mountain ranges and hemmed in by the sea, were peoples possessed of one of the most distinctive and singular cultural systems of North America. Of all the more productive or "high" culture areas of North America, it was the only one that was not ultimately derived from or related to the great civilizations of Mesoamerica; instead, it had affinities with the Orient. The area's coastal environment was also one of the richest, most bountiful, and most readily exploitable in the world, so that despite the wild food nature of subsistence, the social and ceremonial aspects of Northwest Coast culture were more in keeping with peoples having developed agricultural subsistence patterns than with hunters and gatherers.

The Northwest Coast area stretches in a narrow ribbon for some 1,500 miles along the Pacific, from the northwestern corner of California to Yakutat Bay in southeastern Alaska. From southern Alaska to the vicinity of Puget Sound, the Coast Range plunges abruptly into the Pacific. Tumbling streams, often flowing through deep canyons gouged by glacial ice, rush down from the rugged mountain heights, and great rivers cut through the mountains to the sea—the Stikine, the Skeena, the Fraser, and others. Ancient subsidence of the earth's crust has created a drowned coastline with sheer cliffs rising from narrow fiords, with a jumble of irregular large and small islands lying off the tortured coast. South of Puget Sound and the Olympic Peninsula, the coastal plain widens, jagged mountains give way to rounded hills, and the shallower gradients of the rivers have built up estuaries at their mouths. And here the mighty Columbia River cuts through the Cascade Range to find its way to the sea.

A branch of the Japanese Current swings southward from the north Pacific to have a moderating effect on the climate, even along the more northerly parts of the Northwest Coast. The prevailing westerly winds pick up large amounts of moisture from the warm current, and as it rises and cools against the Coast Range and the Cascades, it condenses and falls as abundant rain. In places along the coast, annual precipitation is as much as 100 inches—over 8 feet. The heavy rainfall produces a dense, heavy cover of vegetation, in a real sense a temperate rain forest jungle. Its coniferous forests include red and yellow cedar, hemlock, Douglas fir, spruce, yew, and, toward the south, redwood; there are also maples and oaks and other species of deciduous trees. It is also rich in its diversity of shrubs and bushes, and there is an abundance of berries and edible roots.

Not only do brooding forests blanket the land, but some of its trees are enormous. They would be out of proportion in a lesser land; here they seem right. Though the really large Douglas firs are gone now, before the lumberman's ax took its toll, stands of trees 200–300 feet tall were common, with butt diameters up to 12 feet and with a clear span of 40–50 feet to the lower limbs. But for stone-age woodworkers, the tough wood of the Douglas fir was too demanding. They turned to the cedars whose wood was soft, straight-grained, lightweight, durable in the damp climate, and easily split into planks.

The Northwest Coast is also well endowed with animal life. Larger game animals found in the region are deer, elk, mountain goats, bears, and many smaller animals. Much of it lies within the Pacific flyway and great numbers of waterfowl are present seasonally. But the most important source of food was found in the incredibly rich waters of the Pacific and the many rivers flowing into it. Particularly important were the fish that made annual runs from the sea up the rivers to spawn. These included five species of salmon, as well as herring, smelt, and, in the more northerly rivers, the olachen or candle fish, which is so oily it will burn like a candle when a wick is run through its body. Nobody really knows how numerous the salmon were in the days before the white man's commercial fishery and his dams on the rivers drastically depleted their numbers. But the accounts of major rivers being so jammed with salmon bound upriver to spawn that a man could cross over on their backs, while apocryphal, gives some hint of their numbers. The coastal waters were also rich in cod, halibut, other fish, shellfish, and a number of marine mammals, including seals, sea lions, porpoises, sea otters, and whales. The Northwest Coast was, in short, a fantastically rich region, and once the problems of preserving and storing its seasonally abundant foods were solved, it was an especially attractive and rewarding one for man.

Scattered out along this narrow coastal strip on suitable beaches, coves, and islands, and in river valleys, were the villages of its native Indians. Because of the rugged terrain and the heavy forest cover, communication was primarily by boat. Though one might suspect from their dispersal over such a great length of coast that there would be substantial cultural differences separating its people, this was not the case. In an overall sense, Northwest Coast culture was remarkably uniform, although there were some significant cultural divergencies and considerable linguistic diversity. The more northerly tribes are often reckoned as being the most typical in the area, while along the southern coast the characteristic traits of this cultural pattern fall away, so that the peoples of northwestern California and southern Oregon can be discussed with the California gatherers, as has been done here (Chapter 9).

Apart from the marginal tribes of the south, three Northwest Coast subareas are usually distinguished: a Northern, a Wakashan or Central, and a Coast Salish-Chinook. The Northern subarea extended from Yakutat Bay in Alaska southward to include the Queen Charlotte Islands, Hecate Strait, and the adjacent mainland. The most northerly groups spoke languages of the Na-Déné family, distantly related to Athapascan. Of these, the Tlingits, with fourteen subdivisions, occupied the coast as far south as Cape Fox, and in the protohistoric period were expanding their territory at the expense of nearby Eskimo peoples. The Haidas, who spoke a language related to Tlingit, lived on the Queen Charlotte Islands, and another division of Haidas, known as Kaiganis, inhabited the southern portion of Alaska's Prince of Wales Island. The Tsimshian peoples, speakers of a Penutian language, were subdivided dialectically and culturally into three groups: on the mainland to the north were the Nass River tribes, or the Niskas; on the lower Skeena River were fourteen tribes of Coast Tsimshians; and above the canyon of the Skeena were villages of the Gitksans, the third division.[1]

The Central or Wakashan subarea included geographically Queen Charlotte Sound and most of Vancouver Island. The bulk of its people spoke languages that are lumped together in a Wakashan group of languages. These include Kwakiutl, which has three dialects: Haisla in the north along Gardner and Douglas channels; Heiltsuk, spoken by the warlike Bella Bellas of Milbanke Sound, the Wikenos of Rivers Inlet, and others; and the Southern Kwakiutl, or Kwakiutl proper. The many local groups of Southern Kwakiutl occupied the inlets and coves of Queen Charlotte Sound and the northern end of Vancouver Island. On the southwestern coast of the island were the Nootkas, speakers of a distinct but distantly related language, which also existed in several dialects. The only non-Wakashan-speaking peoples of the Central subarea were the Bella Coolas, speakers of a Salishan language, who occupied a number of villages in the lower Bella Coola River valley and the upper parts of the Dean and Burke channels of British Columbia. They appear to have split off at some unknown time in the past from the more southerly Coast Salish with whom they are closely related linguistically.

The Coast Salish-Chinook subarea embraced the Gulf of Georgia to the east of the Wakashan subarea, the southeastern shores of Vancouver Island, and the region to the south, including the coast of Washington and Oregon. The Coast Salish, composed of a large number of dialectically varied villages, occupied much of this territory, including the shores of the Gulf of Georgia, Puget Sound, much of the Olympic Peninsula, and western Washington. The most southerly of the Salishan speakers, the Tillamooks, lived on the Oregon coast south of the Columbia. The homeland of the Salishan speakers is generally supposed to have been in the plateau country east of the Cascades. It is thought that they invaded the coast country by coming down the Fraser River through the Cascades in relatively recent times. The Salishan languages are distantly related to the Wakashan languages, and they are often grouped together in a Mosan phylum. It has been suggested, though not yet firmly established, that Mosan is distantly related to Algonquian. Living along the lower Columbia River in Washington were the Chinooks, who, like the Tsimshian tribes far to the north and many groups in California, spoke a Penutian language. The Chinooks were great traders and middlemen, trading up and down the coast and with interior tribes as well. As a result, "Chinook jargon," became a lingua franca for the Northwest Coast.

PREHISTORY

The prehistory of the Northwest Coast is not as well known as that of many areas of North America, partly because of the remoteness and inaccessibility of much of it, and partly because of the perishable nature of the material culture of its peoples. Many of them were probably skilled in fashioning wooden articles, most of which have long since disappeared, and they did not make pottery, which is so useful to archeologists in differentiating cultural complexes. Despite or perhaps because of the paucity of factual knowledge about the origins, derivation, and relationships of prehistoric Northwest Coast peoples, there has been considerable speculation about them. Particularly fascinating are the theories about the source of the Asiatic strain in its cultural heritage. There is little doubt, for example, that slat armor, tambourine drums, and the compound bow, to mention some of the more obvious items, originated in Asia. Willey[2] has even suggested that "much of the Northwest Coast's material richness and probably some of its color and flamboyance was owed to its Asiatic ancestry." He proposes the Siberian Mesolithic and Neolithic complexes as ancestral, dating from the period 4000 to 1000 B.C. But how and by what route or routes these influences spread to the Northwest Coast is as yet unclear.

One view has held that Arctic Eskimo and/or Asiatic influences spread down the coast, and the role of Eskimo or Eskimoid cultures as transmitters, barriers to, or recipients of these Asiatic influences is central to the problem. Other views, which seem to be somewhat better substantiated archeologically, have it that the Northwest Coast was populated by peoples moving down the river valleys to the coast country from the interior, and that they too may have been bearers of Asiatically derived traits. Both views probably are, to some degree, correct, the historic tribes representing a probable mixture and synthesis of differing cultural traditions and geographical origins, distinctly adapted to the special conditions of the Northwest Coast.

The earliest people known to have inhabited at least portions of the Northwest Coast, and from whom subsequent cultures were at least partially derived, were of the Old Cordilleran tradition. It will be re-called (Chapter 1) that this archeological complex was first recognized at several sites in the Columbia and Fraser valleys, actually on the western margins of the interior plateau, and not in the coastal region. But when these sites were first occupied, they were much closer to the sea than they are today. Besides hunting land animals, the people made considerable use of salmon, and the discovery of barbed harpoon points at some sites suggests that they also hunted sea mammals. In short, the utilization of the basic resources of the coastal areas appears to have been made at the very outset.

At the latest, these sites date between 7000 and 5000 B.C., and they may have been occupied several thousand years earlier.[3] In other sec-tions of the Northwest Coast, the lower and earlier strata of archeologi-cal sites characteristically contain the leaf-shaped points of the Old Cordilleran tradition, but the transition and/or development from it to later complexes on the Northwest Coast is imperfectly understood. There seems to be a gap in the record of several thousand years between about 6000 and 1000 B.C., after which the course of development be-comes clearer.

The subsequent emergence of the distinctive Northwest Coast cul-ture is best seen on the delta of the Fraser River. Here, in what Borden[4] calls a Locarno Beach phase, beginning about 1000 B.C., sea mammals were hunted, its people possessing an artifact inventory that included toggled antler harpoons; mussel shells, bone, and antler were utilized in the manufacture of points, some of which were barbed, as well as knives and scrapers. Chipped stone artifacts were uncommon, though those they did possess were leaf-shaped and stemless. Many points and knives were made of ground slate, and small ground or polished chisels and adzes of nephrite were manufactured. These were undoubtedly used for woodworking, but they were not heavy enough for hacking out dugout canoes, leading Borden to suggest that skin boats rather than dugouts were employed.

During a Marpole phase, from 300 B.C. to A.D. 400, villages covered several acres, and the artifact inventory was somewhat different from that of the Locarno Beach phase. Small sculptured stone bowls, vaguely suggestive of the later artistic style of the Northwest Coast, appeared, as did large stone adzes and mauls. These made possible the construction of dugout canoes and the plank houses that were to characterize the area in historic times. Caches of beads and native copper ornaments, and the special burial treatment accorded some persons indicate preoccupation with wealth and social differentiation, foreshadowing customs of the region's historic tribes. The Marpole phase was not a direct development of Locarno Beach, both probably representing differing cultural groups that occupied the delta at different times. But a subsequent Whalen II phase, dated from A.D. 300–700, represents a synthesis of elements of the earlier phases, though, curiously, slate artifacts and stone sculpture disappeared. The Whalen II phase was succeeded by a Stselax phase and represented the late prehistoric remains of the Coast Salish.

The Fraser River valley was also a prehistoric center for steatite and other stone carvings that foreshadowed stylistically the wood sculpture of its historic peoples, particularly in the Wakashan subarea. Many objects, including pipes, figurines, and labrets, have been recovered, but the most intriguing are human effigies holding bowls. Stone bowls were first found in the Marpole phase, as has been mentioned, and historic Salish shamans continued to use effigy vessels ritually, the effigies representing guardian spirits.[5]

In sum, the basic cultural pattern of the Northwest Coast was an ancient one, having developed its essential form by the first millenium B.C. By the end of the first millenium A.D., it had spread throughout the region. Oddly, what is usually described as its most typical manifestation was found on the northern part of the coast among the Athapascan-speaking Tlingits and Haidas, who were relative latecomers to the region from the interior and who could hardly have been responsible for its earlier development.

HISTORY

Insulated by the breadth of the continent behind them and shielded by the world's mightiest ocean to their front, the scattered villages of the Northwest Coast peoples did not come to the attention of Europeans and Americans until the eighteenth century was well under way. Then initial explorations were made by the Russians. In 1741 Vitus Bering, a Dane sailing in the *St. Peter* for the Russian tsar, and accompanied by Alexei Chirikov in the *St. Paul*, left the port of Petropavlosk on the Kamchatka peninsula to explore the American continent. A storm parted the two ships, and Chirikov reached the Alaskan coast first, anchoring off Chicagof Island. He sent a boat ashore, and when it did not return in two days' time, he sent his only other boat after it. It also failed to return, and after what he interpreted as a hostile demonstration from two canoes manned by Tlingit Indians, he was forced to abandon his lost boats and sail for home. Bering sighted land several days after Chirikov, and sent a party ashore on Kayak Island; they found many evidences of human occupation but no people. On the homeward voyage Bering's ship was wrecked on one of the Commander islands between Alaska and Kamchatka, and he died there. But the survivors found sea otters, ate them, and took the pelts back to Kamchatka where they fetched high prices. Free-booting Siberian hunters, known as *promyshleniki*, seized this welcome information and soon followed the Aleutian Island stepping-stones eastward in the avid pursuit of sea otters and other furbearers.

The Spaniards, alarmed at a possible Russian threat to their California possessions, dispatched expeditions to explore and take possession of the northern Pacific coasts in 1774 and 1775. They explored as far north as Alaska, reaching Tlingit territory, but the significance of their expeditions lies in a journal kept by a pilot that was soon published in English and German. Shortly afterward, in 1778, an Englishman, Captain James Cook, anchored in Nootka Sound on Vancouver Island's western coast. After trading with the local Nootkas, and obtaining some sea otter skins, he sailed north along the coast to Alaska before returning to the Hawaiian Islands, where he was killed. His ships ultimately visited China to discover that the Chinese prized sea otter fur and were willing to pay fabulous prices for it. More importantly, the furs they brought home and the prompt publication of the results of Cook's last voyage, broadcast the news of the wealth that was to be had on the northwest coast of America.

In the next two decades, ships of France, Spain, England, and American Yankees, mostly out of Boston, entered into a brisk and roughhouse competition for the wealth of furs in this distant land. The English and Americans came to dominate the seaborne trade, and many Americans became wealthy in one voyage, trading cheap iron tools, glass beads, and other items for furs on the Northwest Coast, then sailing to China to exchange them for silk, tea, and spices, which in turn fetched a handsome price in Boston. The advent of European and American traders was not an unmixed blessing; since most of them made only one voyage to the coast, they made no attempt to cultivate the natives' friendship or trust. Had the Indians not been militant, suspicious, hard-nosed traders, they would have been exploited and robbed unmercifully. As it was, considerable bloodshed and violence accompanied the on-slaught of the traders.

To the north the Russians occupied a good competitive position in the fur trade, for they could take their furs directly to the markets of north China, and unlike Americans or the other Europeans, they established permanent trading posts and employed Aleut hunters to sweep the country clean of its riches. By 1789 the Russian American Company, given monopoly rights to exploit this new land, supplanting the ruthless, independent *promyshleniki*, had established a base on Kodiak Island, and a few years later the company expanded into Tlingit country. In 1799 Fort Archangel was built near Sitka, but two years later the Tlingits attacked and destroyed it. The Russians returned and built a new fort near the old one. They were able to hold it, but they never were able to subdue the tough and resolute Tlingits.

In the south, in 1789, two Spanish warships under Esteban José Martinez seized the ships of a British trader, John Meares, in Nootka Sound and sailed them to Mexico. Meares rushed home to complain, and the British government seized the opportunity to threaten and intimidate Spain. Tension between the two countries ran high for a time, but a convention in 1790 resolved the issue, restoring British property and guaranteeing their right to trade with the natives of the Northwest Coast. In effect, the Spaniards relinquished their claim to lands north of San Francisco Bay. In the following year George Van-couver, who had been with Cook, was sent to continue Cook's explora-tion of the Northwest Coast and to settle the remaining problems with the Spaniards on Nootka Sound. His careful and extensive surveys com-pleted the initial exploration of the coast, and among other things, he determined that there was no eastern passage into Hudson Bay.[6]

By the beginning of the nineteenth century, the fur-bearing animals of the Northwest Coast had been drastically depleted, and the sea otter, in particular, was almost exterminated by the relentless pursuit of white and Indian hunters. But for a time after the exhaustion of the coastal furbearers, some of its natives were able to sustain their former status by controlling the fur trade of the interior. Acting as middlemen, they traded the furs they collected from the interior to shipbound Yankees and other seafaring traders. But their favorable trading arrangements were ultimately challenged as British and American fur-trading compa-nies breeched their inland preserves. As early as 1793, Alexander Mack-enzie, of the North-West Company, made his way across the continent to the Pacific, and in 1805 Lewis and Clark also succeeded in crossing the mountains to descend the Columbia to the Pacific.

The bitter rivalry of the North-West Company and Hudson's Bay Company was ended in 1821 with their amalgamation, and within a few years a chain of posts was established along the coast as a counter to the inroads of American traders. They extended from the company's headquarters at Fort Vancouver northward to the Portland Canal, which had been established as the southern boundary of the territory claimed by the Russians. In 1867 the United States purchased Alaska from Russia, but its native residents, including those inhabiting its coastal fringe, were all but ignored in the transaction.

As a result of the influx of metal tools and other goods during the fur trade years, the tribes of the Northwest Coast flourished. Their woodworking skills were liberated by steel adzes and axes, and their artistic creations blossomed, reaching their spectacular zenith in the early decades of the nineteenth century. Hordes of settlers did not descend on them to usurp their lands, and their descendants remain today in their old homelands. Largely ignored by their governments, the assaults on their cultures were not as direct or as purposeful as they were for those who were ignominiously dumped on reservations. But the Northwest Coast peoples did not escape the consequences of the European and American conquest. Their dependence on European tools and weapons unknowingly started the process that would unravel the integrity of their ancient heritage. The inevitable epidemic diseases took a terrible toll among them, and the decline and weakening of their traditional ways of life has been reflected in alcoholism, demoralization, and other ills. They survive, but with shattered cultures, marginal minorities in the industrial Western world.[7]

CULTURAL SUMMARY

Subsistence and Material Culture

The peoples of the Northwest Coast made their living from the sea and the rivers that ran into it, supplemented by land animals and plant foods. Annual spawning runs of the various species of salmon enabled many of its peoples, with a few weeks of intensive labor, to harvest enough fish to last all year. Smelt, herring, and olachen congregated in prodigious numbers during their spawning season and were also taken in great numbers.

Cylindrical, basketlike traps with pole and sapling weirs leading to them were constructed in favorable places to catch salmon; nets of various kinds and meshes were employed for scooping large and small fish from the water; and even large bags for trawling from canoes were used by the Coast Salish and other southerly peoples. Nets, including gill nets, were widely employed, as were harpoons, some with detachable heads, two prongs, and other variations. Angling was also a common way of catching fish, salmon taking hooks while still in salt water, as did many other fish.

Extensive use was also made of clams, mussels, abalones, oysters, limpets, other gastropods, and crabs. Their gathering was women's work, but they were not an insignificant part of the diet. Seals, sea lions, and porpoises were hunted from fast canoes. The outstanding sea mammal hunters were the Nootkas, who hunted whales in the open ocean. A number of other Northwest Coast people consumed dead whales that washed ashore, however advanced their decomposition. Caribou were hunted by some of the northerly Tlingits, and mountain goats by such tribes as the Chilkats, who sought their wool to weave into distinctive blankets. Deer, bear, and many smaller animals were also hunted. Nowhere did vegetable foods loom as a very important part of the diet, though they were a welcome addition to the monotony of the high protein and fat regimen. Berries and fruits of many kinds were abundant and were preserved in various ways. In the southern part of the area, the starchy roots of the camas were gathered, and a number of other roots, tubers, and greens were utilized.

Had the peoples of the Northwest Coast failed to develop effective means of preserving their seasonally abundant food supply, their cultures would have been limited and much less elaborated. But they managed to develop techniques for preserving quick-to-spoil fish, ensuring themselves of a plentiful year-round food supply. Fish were split open, dried or smoked on racks, and then baled or boxed in oil. Fresh fish were consumed raw, but more often broiled or stone-boiled in watertight baskets or boxes. A few foods were steamed by placing them on layers of seaweed over heated rocks. Salmon, roe, and halibut heads were, as among the Nootkas, sometimes allowed to ripen in boxes as a special delicacy. The houses and villages of the Northwest Coast Indians had a well-deserved reputation among traders as being filthy and reeking of fish and other food in various stages of preservation or putrefaction.

The skill of Northwest Coast tribes in woodworking was remarkable in view of the limitations of the stone, shell, and bone tools they commanded. Adept at using fire to hollow out canoes, they employed hot water to bend wood, were experts in mortising and joining wood, and used sharkskin to smooth surfaces. They manufactured a variety of boxes and containers, some beautifully carved and painted. They were also skilled in basketry, manufacturing twined and coiled products. They were inveterate carvers, from sculptured food dishes and bowls, to masks and the intricately carved corner and central posts of their houses. Best known of their carvings are "totem poles," which, along with feather bonnets of Plains warriors, have come to stand as symbols for all Indians. The figures carved on totem poles were not venerated, but represented narrative family histories. Their spectacular nineteenth-century totem poles developed out of the ancient and widespread custom of erecting a post or pole at or near the grave of a person whose survivors wanted to honor and commemorate him. On the Northwest Coast this had been tremendously elaborated, and besides their use as mortuary posts, they served as visible statements of status and as symbols of special privileges.[8]

The artistic works of the Northwest Coast are highly distinctive and, as has been noted, had an ancient origin and development in the area. Their forte was in carving in relief and in the round, and secondarily in painting. They depicted the supernatural creatures, in animal and human guises, who were lineage or family ancestors or who were associated with them. Their purpose was to proclaim their ancestry, or more immediately to glorify individual and family social status. It was, then, a heraldric art, and family crests, like the rancher's brand that appears on everything from his cattle to his boots and linen, adorned their canoes, house fronts, totem poles, and even eating utensils. Although some stylistic differences can be discerned among the Northwest Coast subareas, overall it was a uniform art, characterized by studied symmetry and balanced designs. Their infatuation with symmetry is best seen in two-dimensional designs where animals are split and spread out in ways that are intriguing and odd to the Western eye. Northwest Coast artists also had a strong tendency to fill up blank spaces, so that figures are interlocked and intertwined in complex ways. Adapted to the object it was to decorate, often conventionalized to emphasize only those parts of a creature the artist thought important, Northwest Coast art once seen is thereafter unforgettable.[9]

Northwest Coast artisans were superb canoe builders, the craft reaching its heights among the Haidas and Nootkas, who found an eager market for their vessels among other tribes. From giant red cedars the Haidas charred and chopped out canoes more than fifty feet long and seven to eight feet in the beam. Their round-bottomed northern type of canoe had a high projecting bow and stern, often elaborately painted, with bowsprits bearing carved designs of family crests. The Nootkas built exceptional canoes that differed from the northern type in having a squared-off, low stern and a flat-bottomed hull with graceful and practical sheered sides, which, according to Drucker,[10] "made it one of the finest seagoing vessels built by any primitive people." It is even said that the famous American clipper ships borrowed their sleek, racy bow lines from Nootka canoes.

Northwest Coast peoples had a formidable arsenal of weapons, including both the sinew-backed bow and the self-bow, which were held horizontally when shooting. Short, heavy pikes, clubs, slings, and "slave-killers," that looked like short-handled picks, were used in warfare. Distinctive double-bladed iron daggers were in use when Europeans first arrived, apparently secured through trade with Siberia. Defensive equipment included intricately carved wooden helmets with wooden visors, and wood slat, body armor.

Dwellings varied somewhat; typical of the Northern subarea were rectangular plank houses with gabled roofs. Round or oval doorways were in the gabled end facing the sea or beach. Pits were often dug some distance inside, sometimes with a series of steps or benches leading downward. Along the back or sides were family sleeping compartments, often duplicating in miniature the gabled house itself. In the Central subarea, gables were often so low that the houses appeared to be flat-roofed, and the side and roof planking was but loosely tied into the framework since it was transported back and forth between summer fishing stations and winter villages. Among various Salish groups, tremendously long shed-roof houses were characteristic, and in this southern section of the coast, plank houses set in pits also were built.

In warm weather men often wore nothing, save perhaps a few ornaments. Women always wore a brief, shredded cedar-bark apron or skirt. In cold weather a robe of woven or shredded cedar bark was added. The Chilkat blanket was an elaboration of these robes, woven of mountain-goat wool and yellow-cedar-bark twine on a half-loom, and highly decorated. In the south the Salish tribes used a variety of materials in their weaving, including, in addition to mountain-goat wool, hair of a small breed of woolly dogs, duck and goose down, and other materials. For rainwear, bark capes and conical hats kept people tolerably dry. Most people went barefoot during all seasons, and basketry hats with painted and woven designs were worn by many groups.

For ceremonial and festive occasions, the finest robes were worn, and masks and headdresses were a colorful part of attire. Ornamentation was varied and often quite elaborate. Earrings, nasal ornaments, and labrets were common, the latter being oval, grooved plugs of wood or bone worn by women in the lower lip, especially in the Northern subarea. Anklets and bracelets of sea otter fur were popular with young Kwakiutl and Nootka women. Face painting was elaborate for festive occasions, and in northern portions of the coast, designs were drawn from the family crests. Tattooing was widely practiced, and was extensive on the bodies of high-ranking persons. Head deformation of several varieties was practiced by all but the most northerly tribes. Before race mixture could have occurred, explorers reported that some Northwest Coast people were lighter in skin color and sometimes in eye color than most Indians, and mustaches and beards occasionally adorned men's faces. It raises the possibility that the peoples of the Northwest Coast shared, to some extent, the same genetic background as the hirsute "archaic white" peoples of Asia, such as the Ainus of northern Japan.

Social Organization

Throughout the Northwest Coast the fundamental unit of society, beyond the nuclear family, was an autonomous local group. In the north among the Tlingits, Haidas, Tsimshians, and Haislas, it was a lineage matrilineally reckoned (that is, a group of relatives who traced their descent through the female line to a common ancestor). Elsewhere the local group was an extended family that did not figure descent from a common ancestor, although descent through the male line was emphasized, or descent was calculated on an essentially bilateral basis. Local groups were economically cooperative entities, each having its own chief, ceremonies, ceremonial prerogatives, and crests (representations of animals and supernatural beings who were regarded as ancestral or who had assisted their ancestors). Local groups might temporarily join forces in warfare or on ceremonial occasions, but they never yielded their basic independence or their jealously guarded rights and prerogatives.

The northern matrilineal groups had various combinations of moieties and clans, which, through mutual obligations and reciprocal duties, drew local groups together. But they were lacking among all of the southern peoples, and nowhere on the Northwest Coast did large, viable political structures develop. The Tlingits were subdivided into fourteen, leaderless territorial divisions, usually designated as tribes. The Coast Tsimshians also counted fourteen tribes, but they were somewhat better integrated than those of the Tlingits in that lineage chiefs were ranked with respect to others, the ranking local chief serving as tribal chief. Among the Bella Bellas, local groups congregated in winter villages as tribes. The chiefs of the local groups were ranked with respect to one another, and they held joint ceremonies and joined together in warfare. A few other groups, such as some of the northern Nootkas, carried this tendency a step further to develop rather fragile confederacies in which tribal chiefs were ranked with respect to one another. But, in general, organization and cooperative activity beyond the local group level was weakly developed. It is misleading, then, though probably inevitable, to use blanket designations such as "Nootkas" or "Tlingits." Though culturally and linguistically homogeneous, they were composed of innumerable, essentially independent groups, weakly, if at all, linked together in any political sense.

Basically the structure of Northwest Coast society was like that of many other North American Indians. But it was distinctive for a social system based on kinship in that it emphasized social inequality. In this regard it was similar to social systems found in Polynesia and parts of Asia. Every person occupied a graded position or rank, higher or lower than everybody else. Those who occupied the higher rungs of the social ladder were treated with deference and had many prerogatives and rights, and their station was visibly proclaimed in many ways. It is convenient to employ the familiar categories of chiefs, nobles, and commoners to this system, but it is a mistake to equate it with the classes of Western civilization in anything but external appearances. There were no formal dividing lines separating, for example, higher-ranking from middle-ranking persons. One class did not live by the labor of another; even the lowest-ranking person was a relative of the higher, and there was a variable amount of upward and downward mobility. The only people who stood apart were the so-called slaves, and, in a sense, they were not counted as a part of society at all. In essentials, the ranking system was simple; it was based on a person's proximity in the direct line of descent to the lineage or extended family ancestor. The man who was the closest direct descendant was the local group's chief; the lowest-ranking was the person most distantly related to the family ancestor.[11]

Northward from Vancouver Island, the emphasis on rank was strongest, but even here there was some mobility. Chiefs recognized successful warriors and skilled craftsmen by bestowing on them certain prerogatives. These might be a higher-ranking name and title, the use of some special crest, or particular fishing rights. On the other hand, people who fell out of favor with a chief could expect to receive few honors or material benefits. In the southern sections of the region, less emphasis was placed on rank, and far fewer titles and crests existed to indicate differences in rank. The advent of Europeans served to warp the aboriginal systems by making easily available to high- and low-ranked persons all sorts of material goods necessary for the ceremonies that enhanced prestige. Coupled with the drastic reduction in population, which freed many rungs on the status ladder, it resulted in a competitive scramble of individuals to assert their prestige and status, greatly magnifying and confusing the aboriginal situation.

Although born to his rank, a person did not automatically assume it. He had to establish it through the name he acquired from the family's stock of names, by the formal assumption of titles, and by the display of family and other crests to which he was entitled. The ceremony by which the prerogatives associated with status were validated and assumed is known as a potlatch, after the word for it in Chinook jargon, which was borrowed from a Nootka word meaning "giving." There were many variations in the potlatch ceremonies of different Northwest Coast peoples, but they invariably included the giving away of valuable goods, and in later years when the complex had been distorted, by the destruction of much wealth. In a sense, status depended on both heredity and wealth, since status could not be assumed without the distribution of wealth. Besides lavish feasting during a potlatch, much food was distributed to guests, as well as blankets and other objects, including "coppers." These were originally shieldlike sheets of native copper and were the most highly prized of all possessions. Among the Southern Kwakiutls, their value increased each time they were given away during a potlatch or as a bride price, and some came to be tremendously valuable. Among some of the more northerly tribes, they were thrown into the sea or into a fire in potlatches honoring deceased chiefs.

The reasons for holding a potlatch varied; among the Tlingits it consisted of a series of events, spread over several year's time, that mourned the passing of a chief. The Tsimshians held a potlatch for similar reasons, though stressing the assumption of a heir to the chiefly office. The Haidas, Kwakiutls, and Nootkas, to mention a few, gave potlatches to establish the status of a young person as an heir. In bare outline, the presumptive heir was formally presented to the potlatch guests, and his genealogy explained; the chief then bestowed the appropriate names and crests on him. The guests served as witnesses to these events and as a reward for this service were feasted and loaded with gifts.

Potlatches were not merely a ceremonial way of asserting an individual's or a chief's status. All of the group benefited and participated in a local chief's potlatching by helping to collect the necessary goods and food, by performing the dances, singing, and doing other things. By so doing they demonstrated their membership in the group and shared in the prestige that attended the lavish display and dispersal of their wealth; during the festivities, honors and titles were often bestowed on them. Nor were potlatches without economic overtones, for they served to redistribute the wealth that high-ranking people accumulated, indirectly downward through the ranks, outward to other groups who were their potlatch guests, to flow back again when they were guests at a potlatch.[12]

Birth among Northwest Coast tribes was marked by a number of magical procedures to ensure a long and successful life for the child, many involving the burial of the afterbirth. The mother, a potentially dangerous source of contamination, was generally isolated for some days after the birth of her child, and was required to observe various dietary prohibitions. Among some groups the child's father was similarly restricted in activity and diet. Parents were generally indulgent, and physical punishment of children was rare. Children of high-ranking parents, particularly the oldest sons, were quickly involved in potlatch activities, which celebrated various phases of their growth and development. Girls at the onset of puberty were isolated, were barred from eating fish and meat, and were required to stay away from water, since it was believed that their condition would alienate the spirits of these animals. A girl's behavior at this time was particularly significant, since it reflected how she would act in later life.

Soon after puberty, parents arranged marriages for their children. Ideally, they were arranged between persons of similar rank, and this was particularly desirable for the children of very-high-ranking families. Throughout the Northwest Coast, an essential part of marriage was the payment of a bride price by the groom's family. The bride price was not a closely haggled amount; on the contrary, the groom's family gave as much as they could afford, since it reflected on their prestige. The transaction should not be viewed as an economic one, however, as return gifts by the bride's family were customary. Cross-cousin marriage of a man to his mother's brother's daughter was common among the matrilineal northerners, particularly among high-ranking families. From a chief's point of view, such an arrangement was desirable; since maternal nephews were going to inherit his properties, his daughter's marriage to one of them was a practical, self-serving matter. Elsewhere marriages were often arranged with an eye to retaining or acquiring various prerogatives and strengthening alliances with other groups. Generally, those peoples who did not reckon descent unilaterally had no need to marry close relatives. Polyandry was unknown; polygyny was practiced only by high-ranking men, plural wives being regarded as symbols of wealth.

Throughout much of the Northwest Coast there was considerable apprehension about the ghosts of the dead, with the result that bodies, particularly in the southern sections of the coast, were disposed of as rapidly as possible after death, and sometimes apparently even before it. Everywhere mourners cut their hair short, and among some, women scratched their faces in grief. In the Northern subarea, the dead were cremated, although shaman's bodies were interred in small houses on a point of land overlooking the sea. Among the Haidas, the bodies of chiefs were placed in niches in the mortuary poles raised for them, or in boxes on top of them. Among the Central tribes, corpses were often placed in wooden coffins or wrapped in cedar-bark mats and tied in trees, buried in the ground, or placed in caves. In the Southern subarea, burial in a canoe placed on a scaffold was customary. A dead person's property was burned, buried with him, or left at his grave. The mortuary potlatches of the northerly tribes have already been noted, in which a dead person's wealth was distributed among members of the opposite moiety or clan that had taken care of the corpse and performed other mortuary functions.

Warfare

Many of the Northwest Coast peoples had passed beyond warfare characterized by noneconomic raiding and trophy-taking to wars aimed at acquiring territory and wealth. This was particularly true of the more northerly peoples, from the Tlingits who seized Kayak Island from Eskimos, to the Nootkas who engaged in fierce territorial wars and plundered as far away as Puget Sound. To their south among the Coast Salish and Chinooks, economically motivated warfare was much less important, though feuding was common. Ownership, or perhaps more accurately, the right to manage and exploit fishing stations, berry patches, and other resources by local groups no doubt stimulated strife, as did the emphasis on the accumulation of wealth for potlatches. They had the leisure and the necessary food supplies to engage in extensive forays, though they lacked the large, well-organized political units that could have raised and directed armies and carried on campaigns rather than single battles. Nowhere on the Northwest Coast were the military victors able to establish anything resembling conquest states.

Attacks on enemies were ordinarily well planned and organized, and included practical training as well as ritual preparations. If the object of a raid was territory, every attempt was made to surprise the enemy and wipe him out—men, women, and children. Commonly, the severed heads were carried home to be mounted on poles for display in front of the houses; only the Tlingits scalped their fallen foe. Captives were often taken, and, in fact, captives were viewed as one of the chief forms of plunder. They are generally termed slaves, though they bore little resemblance to the slaves of Western civilization. They were regarded as trophies of war and esteemed as possessions, signifying that their owner was a man of means. They were not sought or taken for the labor they could be forced to do. They ordinarily lived in the owner's house, ate the same foods he did, and worked at the same tasks, though naturally they were given the meanest and most unpleasant ones. When the owner's social rank and ceremonial prerogatives were involved, the slave's status became clear; like other property, he might be destroyed at a potlatch, given away, or buried under a house post when a new house was being constructed. If he was fortunate, he might be ransomed by his people.

Feuding was also widespread on the Northwest Coast and controlled among most tribes by payment to the victim's family of enough goods to embarrass the aggressor's family. The blood money price was established by intermediaries who negotiated the settlement. Among the Tlingits, when no settlement could be agreed upon, a person who approximated the rank of the victim might offer himself up in dramatic and ceremonious fashion. Dressed in his most elegant attire and performing a dance of his lineage, he was permitted to approach within a few yards of the dead man's family before they killed him, thus settling the score.

Religious and Ceremonial Life

Among the Northwest Coast people there were only vague beliefs in powerful and omnipotent supernatural beings, and no widely shared concepts about the origins and nature of the real or supernatural world. Instead, major religious concerns centered around the annual return of animals, particularly salmon. The ritual activities that ensured the return or continued abundance of various animals were varied and, among many tribes, quite complex. Creation and origin stories, though rich and imaginative, were, like society, fragmented and anarchic in that each local group had its own concepts and ideas, often strikingly different from those of their neighbors. Individual assistance through life by guardian spirits was also emphasized throughout the Northwest Coast. While they were an intensely religious people and religious activities were an essential part of virtually every undertaking, from hunting to house-building, the attitudes about the supernatural world were not characterized by reverence and awe, but were rather more mechanical and frequently aimed at not giving offense to supernatural spirits.

The beliefs about the economically important animals, specifically salmon, were that they were immortal, supernatural creatures who lived in a tremendous house under the sea. They lived there as men did on earth, but when it came time for the annual "run," they dressed themselves as salmon for their bodily sacrifice. After they died, their spirits returned to their home under the sea. Humans had to take care that they did not in some way offend the salmon-people, who, if angered, might not return. The result was that there were a great many rules and regulations about how salmon and other animals might be treated. Everywhere on the Northwest Coast, there were First Salmon ceremonies, held to welcome the arrival each year of the first salmon. The fish were usually addressed as if they were honored guests, and were given various offerings; they were consumed with much ceremonial protocol. Many other fish were accorded similar rituals, and all game was carefully treated so that its spirit would return again to the hunter in another body.

The accumulated ritualistic burden of the First Salmon and other rites had become so complex and demanding that specialists performed them. The First Salmon rituals, as well as those dealing with less economically important animals, were the property of individuals, passed down in family lines. Thus, a Nootka chief ritually purified himself and performed the complicated rituals of the First Salmon Ceremony as part of his chiefly duties. Those who hunted bears, on the other hand, had passed on to them through their families the arcane knowledge of how to successfully hunt bears, and this was employed for private, not public benefit.

The belief that the assistance of guardian spirits was necessary to a successful life was widespread. Individuals prepared themselves to receive such supernatural assistance by fasting, bathing in cold water, being sexually continent, mortifying the flesh with nettles, and the like. Among the more northerly peoples, such as the Tlingits and Haidas, the spirit helpers that came to a person's aid were associated with or belonged to his maternal lineage. The guardian spirits conferred different kinds of power on individuals, and it was said that they also gave men the highly prized crests. The most powerful guardian spirits, and the spirits that were frequently sought by ambitious men of low rank or younger sons of high-ranking men, were those that gave power to cure illness and to cause it. This was, obviously, an avenue to wealth and power otherwise denied to them. But this course was not undertaken by the timid, since a person had to learn to control and overcome the guardian being; if unsuccessful, a person might die or go mad.

It was believed that illness was caused by foreign objects that had been driven into the body, by witchcraft, by soul loss, and by contamination from a ghost. The shaman, after summoning his spiritual helper through singing and dancing, removed the foreign object in the patient's body, discovered the cause of illness, and treated it or prescribed a course of action. His fee, it was said, was set by his spirit helper; should the gifts or payment be insufficient, the spirit helper declined to aid the shaman further. Successful shamans often became quite wealthy, though seldom could they challenge the wealth or prestige of local chiefs.

Shamanistic curing rites performed at night beside flickering fires were exciting and drew crowds of onlookers. But the most popular and dramatic ceremonial performances were put on by secret societies. Their center of development was among the Wakashan-speaking peoples, where they were built around a plot in which a supernatural spirit kidnapped a person and conferred on him supernatural powers and then returned him to his village. Spectacular dramas were built around this theme, and their effects were tremendously heightened by the elaborate costuming and masking of the actors, and by a number of stage devices that served to mystify the audience. Tunnels were dug under house floors so that actors could, as if by magic, appear and disappear, speaking tubes allowed voices to be heard from strange places, and puppets and other devices flew through the air on strings. Performed at night by the light of the central fire, these dramas were often awesome and always impressive.

NOTES

[1] Sources of information on the Northwest Coast area are scattered but extensive. Drucker's (1955a) widely available general summary has been relied on heavily here. See also McFeat (1966); Underhill (1944). For specific tribes, see the following: Nootka: Drucker (1951); Kwakiutl: Boas (1909), Codere (1950; 1957), Drucker and Heizer (1967); Tsimshian: Garfield (1939); Bella Coola: McIlwraith (1948); Tlingit: Krause (1956), Laguna (1952; 1960); Haida: Swanton (1909); Makah: Colson (1953); Coast Salish: Barnett (1955).

[2] Willey (1966, 385). For the prehistory of the area, see Drucker (1955b); Osbourne et al. (1956); Cressman et al. (1960); Daugherty (1962); Borden (1962).

[3] Borden (1962); Butler (1959); Cressman et al. (1960).

[4] Borden (1962).

[5] Duff (1956).

[6] For early historic works, see Drucker's (1955a) bibliography.

[7] Drucker (1958).

[8] See Keithahn (1963) for a study of the origins and development of totem poles.

[9] For works on the area's art, see Davis et al. (1949); Hawthorne (1967); Holm (1965); Inverarity (1950).

[10] Drucker (1955a, 73).

[11] See White (1959, 199–203) for a succinct discussion of rank in primitive society.

[12] The potlatch has been much discussed. For varying viewpoints, see particularly Barnett (1938); Codere (1950; 1956); Suttles (1960); Drucker and Heizer (1967).

ELEVEN

A COMPARATIVE SUMMARY

An enormous continent, stretching away rich and unspoiled, awaited the first men to reach North America. It embraced almost every kind of natural environment found elsewhere in the world, from scorching deserts to lush tropical forests, massive mountain chains to sweeping plains, and tremendous fresh water lakes to seacoasts of every description. Some regions were promising and easily exploited; others were unpromising, harsh and difficult. Plant resources were many and varied, and the potential of some for domestication was excellent. Animal life was diverse and often extremely abundant, though only a few species were suitable for domestication. Men prospered and flourished in this primeval land, and they apparently reached its farthest limits in less than a millennium. Ten or more millennia later, their descendants, and those who came later, numbered in the millions.

So far as it is possible to judge, the earliest of these men, as well as their descendants, were biologically of the modern species, born with the same inherent capabilities as are other groups of men. Compared with other human populations, spread over a large and diverse area, the American Indians are a homogeneous group. Their homogeneity suggests that they were derived from one or more fairly uniform ancestral populations that had not been in America long enough for the forces of evolution to produce much variability. This essential biological oneness is probably the best testimony in the world to the idea that "race" is not a determinant of cultural type, that the two are independent variables. If the racist argument were true, American Indians would have been restricted to one slightly varied cultural type; but in North America alone, as this book attests, there were numerous culturally differing tribes and nations. The explanations for the differences in the customs, attitudes, and traditions of American Indians, as for other peoples, must be sought elsewhere than through recourse to assumed differences in biological capacities for culture.

The earliest well-authenticated evidence of people in North America indicates that they were hunters of big game animals, but the diversification of culture soon began as men spread into the varied regions of the continent to adapt in a multitude of ways to differing environmental conditions. The great continental glaciers receded, and soon many of the ice-age game animals became extinct, perhaps hurried to oblivion by the hunters who then were forced to readjust their ways of gaining a livelihood. Through the centuries, climatic conditions continued to be dynamic, often stimulating migrations and sparking cultural adjustments and innovations. In parts of North America the wealth of game and other wild food allowed populations to become relatively dense and sedentary. In others that lacked abundant resources or where the people lacked knowledge of how to exploit the resources, sparse, wandering populations eked out a bare livelihood. Ultimately, in South America and Mesoamerica, men began to raise crops instead of merely gathering wild plant and animal foods, thus initiating the process that culminated in the development of the great, populous, advanced civilizations of the New World. Their influences spread far and wide, and their effect on the nature and development of a number of North American cultures was profound.

At one end of the cultural spectrum in aboriginal North America were the scattered peoples of the deserts and semideserts of the West. By consuming virtually every available foodstuff a marvelously rugged and markedly omnivorous digestive apparatus could utilize, aided by the custom of grinding or milling otherwise inedible materials into consumable form, men were able to inhabit these lands for thousands of years. So scant were foodstuffs in the more barren wastes that nomadic populations were very thinly scattered, and nowhere were the desert gatherers sedentary or numerous. Under such conditions, life was reduced to essentials; at the extreme the simple family was the sum and total of human society. So lacking were they in the innumerable social groups in which modern men are immersed—occupational, recreational, ceremonial, political, and so on—that the atomistic, individualistic essence of their life may be all but incomprehensible to modern urban men. At least in imagination one can adjust to the dietary regimen of the desert wanderers, but the idea of total reliance for months on end on one's self, a spouse, small children, and perhaps few if any other human beings for all of life's necessities and pleasures is a staggering one.

But there was some compensation or seeming compensation for the brief, lonely, sometimes desperate struggle for survival. Unfettered by the constraints imposed by men living closely packed in large groups, they were free. Distinguished from others not by occupation, class, or wealth, but only by sex, age, and personal attributes, all men were equals. Though all men were not literally brothers, almost all were kinsmen. Envied by none, lacking riches, and sometimes even lacking territories to defend, they were not victims of aggression, nor were they capable of it; they were at peace. The cultures of the Desert gatherers stand, then, in stark contrast to our own—certainly not to be envied, but perhaps to be appreciated as rare examples of elemental, indomitable humanity.

The hunters and fishermen of the subarctic forests commanded a more extensive and complex tool kit than did Desert gatherers, and they inhabited a natural environment that was very different, though also harsh and severe. In basic ways the two cultures were, nevertheless, quite similar. The precarious and often minimal food supply available in the Subarctic meant that, for the most part, its people were scattered, hunting and foraging in small, essentially autonomous family groups. Only some groups during some seasons were able to join forces for such activities as communal caribou hunts. Like the Desert gatherers, their largest political groupings were rather amorphous bands. Apart from occasional raids and feuds, apparently most often brought on by charges of witchcraft, they also seem to have been a peaceable folk. Dangerous supernatural forces and spirits lurked everywhere, to be easily provoked by the careless or foolish. Concepts of the supernatural were vague and unstructured. A few individuals, by virtue of special supernatural gifts, diagnosed and treated the misfortunes and ills to which others were prone, but there could be few shared religious observances. Though the lack of information about Subarctic peoples prior to the cultural deterioration and disorganization wrought by the fur trade obscures our picture of them, their ancient way of life may be summed up as austere, even barren, focused on the small family group and its resourcefulness, alone in a land where existence was a difficult and often brief struggle.

The peoples of the Columbia-Fraser Plateau led a more settled, secure life than Desert gatherers or Subarctic hunters, since they were able to depend on relatively abundant natural resources, including salmon, camas, cous, other nutritious roots and tubers, and game. Though the basic foods were seasonal, there were well-developed techniques to preserve and store them. The small, semipermanent Plateau villages, frequently with substantial dwellings, were concentrated along streams at good fishing sites. They contrast markedly with the small, shifting, temporary camps of the peoples of the desert and subarctic. But the subsistence quest of Plateau peoples did not lead to large or complex social groups; neighboring villages and hamlets maintained social and ceremonial relationships, but autonomous villages were the largest political entities. Small-scale raiding was known, though most Plateau tribes apparently were without serious conflict before the introduction of horses. In their religions, the guardian spirit quest was emphasized and central to annual group ceremonies. Shamans were active as curers and played important roles in critical undertakings. Many of the geographically marginal peoples of the area were influenced by the cultures of adjacent regions, and some adopted a Plains or quasi-Plains culture after the diffusion of horses, so that the essential character of aboriginal Plateau culture is somewhat veiled. The area is probably best characterized culturally as a somewhat more affluent, variant expression of the widespread way of life of wild-food gatherers of the West and as a culture area that did not develop any very distinctive thrust or bent.

Of all the regions of North America in which men existed by relying on wild plant foods, California had the mildest climate and the largest supply of food, and it supported the most populous, assured, and stable cultures. Acorns were the basic and an almost ideal food source, supplemented by a variety of other wild foods. Material culture was about as simple and uncomplicated as among Desert gatherers, though it was a region of some of the finest basketmakers in the world. Housing was simple and minimal, as was dress, except for special occasions. Dwelling in fairly permanent villages, politically autonomous "tribelets" had a strong sense of proprietorship over the resources of their adjacent lands. They were led by headmen whose principal duties were to resolve disputes, entertain visitors, give economic advice, and serve as the chief administrators for social and ceremonial affairs. Family and group rituals and ceremonies were well developed, and secret societies were present. Despite a relatively dense population, considerable linguistic diversity, and many small, politically distinct societies, Californians were a peaceable folk. The relatively abundant natural resources of California and their effective exploitation led to a settled life and to many social and ceremonial embellishments that were rare or absent among other North American wild-plant gatherers.

The Northwest Coast was the only area of North America where men were able to make an easy, richly rewarding living predominantly from fish and other marine life. Their fishery was so productive and their techniques for taking and preserving fish so good that they were able to lead a settled, stable, village existence. They possessed a relatively complex technology, including a developed woodworking tradition, with highly skilled artisans and craftsmen, and a distinctive, well-developed artistic tradition. Socially, the Northwest Coast was an area of autonomous local kinship groups, weakly linked in various ways.

Politically, it was the only area of North America characterized by chiefdoms, that is, by societies with hereditary leaders at the apexes of ranked social systems. Such affluent tribes could afford the luxury of warfare, and did so for territorial aggrandizement, captives, and goods. They developed an elaborate religious life, with highly dramatic rituals, dances, and ceremonies. Northwest Coast culture was, in an overall sense, more like those of productive food-producing peoples than of societies dependent upon the vagaries of subsistence on wild foods. Compared with the low-keyed, placid, and bland Californian acorn gatherers, the ways of life of the Northwest Coast stand out as vigorous, competitive, aggressive, and warped toward the attainment of social status and power through the accumulation and distribution of wealth.

Everywhere east of the Rockies where environmental conditions permitted, native peoples were food producers, combining gardening with hunting and collecting in a kaleidoscopic assortment of ways. The heterogeneity of cultures was greatest in the Northeast Woodlands where, on its northern fringes, the brief growing season severely limited or precluded horticulture, and the cultures of its partly or wholly hunting and fishing peoples faded into those of the Subarctic. Southward, with a longer growing season, the importance of gardening increased, to become the principal means of subsistence of the Iroquoians, a number of Coastal Algonkians, and perhaps some of the Central Algonkians. Special resources, such as wild rice, or special techniques for exploiting potential resources, such as maple-sugaring, also contributed to cultural heterogeneity. As the nature and means of exploiting a diverse environment varied, so did other aspects of Northeast Woodland cultures. Some were culturally little different from the simplest societies of wild-food hunters and gatherers. But the more economically productive tribes of the Northeast Woodlands led a sedentary or semisedentary village life, were well organized by varied extensions of kinship, and were united into tribes governed by chiefs and councils. Warfare of a ritualized nature was widespread among them, and confederacies of tribes had appeared. Among some tribes a series of annual religious ceremonies, as well as other customs, bespoke ties to the Southeast.

At the summit of the varied cultures of the Eastern Woodlands were the intensive agriculturalists of the Southeast. In fact, in terms of technological productivity, wealth, population, social complexity, or any other objective measure, the highest and most advanced tribes and confederacies north of Mexico were found in the Southeast. Ultimately drawing much of their inspiration from Mesoamerican sources, their villages, or towns, numbered in the tens of thousands; their ceremonial centers were unparalleled in North America, and some rivaled in size even those of Mesoamerica. Though anchored in kinship, their societies were complex; some were stratified in distinctive ways, and occupational classes had appeared. Priest-kings sanctioned by celestial and other deities, and supported by a hierarchy of officials, provided an effective and relatively centralized source of governmental and religious authority. Tribes were gathered into alliances and confederacies, and it is likely that conquest states had arisen prehistorically, though none seems to have survived into historic times. In short, all the ingredients of what is often defined as civilization, save that none of its peoples were literate, had appeared in the wealthy, imposing, elaborate cultures of the Southeast.

Westward across the Mississippi, and, at times in the past, extending up the river valleys almost across the Plains, were a series of semisedentary, village-dwelling tribes who combined a productive gardening economy with bison hunting. Their ancestral connections lay with farming peoples to the east, but their adaptation to the changeable environment of the Plains, and particularly their exploitation of bison, gave a distinctive cast to their cultures. With a flexible, dual economy and a society tightly organized on a village level, they were for centuries the dominant and most successful people in the Plains.

But with the spread of Spanish-introduced horses, a new and highly distinctive cultural system took shape in the Plains. It flared brightly for a time, dominating the region until the bison herds were depleted and its peoples overwhelmed by white settlers and soldiers. The rapidity with which peoples of widely varied backgrounds adopted an essentially common Plains culture is indicative of how powerful and persuasive ecological conditions can be. Hunting bison on horseback was attractive and richly rewarding, and the nature and habits of bison led or forced those who depended on them to join together in summer for great communal hunts, dispersing during other seasons. Such a cycle demanded a flexible social and political organization with institutions of control and leadership operative during the season of togetherness, but absent during most of the year, when family and other small groups led an independent existence. Thus, the more rigid clan and related organizations of former horticultural village-dwellers tended to disappear, and more fluid kinds of institutions replaced them. The great tribal and band festivities and ceremonials—of necessity held during the summer——emphasized in important ways tribal unity and cohesion, thus countering the centrifugal forces of their seasonal dispersal. The competition between Plains tribes for horses, guns, and good hunting grounds also fostered warfare, and a widely shared and distinctive form of conflict developed. In sum, the introduction of horses to the Plains of North America initiated a cultural revolution among its old residents as well as among the newcomers who had been attracted to or forced into it. Though most of the traits of the Plains culture were ancient, their recombination under different circumstances led to a new kind of cultural system—flamboyant, vigorous, unique, and, for a time, highly successful.

Like the productive tribes and confederacies of the Southeast, the Pueblo Indians of the Southwest were successful farmers, sedentary village-dwellers, and ingenious builders, much of whose culture was ultimately derived from Mexican sources. But there were few other similarities. Their culture was uniquely their own, not a provincial reflection of some Mesoamerican model, and it was quite unlike that of the Southeast. Developing over the centuries in a difficult desert land, each pueblo became a fiercely independent, self-governing, tightly-knit community. Leading a highly ritualized existence, they seem to have been preoccupied with their world and its endless round of seasonal and ceremonial rhythms. They succeeded and endured in a land of adversity, and their struggles equipped them well, it appears, to withstand the assaults of alien peoples. In any case they exist today, colorful enclaves within a very different civilization, and poignant reminders of an often forgotten world.

In a sense the Athapascan newcomers to the Southwest, particularly the Navajos, are comparable to the Plains tribes, since their cultures are also recent syntheses, derived from Western civilization and various aboriginal sources. As was the case in the Plains, the farming-herding culture that developed is distinctive and quite different from its antecedents. But unlike the Plains cultures, those of the Navajos have survived—dynamic, expanding, persisting in an often antagonistic white world.

The major cultural systems of native North America described in this book encompass most of the categories of preindustrial cultures of the entire world. This striking, rainbow assortment of cultures faded in the maelstrom of European invasion, conquered by men with superior equipment, know-how, and ultimately overwhelming numbers. The detailed story of this conquest and its aftermath, and of the plight of today's Indians is peripheral to the aims of this book, however critical its importance to the comprehension of the nature and problems of Indians and modern America. Most North American Indians are now no more than lingering memories, but the part they played in the emergence of a great new nation and their contributions to it have been immense. Their sun may have set, but the lands on which they so long trod are still warmed by their touch.

APPENDIX

BIBLIOGRAPHY

Aberle, S. D.
  1948 The Pueblo Indians of New Mexico: their land, economy, and civil organization. American Anthropological Association, Memoir 70.

Adams, R. M.
  1966 Evolution of urban society: early Mesopotamia and pre-Hispanic Mexico. Chicago: Aldine.

Albers, Patricia, and Seymour Parker
  1971 The Plains vision experience: a study of power and privilege. Southwestern Journal of Anthropology, 27:203–33.

Bahti, Tom
  1968 Southwestern Indian tribes. Flagstaff, Ariz.: KC Publications.

Barnett, Homer G.
  1938 The nature of the potlatch. American Anthropologist, 40:349–58.
  1955 The Coast Salish of British Columbia. Eugene, Ore.: University of Oregon Press.

Beals, Ralph L.
  1932 The comparative ethnology of northern Mexico before 1750. Ibero-Americana, 2:92–225.
  1943 Northern Mexico and the Southwest, pp. 191–99, in El norte de Mexico el sur de Estados Unidos Tercera Reunion de Mesa Redondo Sobre Problemas Anthropologicas de Mexico y Central America, Mexico, D.F.

Beardsley, R. K.
  1948 Culture sequences in central California. American Antiquity, 14:1–28.

Beauchamp, W. M.
  1905 History of the Iroquois. Albany: New York State Museum Bulletin.

236

Benedict, Ruth
1922 The vision in Plains culture. American Anthropologist, 24:1–23.
1923 The concept of the guardian spirit in North America. American Anthropological Association, Memoir 29.
1934 Patterns of culture. Boston: Houghton Mifflin.

Bennett, W. C., and R. M. Zingg
1935 The Tarahumara, an inland tribe of northern Mexico. Chicago: University of Chicago Press.

Bergsland, Knut, and Hans Vogt
1962 On the validity of glottochronology. Current Anthropology, 3:115–53.

Berreman, Joel V.
1937 Tribal distribution in Oregon. American Anthropological Association, Memoir 47.

Birket-Smith, Kaj
1930 Contributions to Chipewyan ethnology. Report of the Fifth Thule Expedition, vol. 6, no. 3.

Bloomfield, Leonard
1946 Algonquian, pp. 85–129, in Harry Hoijer et al., Linguistic structures of native America. Viking Fund Publications in Anthropology, no. 6.

Boas, Franz
1909 Kwakiutl of Vancouver Island. American Museum of Natural History, Memoir.

Borden, C. E.
1962 West Coast Crossties with Alaska, pp. 9–19, in J.M. Campbell, ed., Prehistoric cultural relations between the arctic and temperate zones of North America. Technical Papers, no. 11, Arctic Institute of North America, Montreal.

Bunzel, R. L.
1932 An introduction to Zuni ceremonialism. 47th Annual Report, Bureau of American Ethnology, Smithsonian Institution, Washington, D.C.

Butler, B. R.
1959 Lower Columbia Valley archaeology: a survey and appraisal of some major archaeological resources, Tebiwa, 2:6–24.
1961 The Old Cordilleran culture in the Pacific Northwest. Occasional Papers, no. 5, Idaho State University Museum, Pocatello.
1968 A guide to understanding Idaho archaeology. 2d rev. ed., Idaho State University Museum, Pocatello.

Byers, Douglas D. (ed.)
1967 The prehistory of the Tehuacan Valley, volume I, environment and subsistence. Austin: University of Texas Press.

Caldwell, Joseph R.
1958 Trend and tradition in the prehistory of the eastern United States. Scientific Papers, vol. 10, Illinois State Museum, Springfield; and American Anthropological Association, Memoir 88.

Callender, C.
1962 Social organization of the Central Algonkian Indians. Milwaukee Public Museum Publications in Anthropology, no. 7.

Castetter, E. F., and W. H. Bell
1942 Pima and Papago Indian agriculture. Albuquerque: Inter-American Studies, no. 1.
1951 Yuman Indian agriculture. Albuquerque: University Of New Mexico Press.

Chamberlain, A. F.
1892 Report on the Kootenay Indians. British Association for the Advancement Of Science, 62:549–617.

Champe, J. L.
1946 Ash Hollow Cave, a study of stratigraphic sequences in the central Great Plains. University of Nebraska Studies, n s, no. 1
1949 White Cat Village. American Antiquity, 14:285–92.

Childe, V. G.
1946 What happened in history. New York: Pelican.

Chittenden, H. M.
1902 The American fur trade of the far West. 3 vols. New York: Harper.

Chretien, C. Douglas
1962 The mathematical models of glottochronology. Language, 38:11–37.

Codere, H.
1950 Fighting with property, a study of Kwakiutl potlatching and warfare, 1792–1930. Monographs of the American Ethnological Society, 18. New York: Augustin.
1956 The amiable side of Kwatkiutl life. American Anthropologist, 58:334–51.
1957 Kwakiutl society: rank without class. American Anthropologist, 59:473–86.

Colson, E.
1953 The Makah Indians. Minneapolis: University of Minnesota Press.

Colton, H. S.
1945 The Patayan problem in the Colorado River valley. Southwestern Journal of Anthropology, 1:114–21.

Comas, Juan
1955 Review of: catalogue des hommes fossiles, ed. Vallois and Movius. Boletin Bibliográfico de Antropología Americana, 17:252–54.

Cook, S. F.
  1971   The aboriginal population of upper California, pp. 66–83, in The California Indians, a source book, comp. and ed. R. F. Heizer and M. A. Whipple. 2d ed. revised and enlarged. Berkeley and Los Angeles: University of California Press.

Coon, C. S.
  1948   A Reader in general anthropology. New York: Henry Holt & Co.

Cooper, John M.
  1939   Is the Algonquian family hunting ground system pre-Columbian? American Anthropologist, 41:66–90.

Crabtree, Donald
  1969   A technological description of artifacts in Assemblage I, Wilson Butte Cave, Idaho. Current Anthropology, 10:366–67.

Crane, Leo
  1928   Desert drums: the Pueblo Indians of New Mexico, 1540–1928. Boston: Little, Brown.

Cressman, L. S.
  1960   Cultural sequences at The Dalles, Oregon. Transactions, American Philosophical Society, Philadelphia, vol. 50, pt. 10.

Crook, Wilson W., Jr., and R. K. Harris
  1957   Hearths and artifacts of early man near Lewisville, Texas, and associated faunal material. Bulletin of the Texas Archeological Society, 28:7–97.
  1958   A Pleistocene campsite near Lewisville, Texas. American Antiquity, 23:233–46.

Daugherty, R. D.
  1956   Archaeology of the Lind Coulee Site, Washington. Proceedings, American Philosophical Society, Philadelphia, vol. 100, no. 2.
  1962   The Intermontane western tradition. American Antiquity, 28:144–50.

Davis, Robert T.
  1949   Native arts of the Pacific Northwest. Stanford, Calif.: Stanford University Press.

Debo, Angie
  1940   And still the waters run. Princeton, N.J.: Princeton University Press.

Denhardt, Robert M.
  1947   The horse of the Americas. Norman: University of Oklahoma Press.

De Terra, Helmut, Javier Romero, and T. D. Stewart
  1949   Tepexpan man. Viking Fund Publications in Anthropology, no. 11.

DeVoto, Bernard
  1947   Across the wide Missouri. Boston: Houghton Mifflin.

DeVoto, Bernard (ed.)
1953 The journals of Lewis and Clark. Boston: Houghton Mifflin.

Dixon, R. B.
1905 The Northern Maidu. American Museum of Natural History, Bulletin 18.
1923 The racial history of man. New York: Scribner's.

Dobie, J. F.
1952 The Mustangs. Boston: Little, Brown.

Dobyns, Henry F.
1966 Estimating aboriginal American population, an appraisal of techniques with a new hemispheric estimate. Current Anthropology, 7: 395–449.

Dole, G. E., and R. L. Carneiro (eds.)
1960 Essays in the science of culture in honor of Leslie A. White. New York: T. Y. Crowell.

Downs, James F.
1971 California, pp. 289–316, in North American Indians in historical perspective, ed. Eleanor Burke Leacock and Nancy Oestreich Lurie. New York: Random House.

Dozier, E. P.
1964 Pueblo Indians of the Southwest. Current Anthropology, 5:79–97.
1966 Hano, a Tewa Indian community in Arizona. New York: Holt, Rinehart and Winston.
1970 The Pueblo Indians of North America. New York: Holt, Rinehart and Winston.

Driver, Harold E.
1961 Indians of North America. 2d rev. ed. Chicago: University Of Chicago Press.

Drucker, Philip
1951 The Northern and Central Nootkan tribes. Bulletin 144, Bureau of American Ethnology. Smithsonian Institution, Washington, D.C.
1955a Indians of the Northwest Coast. New York: McGraw-Hill.
1955b Sources of Northwest Coast culture, pp. 59–81, in New interpretations of aboriginal American culture history: 75th Anniversary Volume of the Anthropological Society of Washington.
1958 The native brotherhoods. Bulletin 168, Bureau of American Ethnology, Smithsonian Institution, Washington, D. C.

Drucker, P., and R. F. Heizer
1967 To make my name good: a reexamination of the Southern Kwakiutl potlatch. Berkeley and Los Angeles: University of California Press.

Drury, E. M.
1936 Henry Harmon Spalding. Caldwell, Ida.: Caxton Printers.

Duff, Wilson
  1956 Prehistoric stone sculpture of the Fraser River and Gulf of Georgia. Anthropology in British Columbia, no. 5, pp. 15–151. Department of Education, British Columbia Provincial Museum, Victoria, B. C.

Egan, Major Howard R.
  1917 Pioneering the West, 1846 to 1878, ed. William M. Egan, Salt Lake City, Utah.

Eggan, Fred
  1937 The Cheyenne and Arapaho kinship system, pp. 35–95, in Social anthropology of North American tribes, ed. Fred Eggan. Chicago: University of Chicago Press. (Enlarged ed., 1955.)
  1950 Social organization of the Western Pueblos. Chicago: University of Chicago Press.
  1952 The ethnological cultures and their archeological background, pp. 35–45, in Archeology of the eastern United States, ed. J. B. Griffin. Chicago: University of Chicago Press.
  1966 The American Indian, perspectives for the study of social change. Chicago: Aldine.

Eiseley, Loren C.
  1947 Land tenure in the Northeast: a note on the history of a concept. American Anthropologist, 49:680–81.

Ekholm, G. F.
  1944 Excavations of Tampico and Panuco in the Huasteca, Mexico. Anthropological Papers, vol. 38, pt. 5. American Museum of Natural History, New York.

Ellis, Florence Hawley
  1951 Patterns of aggression and the war cult in Southwestern Pueblos. Southwestern Journal of Anthropology, 7:177–201.

Euler, Robert C.
  1966 Southern Paiute ethnohistory. University of Utah Anthropological Papers, no. 78.

Evans, Glen L.
  1961 The Friesenhahn Cave, part I. Bulletin of the Texas Memorial Museum, no. 2.

Ewers, John C.
  1948 Gustavus Sohon's portraits of Flathead and Pend d'Oreille Indians, 1854. Smithsonian Miscellaneous Collections, 110:1–68.
  1955 The horse in Blackfoot Indian culture. Bulletin 159, Bureau of American Ethnology, Smithsonian Institution, Washington, D.C.
  1958 The Blackfoot. Norman: University of Oklahoma Press.

Fairbanks, C. H.
  1949 A general survey of Southeastern prehistory, pp. 55–76, in J. W. Griffin, ed., The Florida Indian and his neighbors. Winter Park, Fla: Rollins College.

Farb, Peter
1968 Man's rise to civilization as shown by the Indians of North America from primeval times to the coming of the industrial state. New York: Dutton.

Fenton, W. N.
1940 Problems arising from the historic northeastern position of the Iroquois. Smithsonian Miscellaneous Collections, 100:159-251.
1941 Tonawanda longhouse ceremonies: ninety years after Lewis Henry Morgan. Bulletin 128, Bureau of American Ethnology, Anthropological Papers, no. 15, pp. 139-65, Smithsonian Institution, Washington, D.C.
1953 The Iroquois Eagle Dance. Bulletin 136, Bureau of American Ethnology. Smithsonian Institution, Washington, D.C.

Fisher, M. W.
1946 The mythology of the Northern and Northeastern Algonkians. Papers of the Robert S. Peabody Foundation for Archaeology, III:226-62, Andover, Mass.

Flannery, Regina
1939 An analysis of Coastal Algonquian culture. Catholic University of America, Anthropology Series, 7:1-219.

Forbes, Jack D.
1960 Apache, Navaho, and Spaniard. Norman: University of Oklahoma Press.
1965 Warriors of the Colorado: the Yumas of the Quechan Nation and their neighbors. Norman: University of Oklahoma Press.
1967 Nevada Indians speak. Reno: University of Nevada Press.

Ford, J. A.,and G. R. Willey
1941 An interpretation of the prehistory of the eastern United States. American Anthropologist, 43:325-63.

Forde, C. D.
1931 Ethnography of the Yuma Indians. University of California Publications in American Archaeology and Ethnology, 28:83-278.

Fortune, Reo
1932 Omaha secret societies. Columbia University Contributions To Anthropology, no. 15.

Fowler, Don D.
1966 Great Basin social organization, pp. 57-74, in W. L. d'Azevedo et al., eds., Current status of anthropological research in the Great Basin: 1964. Desert Research Institute, Publications in the Social Sciences and Humanities, no. 1.

Fowler, Don D., and Catherine S. Fowler (eds.)
1971 Anthropology of the Numa: John Wesley Powell's manuscripts on the numic peoples of western North America, 1868-1880. Smithsonian Contributions to Anthropology, no. 14.

Fox, J. R.
1967 The Keresan Bridge. London School of Economics Monographs on Social Anthropology, no. 35. The Athlone Press, University of London. New York: Humanities Press.

Garfield, V. E.
1939 Tsimshian clan and society. University of Washington Publications in Anthropology, 7:167–349.

Garretson, M. S.
1938 The American bison. New York: New York Zoological Society.

Goddard, Pliny E.
1913 Indians of the Southwest. New York: American Museum of Natural History.

Goldfrank, Esther
1945 Socialization, personality, and the structure of the Pueblo society. American Anthropologist, 47:516–39.

Green, F. E.
1963 The Clovis blades: an important addition to the Llano complex. American Antiquity, 29:145–65.

Greenberg, J. H.
1960 The general classification of Central and South American languages, pp. 791–94, in A. F. C. Wallace, ed., Men and cultures, Selected Papers, 5th International Congress of Anthropological and Ethnological Sciences. Philadelphia: University of Pennsylvania Press.

Griffin, J. B.
1944 The Iroquois in American prehistory. Papers, Michigan Academy of Sciences, Arts, Letters, 29:35–374.
1946 Cultural change and continuity in eastern United States archaeology, pp. 37–95, in F. Johnson, ed., Man in northeastern North America, Papers of the Robert S. Peabody Foundation for Archaeology, vol. 33, Andover, Mass.
1952 Culture periods in eastern United States archaeology, pp. 352–64, in J. B. Griffin, ed., Archaeology of eastern United States, Chicago: University of Chicago Press.

Gruhn, Ruth
1961 The archaeology of Wilson Butte Cave, south-central Idaho. Occasional Papers of the Idaho State College Museum, no. 6.
1965 Two early radiocarbon dates from the lower levels of Wilson Butte Cave, south-central Idaho. Tebiwa, 8:57.

Gunnerson, J. H.
1960 An introduction to Plains Apache archeology—the Dismal River Aspect. Bulletin 173, Bureau of American Ethnology, pp. 131–260, Smithsonian Institution, Washington, D.C.
1968 Plains Apache archeology: a review. Plains Anthropologist, 13:167–89.

Gunnerson, James H., and Dolores A. Gunnerson

1971 Apachean culture: A study in unity and diversity, chap. 2, in Apachean culture history and ethnology, ed. Kieth H. Basso and Morris E. Opler. Anthropological Papers of the University of Arizona, no. 21.

Haag, William G.

1962 The Bering Strait land bridge. Scientific American, 206:112–23.

Haas, Mary R.

1939 Natchez and Chitimacha clans and kinship terminology. American Anthropologist, 41:597–610.

1941 The classification of the Muskogean languages, pp. 41–58, in L. Spier et al., eds., Language, culture, and personality. Essays in memory of Edward Sapir. Menasha, Wis.: Sapir Memorial Publication Fund.

1958a Algonkian-Ritwan: the end of a controversy. International Journal of American Linguistics, 24:159–73.

1958b A new linguistic relationship in North America: Algonkian-Gulf relationships. Southwestern Journal of Anthropology, 14:231–64.

Hack, J. T.

1942 The changing physical environment of the Hopi Indians of Arizona. Papers of the Peabody Museum of American Archaeology and Ethnology, vol. 36, Cambridge, Mass.

Hackenberg, R. A.

1962 Economic alternatives in arid lands: a case of the Pima and Papago Indians. Ethnology, 1:186–96.

Haines, Francis

1938a Where did the Plains Indians get their horses? American Anthropologist, 40:112–17.

1938b The northward spread of horses among the Plains Indians, American Anthropologist, 40:429–37.

1955 The Nez Percés, tribesmen of the Columbia plateau. Norman: University of Oklahoma Press.

1963 Appaloosa, the spotted horse in art and history. Austin: University of Texas Press.

Hallowell, A. I.

1949 The size of Algonkian hunting territories, a function of ecological adjustment. American Anthropologist, 51:35–45.

1957 The impact of the American Indian on American culture. American Anthropologist, 59:201–17.

Hammond, George P., and Agapito Rey

1929 Expedition into New Mexico made by Antonio de Espejo, 1582–1583, as revealed in the journal of Diego Pérez de Luxán, a member of the party. Quivira Society Publications, vol. 1.

Handlin, Oscar
1963   The Americans, a new history of the people of the United States. Boston: Little, Brown.

Hardacre, Emma
1971   The lone woman of San Nicolas Island, pp. 272–84, in The California Indians, a source book, Comp. and ed. R. F. Heizer and M. A. Whipple. 2d ed. revised and enlarged. Berkeley and Los Angeles: University of California Press.

Harper, E. A.
1953a The Taovayas Indians in frontier trade and diplomacy, 1719–1768. The Chronicles of Oklahoma, 31:268–89.
1953b The Taovayas Indians in frontier trade and diplomacy, 1769–1779. Southwestern Historical Quarterly, 57:181–201.
1953c The Taovayas Indians in frontier trade and diplomacy. Panhandle Plains Historical Review, 26:41–72.

Harrington, John P.
1910   A brief description of the Tewa language. American Anthropologist, 12:497–504.

Harrington, M. R.
1948   An ancient site at Borax Lake, California. Southwest Museum Papers, no. 16, Los Angeles.

Harris, Jack S.
1940   The White Knife Shoshoni of Nevada, pp. 39–118, in Ralph Linton, ed., Acculturation in seven American Indian tribes. New York: Appleton-Century-Crofts.

Hart, C. W.
1943   A reconsideration of the Natchez social structure. American Anthropologist, 45:374–86.

Haury, E. W.
1962   The greater American Southwest, pp. 106–31, in R. J. Braidwood and G. R. Willey, eds., Courses toward urban life, Viking Fund Publication in Anthropology, no. 32.

Hawthorn, A.
1967   Art of the Kwakiutl Indians and other Northwest Coast Indian tribes. Seattle: University of Washington Press.

Haynes, C. Vance, Jr.
1964   Fluted projectile points: their age and dispersion. Science, 145:1408–13.
1966   Elephant-hunting in North America. Scientific American, 214:104–12.
1967   Carbon 14 dates and early man in the New World, pp. 267–86, In Pleistocene extinctions, the search for a cause, ed. P. S. Martin and H. E. Wright, Jr. Vol. 6 of the Proceedings of the VII Congress

of the International Association for Quarternary Research. New
Haven: Yale University Press.
1969 Comments on Bryan. Current Anthropology, 10:353–54.

Hearne, Samuel
1795 A journey from Prince of Wale's Fort in Hudson's Bay to the northern ocean. London. 1911 ed. by J. B. Tyrell, The Champlain Society;
1958 ed. by Richard Glover, MacMillan.

Heizer, R. F.
1947 Francis Drake and the California Indians, 1579. Berkeley and Los
Angeles: University of California Press.
1964 The western coast of North America, pp. 117–48, in J. G. Jennings
and E. Norbeck, eds., Prehistoric man in the New World. Chicago:
University of Chicago Press.

Heizer, Robert F., and Richard A. Brooks
1965 Lewisville—ancient campsite or wood rat houses. Southwestern Journal of Anthropology, 21:155–65.

Heizer, R. F., and M. A. Whipple (compiled and edited by)
1971 The California Indians, a source book. 2d ed. revised and enlarged
Berkeley and Los Angeles: University of California Press.

Helm, June, and Eleanor Burke Leacock
1971 The hunting tribes of subarctic Canada, chap. 12, in North American
Indians in historical perspective, ed. Eleanor Burke Leacock and Nancy
Oestreich Lurie. New York: Random House.

Hibben, F. C.
1941 Evidences of early occupation of Sandia Cave, New Mexico, and other
sites in the Sandia-Manzano region, Smithsonian Miscellaneous Collections, vol. 99, no. 23.

Hickerson, Harold
1967 Some implications of the theory of the particularity, or "atomism,"
of Northern Algonkians. Current Anthropology, 8:313–43.

Hodge, Frederick Webb (ed.)
1907– Handbook of American Indians north of Mexico, parts 1 and 2, Bulle-
10   tin 30, Bureau of American Ethnology, Smithsonian Institution.
Washington, D.C.

Hoffman, W. J.
1891 The Midé wiwin or "Grand Medicine Society" of the Ojibwa, pp.
149–299. 7th Annual Report of the Bureau of Ethnology, 1885–1886,
Smithsonian Institution. Washington, D.C.
1893 The Menomini Indians. 15th Annual Report, Bureau of American
Ethnology, Smithsonian Institution, Washington, D.C.

Holm, B.
1965 Northwest Coast Indian art. Seattle: University Of Washington Press.

Honigman, John J.
1946 Ethnography and acculturation of the Fort Nelson slave. Yale University Publications in Anthropology, no. 33, pp. 1–169.

Hopkins, Nicholas A.
1965 Great Basin prehistory and Uto-Aztecan. American Antiquity, 31:48–60.

Hornaday, W. T.
1887 The extermination of the American bison. Annual Report, Smithsonian Institution, Washington, D.C., part II, pp. 367–548.

Howard, Helen A., and D. L. McGrath
1941 War Chief Joseph. Caldwell, Ida.: Caxton Printers.

Howard, James A.
1957 The mescal bean cult of the central and southern Plains: an ancestor of the peyote cult? American Anthropologist, 59:75–87.
1968 The Southeastern Ceremonial complex and its interpretation. Memoir, no. 6, Missouri Archaeological Society, Columbia, Mo.

Howells, W. W.
1967 Mankind in the making, rev. ed. Garden City, N. Y.: Doubleday.

Hunt, George T.
1940 The wars of the Iroquois: a study in intertribal trade relations. Madison: University of Wisconsin Press.

Hyde, George E.
1959 Indians of the High Plains, from the prehistoric period to the coming of Europeans. Norman: University of Oklahoma Press.

Hymes, D. H.
1960 Lexicostatistics so far. Current Anthropology, 1:3–44.

Imbelloni, Jose
1958 Nouveaux apports à la classification de l'homme Américain. Miscellanea Paul Rivet, Octogenaria Dictata, I:107–36. Mexico, D.F.

Inverarity, R. B.
1950 Art of the Northwest Coast Indians. Berkeley and Los Angeles: University of California Press.

Irving, Washington
1961 Astoria, or anecdotes of an enterprise beyond the Rocky Mountains. Garden City, N. Y.: Doubleday, Dolphin Books.

Irwin-Williams, Cynthia
1969 Comments on the association of archaeological materials and extinct fauna in the Valsequillo region, Puebla, Mexico. American Antiquity, 34:82–83.

Jenks, Albert E.
1898 The wild rice gatherers of the upper lakes. 19th Annual Report, Bureau of American Ethnology, Smithsonian Institution. Washington, D.C.

1936   Pleistocene man in Minnesota, a fossil Homo sapiens. Minneapolis: The University of Minnesota Press.

Jenness, Diamond
1934   The Indians of Canada. 2d ed. National Museum of Canada, Bulletin 65, Anthropological Series no. 15.

Jennings, Jesse D.
1956   The American Southwest: a problem in cultural isolation, pp. 59–127, in R. Wauchope, ed., Seminars in archaeology. Society for American Archaeology, Memoir 11.
1968   Prehistory of North America. New York: McGraw-Hill.

Jennings, Jesse D., and Edward Norbeck
1955   Great Basin prehistory: a review. *American Antiquity*, 21:1–11.

Jennings, Jesse D., and Edward Norbeck (eds.)
1964   Prehistoric man in the New World. Chicago: University of Chicago Press.

Johnson, Frederick (ed.)
1946   Man in northeastern North America. Papers of the Robert S. Peabody Foundation for Archaeology, vol. 3, Andover, Mass.

Johnson, O. W.
1969   Flathead and Kootenay, the rivers, the tribes, and the region's traders. Glendale, Calif.: Arthur H. Clark Co.

Josephy, Alvin M., Jr.
1965   The Nez Percé Indians and the opening of the Northwest. New Haven: Yale University Press.
1968   The Indian heritage of America. New York: Knopf.

Keesing, F. M.
1939   The Menomini Indians of Wisconsin. Memoirs of the American Philosophical Society, vol. 10.

Keithahn, Edward L.
1963   Monuments in cedar. rev. ed. Seattle, Wash.: Superior Publishing Co.

Kelley, J. Charles
1955   Juan Sabeata and diffusion in aboriginal Texas. American Anthropologist, 57:981–95.

Kellogg, Louise P.
1925   The French regime in Wisconsin and the Northwest. State Historical Society of Wisconsin, Madison.

Kelly, Isabel T.
1932   Ethnography of the Surprise Valley Paiute. University of California Publications in American Archaeology and Ethnology, vol. 31.
1964   Southern Paiute ethnography. University of Utah Anthropological Papers, no. 69.

Kinietz, W. Vernon
 1940   The Indians of the western Great Lakes, 1615–1760. Occasional Con-
        tributions no. 10, Museum of Anthropology, University of Michigan,
        Ann Arbor. (Reprinted, Ann Arbor: University of Michigan Press,
        Ann Arbor Paperbacks, 1965.)

Kirchoff, Paul
 1954   Gatherers and farmers in the greater Southwest: a problem in clas-
        sification. American Anthropologist, 56:529–50.

Kluckhohn, C., and D. C. Leighton
 1946   The Navaho. Cambridge, Mass.: Harvard University Press.

Knight, Rolf
 1968   Ecological factors in changing economy and social organization
        among the Rupert House Cree. Anthropology Papers of the National
        Museum of Canada, no. 15.

Knowles, Nathaniel
 1940   The torture of captives by the Indians of eastern North America.
        Proceedings of the American Philosophical Society, no. 82, pp.
        151–225.

Krause, Aurel
 1956   The Tlingit Indians, results of a trip to the Northwest Coast of Ameri-
        ca and the Bering Strait, trans. Erna Gunther. Seattle: University of
        Washington Press for the American Ethnological Society.

Krieger, Alex D.
 1948   Importance of the "Gilmore Corridor" in culture contacts between
        Middle America and the eastern United States. Texas Archeological
        and Paleontological Society Bulletin, 19:155–78.
 1953   New World culture history: Anglo-America, pp. 238–64, in A. L.
        Kroeber, ed., Anthropology today, an encyclopedia inventory. Chica-
        go: University of Chicago Press.
 1964   Early man in the New World, pp. 23–81, in Jesse D. Jennings and
        Edward Norbeck, eds., Prehistoric man in the New World. Chicago:
        University of Chicago Press.

Kroeber, A. L.
 1907   Shoshonean dialects of California. University Of California Publica-
        tions in American Archaeology and Ethnology, no. 4.
 1925   Handbook of the Indians of California. Bulletin 78, Bureau of Ameri-
        can Ethnology, Smithsonian Institution, Washington, D.C.
 1928   Native culture of the Southwest. University of California Publications
        in American Archaeology and Ethnology, 23:375–98.
 1937   Athabascan kin term systems. American Anthropologist, 39:602–9.
 1939   Cultural and natural areas of native North America. University of
        California Publications in American Archaeology and Ethnology, vol.
        38.

1948   Anthropology. New York: Harcourt, Brace and Co.

Kroeber, A. L., and Clyde Kluckhohn, with the assistance of Wayne Untereiner
  1952   Culture: a critical review of concepts and definitions. Papers of the Peabody Museum of American Archaeology and Ethnology, vol. 47 (1), Cambridge, Mass.

Kroeber, Theodora
  1961   Ishi in two worlds. Berkeley and Los Angeles: University of California Press.

La Barre, Weston
  1960   Twenty years of peyote studies. Current Anthropology, 1:45–60.
  1969   The peyote cult, enlarged ed. New York: Schocken Books.

Laguna, Frederica de
  1952   Some dynamic forces in Tlingit society. Southwestern Journal of Anthropology, 8:1–12.
  1960   The story of a Tlingit community. Bulletin 172, Bureau of American Ethnology, Smithsonian Institution, Washington, D. C.

Lamb, Sidney M.
  1958   Linguistic prehistory in the Great Basin. International Journal of American Linguistics, 24:95–100.
  1964   The classification of the Uto-Aztecan languages: a historical study. University of California Publications in Linguistics, 34:106–25.

Landes, Ruth
  1937   Ojibwa sociology. Columbia University Contributions To Anthropology, vol. 29.
  1968   Ojibwa religion and the Midewiwin. Madison: University of Wisconsin Press.
  1970   The prairie Potauatomi, tradition and ritual in the twentieth century. Madison: University of Wisconsin Press.

Lange, Charles
  1959   Cochiti: A New Mexico Pueblo past and present. Austin: University of Texas Press.

Leacock, Eleanor B.
  1954   The Montagnais hunting territory and the fur trade, American Anthropological Association, Memoir 78.

Leacock, Eleanor B., and Nancy Oestreich Lurie
  1971   North American Indians in historical perspective. New York: Random House.

Leakey, L. S. B., Ruth De E. Simpson, and T. Clements
  1968   Archaeological excavations in the Calico Mountains, California: Preliminary report. Science, 160:1022–23.

Lees, Robert B.
  1953   The basis of glottochronology. Language, 29:113–27.

Lehmer, D. J.
1954   Archeological investigations in the Oahe Dam area, South Dakota, 1950–1951. Bulletin 158, Bureau of American Ethnology. Smithsonian Institution, Washington, D.C. River basin survey papers, no. 7, pp. 139–40.

Leighton, Dorothea C., and John Adair
1966   People of the middle place: a study of the Zuni Indians. New Haven, Conn.: Human Relations Area Files Press.

Li An-Che
1937   Zuñi: some observations and queries. American Anthropologist, 39:296–300.

Lips, Julius
1947   Naskapi law. Transactions of the American Philosophical Society, vol. 37, pt. 4.

Lorenzo, J. L.
1967   Sobre metodo arqueológico. Boletín, Instituto Nacional de Anthropología e Historía, no. 28.

Lowie, R. H.
1909   The Northern Shoshone. American Museum of Natural History, Anthropological Papers, 2:165–306.
1924   Notes on Shoshonean ethnography. American Museum Of Natural History, Anthropological Papers, 20:187–314.
1963   Indians of the Plains. Garden City, N. J.: Natural History Press. (Reprinted from 1954 ed. New York: McGraw-Hill.)

MacGowan, K., and J. A. Hester
1962   Early man in the New World, Garden City, N. Y.: Doubleday.

MacLeod, William Christie
1928   The American Indian frontier. New York: Knopf.

MacNeish, June Helm
1956   Leadership among the Northeastern Athaabascans. Anthropologica, 2:131–63.

MacNeish, Richard S.
1947   A preliminary report on Coastal Tamaulipas, Mexico. American Antiquity, 13:1–15.
1952   The archaeology of the northeastern United States, pp. 46–57, in J. B. Griffin, ed., Archaeology of eastern United States. Chicago: University of Chicago Press.
1964   Investigations in the southwest Yukon: part II: archaeological excavation, comparisons and speculations. Papers for the Robert S. Peabody Foundation for Archaeology, vol. 6, no. 1, Andover, Mass.

McAllister, J. Gilbert, and W. W. Newcomb, Jr.
1970   Daveko, Kiowa-Apache medicine man, with a summary of Kiowa-

Apache history and culture. Bulletin 17 of the Texas Memorial Museum.

McCombe, L., E. Z. Vogt, and C. Kluckhohn
1951   Navaho means people. Cambridge, Mass.: Harvard University Press.

McFeat, T. (ed.)
1966   Indians of the North Pacific Coast. Seattle: University of Washington Press.

McIlwraith, T. F.
1948   The Bella Coola Indians, 2 vols. Toronto: University of Toronto Press.

McQuown, Norman
1955   Indigenous languages of Latin America. American Anthropologist, 57:501–70.

McWhorter, Lucullus V. (ed.)
1940   Yellow Wolf. Caldwell, Ida.: Caxton Printers.
1952   Hear me, my chiefs! Caldwell, Ida.: Caxton Printers.

Malouf, Carling
1966   Ethnohistory in the Great Basin. Desert Research Institute Publications in the Social Sciences and Humanities, no. 1, pp. 1–39.

Mangelsdorf, P. C., and C. E. Smith, Jr.
1949   New archaeological evidence on evolution in maize. Botanical Museum Leaflets, 13:213–47, Harvard University, Cambridge, Mass.

Martin, Paul S.
1973   The discovery of America. Science, 179:969–74.

Martin, Paul S., W. A. Longacre, and J. N. Hill
1967   Chapters in the prehistory of eastern Arizona, III. Chicago Natural History Museum, Fieldiana: Anthropology, vol. 57.

Martin, Paul S., John B. Rinaldo, Elaine Bluhm, Hugh C. Cutler, and Roger Grange, Jr.
1952   Mogollon cultural continuity and change: the stratigraphic analysis of Tularosa and Cordova caves. Chicago Natural History Museum, Fieldiana: Anthropology, vol. 40.

Mason, J. Alden
1935   The place of Texas in pre-Columbian relationships between the United States and Mexico. Texas Archeological and Paleontological Society Bulletin, 7:29–46.

1937   Further remarks on pre-Columbian relationships between the United States and Mexico. Texas Archeological and Paleontological Society Bulletin, 9:120–29.
1946   Notes on the Indians of the Great Slave Lake area. Yale University Publications in Anthropology, 31:1–46.

Mason, Leonard
1967 The Swampy Cree: a study in acculturation. Anthropology Papers of the National Museum of Canada, no. 13.

Mason, Otis T.
1895 Influence of environment upon human industries or acts. Annual Report, Smithsonian Institution, pp. 639–65.
1907– Environment, pp. 427–30, in F. W. Hodge, ed., Handbook of American
10 Indians. Bulletin 30, Bureau of American Ethnology, Smithsonian Institution, Washington, D.C.

Mason, Ronald J.
1962 The Paleo-Indian tradition in eastern North America. Current Anthropology, 3:227–78.

Meighan, C. W.
1959 California cultures and the concept of an Archaic stage. American Antiquity, 24:289–305.

Michelson, Truman
1934 The identification of the Mascoutens. American Anthropologist, 36:226–33.

Miller, Wick
1966 Anthropological linguistics in the Great Basin. Desert Research Institute Publications in the Social Sciences and Humanities, no. 1, pp. 75–112.

Mirambell, Lorena
1967 Excavaciones en un sitio pleistocénico de Tlapacoya, Mexico. Boletín, Instituto Nacional de Anthropología e Historía, no. 29, pp. 37–41.

Mishkin, Bernard
1940 Rank and warfare among the Plains Indians. Monographs of the American Ethnological Society, vol. 3.

Mooney, James
1928 The aboriginal population of America north of Mexico. Smithsonian Miscellaneous Collections, 80:1–26.

Morgan, Lewis H.
1851 League of the Ho-de-no-sau-nee or Iroquois. Rochester: Sage And Broa. (Reprinted, New York: Corinth Books, 1962.)

Müller-Beck, Hansjürgen
1966 Paleohunters in America: Origins and diffusion. Science, 152:1191–1210.

Mulloy, W.
1952 The northern Plains, pp. 124–38, in J. R. Griffin, ed., Archaeology of Eastern United States. Chicago: University of Chicago Press.

Murdock, G. P.
    1949   Social structure. New York: MacMillan.

Murphy, Robert F., and Yolanda Murphy
    1960   Shoshone-Bannock subsistence and society. University of California, Anthropological Records, 16:293–338.

Neumann, G. K.
    1952   Archaeology and race in the American Indian, pp. 13–34, in J. B. Griffin, ed., Archaeology of eastern United States, Chicago: University of Chicago Press.

Nevins, Allan, and Henry Steele Commager
    1951   The pocket history of the United States, the story of a free people. New York: Pocket Books.

Newcomb, W. W., Jr.
    1950   A re-examination of the causes of Plains warfare. American Anthropologist, 52:317–29.
    1956a   The culture and acculturation of the Delaware Indians. Anthropological Papers, Museum of Anthropology, University of Michigan, no. 10. (Reprinted 1970.)
    1956b   A reappraisal of the "Cultural Sink" of Texas, Southwestern Journal of Anthropology, 12:145–53.
    1960   Toward an understanding of war, pp. 317–36, in Essays in the science of culture in honor of Leslie A. White, ed. G. E. Dole and R. L. Carneiro. New York: T. Y. Crowell.
    1961   The Indians of Texas, from prehistoric to modern times. Austin: University of Texas Press.
    1971   My country 'tis of thee and the interpretation of the past, pp. 45–62, in History and the social studies: an interdisciplinary approach, ed. J. D. Born, Jr., and P. D. Thomas. History Resource Center, Wichita State University, Wichita, Kan.

Newcomb, W. W., Jr., and Forrest Kirkland
    1967   The rock art of Texas Indians. Austin: University of Texas Press.

Newell, H. Perry, and Alex D. Krieger
    1949   The George C. Davis Site, Cherokee County, Texas. Memoirs of the Society of American Archaeology, no. 5.

Newman, M. T.
    1951   The sequence of Indian physical types in South America, pp. 69–97, in W. S. Laughlin, ed., Papers on the physical anthropology of the American Indian. Viking Fund Publications in Anthropology.

Noon, J. A.
    1949   Law and government of the Grand River Iroquois. New York: Viking Fund Publications in Anthropology.

O'Dell, Scott
1960   Island of the blue dolphins. Boston: Houghton Mifflin.

Oliver, Symmes C.
1962   Ecology and cultural continuity as contributing factors in the social organization of the Plains Indians. University of California Publications in American Archaeology and Ethnology, vol. 48, no. 1, pp. 1-90.

Opler, Marvin K.
1940   The Southern Ute of Colorado, pp. 119-206, in Ralph Linton, ed., Acculturation in seven American Indian tribes. New York: Appleton-Century-Crofts.

Orr, P. C.
1956   Radiocarbon dates from Santa Rosa Island, I, Anthropological Bulletin, no. 2, Santa Barbara Museum of Natural History.

Ortiz, Alfonso
1969   The world of the Tewa Indians. Chicago: University of Chicago Press.

Osbourne, Douglas
1957   Excavations in the McNary Reservoir Basin near Umatilla, Oregon. River Basin Survey Papers, no. 8, bulletin 166, Bureau of American Ethnology, Smithsonian Institution, Washington, D.C.

Osbourne, Douglas, W. W. Caldwell, and R. H. Crabtree
1956   The problem of Northwest coastal interior relationships as seen from Seattle. American Antiquity, 22:117-27.

Osgood, Cornelius
1936   The distribution of the Northern Athapaskan Indians. Yale University Publications in Anthropology, no. 7.
1937   The ethnography of the Tanaina. Yale University Publications in Anthropology, no. 16.

Oswalt, Wendell H.
1973   This land was theirs, a study of the North American Indian. 2d ed. New York: Wiley.

Parsons, E. C.
1925   The Pueblo of Jemez. Andover, Mass.: Phillips Academy.
1929   The social organization of the Tewa of New Mexico. American Anthropological Association, Memoir 36.
1939   Pueblo Indian religion. 2 vols. Chicago: University of Chicago Press.

Pennington, Campbell W.
1963   The Tarahumar of Mexico: Their environment and material culture. Salt Lake City: University of Utah Press.

Powell, J. W.
1891   Indian linguistic families of America north of Mexico. 7th Annual Report, Bureau of American Ethnology, Smithsonian Institution, Washington, D.C.

Quimby, G. I.
1942   The Natchezan culture type. American Antiquity, 7:255-75.
1946   Natchez social structure as an instrument of assimilation. American Anthropologist, 48:134-37.
1960   Indian life in the upper Great Lakes. Chicago: University of Chicago Press.

Radin, Paul
1916   The Winnebago tribe. 37th Annual Report, Bureau of American Ethnology, Smithsonian Institution, Washington, D.C.

Ray, Verne F.
1932   The Sanpoil and Nespelem. University of Washington Publications in Anthropology, 5:1-237.
1939   Cultural relations in the plateau of northwestern America. F. W. Hodge Anniversary Fund, Southwest Museum, vol. 3.
1942   The plateau. Culture Element Distributions, XXII. Berkeley and Los Angeles: University of California Press.

Riddell, Francis
1960   Honey Lake Paiute ethnography. Nevada State Museum Anthropological Papers, no. 1.

Ritchie, W. A.
1938   A perspective of northeastern archaeology. American Antiquity, 4:91-112.
1961   Iroquois archaeology and settlement patterns, pp. 27-38, in W. A. Ritchie and John Gulick, eds., Symposium on Cherokee and Iroquois culture. Bulletin 180, Bureau of American Ethnology, Smithsonian Institution, Washington, D.C.

Ritzenthaler, Robert E.
1953   The Potawatomi Indians of Wisconsin. Milwaukee Public Museum Bulletin, vol. 19, no. 3.

Ritzenthaler, Robert E., and Pat Ritzenthaler
1970   The woodland Indians of the western Great Lakes. Garden City, N. Y.: Natural History Press.

Roe, F. G.
1951   The North American buffalo: a critical study of the species in its wild state. Toronto: University of Toronto Press.

Rogers, Edward S.
1963   The hunting group–hunting territory complex among the Mistassini Indians. National Museum of Canada, Bulletin 195.
1965   Leadership among the Indians of eastern subarctic Canada. Anthropologica, 7:263-84.
1966   Subsistence areas of the Cree-Ojibwa of the eastern subarctic: A preliminary study. National Museum of Canada, Bulletin 204, pp. 87-118.
1967   The material culture of the Mistassini. National Museum of Canada, Bulletin 218.

Roosa, William B.

1956 The Lucy Site in central New Mexico. American Antiquity, 21:310.

Russell, F.
1908 The Pima Indians. 26th Annual Report, Bureau of American Ethnology, Smithsonian Institution, Washington, D.C.

Sapir, Edward
1916 Time perspective in aboriginal American culture. Geological Survey of Canada, Memoir 90, Anthropology Series 13.

Sauer, Carl O.
1934 The distribution of aboriginal tribes and languages in northwestern Mexico. Ibero-Americana, V:1–90.
1971 Sixteenth century North America. Berkeley and Los Angeles: University of California Press.

Schroeder, A. H.
1957 The Hakataya cultural tradition. American Antiquity, 23:176–78.

Sellards, E. H.
1952 Early man in America, a study in prehistory. Austin: University of Texas Press.

Service, Elman R.
1966 The hunters. Foundations of Modern Anthropology Series. Englewood Cliffs, N. J.: Prentice-Hall.
1971 Primitive social organization, an evolutionary perspective. 2d ed. New York: Random House.

Shiner, Joel L.
1961 The McNary Reservoir: a study in plateau archaeology. Bulletin 179, Bureau of American Ethnology, Smithsonian Institution, Washington, D.C.

Simpson, George G.
1961 Horses, the story of the horse family in the modern world and through sixty million years of history. Garden City, N. Y.: Doubleday, Anchor Books.

Skinner, Alanson
1913 Social life and ceremonial bundles of the Menomini Indians. Anthropological Papers, American Museum of Natural History, vol. 13.
1921 Material culture of the Menomini. Indian Notes and Monographs, n.s., 20. New York: Museum of the American Indian. Heye Foundation.
1923– Observations of the ethnology of the Sauk Indians. Bulletin of the
25 Public Museum of the City of Milwaukee, 5:1–180.
1924– The Mascoutens or Prairie Potawatomi Indians. Bulletin of the Public
27 Museum of the City of Milwaukee, vol. 6.

Snyderman, George S.
1955 The functions of wampum. Proceedings of the American Philosophical Society, 98:469–94.

Spaulding, A. C.
1952 The origin of the Adena culture of the Ohio Valley. Southwestern Journal of Anthropology, 8:260–68.

Speck, Frank G.
1907 The Creek Indians of Taskigi Town. American Anthropologist, 2:99–164.
1919 Functions of wampum among the Eastern Algonkian. Memoirs of the American Anthropological Association, vol. 6, no. 1.
1926 Land ownership among hunting peoples in primitive America and the world's marginal areas. 22nd International Congress of Americanists, 2:323–32.
1927 Family hunting territories of the Lake St. John Montagnais and neighboring bands. Anthropos, 22:387–403.
1931 A study of the Delaware Indian Big House Ceremony. vol. 2, Publications of the Pennsylvania Historical Commission, Harrisburg.
1940 Penobscot man: The life history of a forest tribe in Maine. Philadelphia: University of Pennsylvania Press.
1944 Midwinter rites of the Cayuga longhouse. Philadelphia: University of Pennsylvania Press.
1955 The Iroquois. Bloomfield Hills, Mich.: Cranbrook Institute of Science.

Speck, Frank G., and Loren C. Eiseley
1939 The significance of the hunting territory systems of the Algonkian in social theory. American Anthropologist, 41:269–80.

Spicer, Edward H.
1940 Pascua: a Yaqui village in Arizona. Chicago: University of Chicago Press.
1954 Potam: a Yaqui village in Sonora. American Anthropological Association, Memoir 77.
1962 Cycles of conquest. Tucson: University of Arizona Press.

Spier, Leslie
1921 The Sun Dance of the Plains Indians. Anthropological Papers of American Museum of Natural History, 16:451–527.
1930 Klamath ethnography. University of California Publications in American Archaeology and Ethnology, vol. 30.
1933 Yuman tribes of the Gila River. Chicago: University of Chicago Press.
1936 Cultural relations of the Gila River and lower Colorado tribes, Yale University Publications in Anthropology, no. 3.

Spier, Leslie, and Edward Sapir
1930 Wishram ethnography. University of Washington Publications In Anthropology, 3:151–300.

Spinden, Herbert J.
 1908 The Nez Perce Indians. American Anthropological Association, Memoirs, vol. 2, pt. 3.

Stevenson, M. C.
 1904 The Zuni Indians. 23rd Annual Report, Bureau of American Ethnology, Smithsonian Institution, Washington, D.C.

Steward, Julian H.
 1938 Basin-plateau aboriginal sociopolitical groups. Bulletin 120, Bureau of American Ethnology, Smithsonian Institution, Washington, D.C.
 1955 Theory of culture change. Urbana: University of Illinois Press.

Stewart, T. D.
 1960 A physical anthropologist's view of the peopling of the New World. Southwestern Journal of Anthropology, 16:259-71.

Strong, W. D.
 1932 An archeological reconnaissance in the Missouri Valley. Explorations and field-work of the Smithsonian Institution in 1931, pp. 151-58.
 1935 An introduction to Nebraska archeology. Smithsonian Miscellaneous Collections, vol. 93, no. 10.

Suhm, Dee Ann, Alex D. Krieger, with E. B. Jelks
 1954 An introductory handbook of Texas archeology, vol. 25, Bulletin of the Texas Archeological Society, Austin.

Suttles, Wayne
 1960 Affinal ties, subsistence, and prestige among the Coast Salish. American Anthropologist, 62:296-305.

Swadesh, Morris
 1952 Lexicostatistic dating of prehistoric ethnic contacts. Proceedings of the American Philosophical Society, 96:452-63.

Swanson, Earl H., Jr.
 1962a Early cultures in northwestern America. American Antiquity, 28:151-58.
 1962b The emergence of Plateau culture. Occasional Papers, no. 8, Idaho State University Museum. Pocatello.

Swanton, John R.
 1909 Contributions to the ethnology of the Haida. Memoir, the American Museum of Natural History.
 1911 Indian tribes of the lower Mississippi Valley and adjacent coast of the Gulf of Mexico, Bulletin 43, Bureau of American Ethnology, Smithsonian Institution, Washington, D.C.
 1928 Aboriginal culture of the Southeast. 42nd Annual Report, Bureau of American Ethnology, Smithsonian Institution, Washington, D.C.
 1946 The Indians of the southeastern United States. Bulletin 137, Bureau of American Ethnology, Smithsonian Institution, Washington, D.C.

1952 The Indian tribes of North America. Bulletin 145, Bureau of American Ethnology, Smithsonian Institution, Washington, D.C.

Swanton, John R. (directed by)
1939 Final report of the United States De Soto Expedition Commission. 76th Congress, House Document no. 71 (10328), Washington, D.C.

Taylor, Walter W.
1961 Archaeology and language in western North America. American Antiquity, 27:71–81.

Teit, James
1898 Traditions of the Thompson River Indians of British Columbia. Memoirs, American Folklore Society, vol. 6, Boston and New York.
1900 The Thompson Indians. Memoirs of the American Museum of Natural History, 2:163–392.
1906 The Lillooet Indians. Memoirs of the American Museum of Natural History, 4:193–300.
1909 The Shuswap. Memoirs of the American Museum of Natural History, 4:447–758.
1930 The Salishan tribes of the western plateau, ed. Franz Boaz. 45th Annual Report, Bureau of American Ethnology, Smithsonian Institution, Washington, D.C.

Thomas, A. B. (tr. and ed. by)
1935 After Coronado: Spanish exploration northeast of New Mexico, 1696–1727. Norman: University of Oklahoma Press.

Thompson, Laura, and Alice Joseph
1944 The Hopi way. Chicago: University of Chicago Press.

Thwaites, Reuben G. (ed.)
1904– Original journals of the Lewis and Clark expedition, 1804–1806. New
5   York: Dodd, Mead & Co.

Titiev, Mischa
1944 Old Oraibi: a study of the Hopi Indians of Third Mesa. Papers of the Peabody Museum of American Archaeology and Ethnology, 22:1–277.

Tooker, Elisabeth
1964 An ethnography of the Huron Indians, 1615–1649. Bulletin 190, Bureau of American Ethnology, Smithsonian Institution, Washington, D.C.

Trager, George L.
1942 The comparative phonology of the Tiwa languages. Studies in Linguistics, 1:1–10.

Trigger, Bruce G.
1969 The Huron, farmers of the North. Case Studies In Cultural Anthropology. New York: Holt, Rinehart and Winston.

Troike, Rudolph C.
1962 The origins of Plains mescalism. American Anthropologist, 64:946–63.

Tunnell, C. D., and W. W. Newcomb, Jr.
1969 A Lipan Apache Mission, San Lorenzo de la Santa Cruz, 1762–1771. Bulletin 14, Texas Memorial Museum, Austin.

Turney-High, H. H.
1937 The Flathead Indians of Montana. American Anthropological Association, Memoir 48.
1941 Ethnography of the Kutenai. American Anthropological Association, Memoir 56.

Underhill, Ruth M.
1939 Social organization of the Papago Indians. Columbia University Contributions to Anthropology, 30:1–280.
1944 Indians of the Pacific Northwest. Bureau of Indian Affairs, Department of the Interior, Washington, D.C.
1946 Papago Indian religion. Columbia University Press:
1956 The Navahos. Norman: University of Oklahoma Press.

Vaillant, G. C.
1962 Aztecs of Mexico: origin, rise and fall of the Aztec Nation. Rev. by S. B. Vaillant. New York: Pelican.

Vallois, Henri V., and Hallam L. Movius, Jr.
1952 Catalogue des hommes fossiles. Extrait du Fascicule V des Comptes rendus de la XIX e Session du Congres Geologique International.

Van der Merwe, Nicholaas J.
1966 New mathematics for glottochronology. Current Anthropology, 7:485–500.

Voegelin, C. F., and E. W. Voegelin
1946 Linguistic considerations in northeastern North America, pp. 178–94, in Man in northeastern North America, ed. Frederick Johnson. Papers of the Robert S. Peabody Foundation for Archaeology, vol. 3.

Vogt, E. Z.
1961 Navaho, pp. 278–336, E. H. Spicer, ed., Perspectives in American Indian culture change. Chicago: University of Chicago Press.

Von Eickstedt, E.
1933– Rassenkunde und rassengeschichte der menschheit, Ferdinand Enke,
34   Verlag, Stuttgart.

Wagner, Henry R.
1926 Sir Francis Drake's voyage around the world: its aims and achievements. San Francisco: J. Howell.

1941 Juan Rodríguez, discoverer of the coast of California. San Francisco: J. Howell.

Wallace, Anthony F. C.
1958 Dreams and the wishes of the South: a type of psychoanalytic theory among the seventeenth century Iroquois. American Anthropologist, 60:234–48.

Wallace, Paul A. W.
1961 Indians in Pennsylvania. The Pennsylvania Historical and Museum Commission, Harrisburg.

Waring, Antonio J., Jr., and Preston Holder
1945 A prehistoric ceremonial complex in southeastern United States. American Anthropologist, 47:1–34.

Wauchope, Robert
1956 Seminars in archaeology. Memoirs of the Society for American Archaeology, no. 11.

Webb, Walter P.
1931 The Great Plains. New York: Grosset and Dunlap.

Weddle, Robert S.
1968 San Juan Bautista, gateway to Spanish Texas. Austin: University of Texas Press.

Wedel, Waldo R.
1942 Archeological remains in central Kansas and their possible bearing on the location of Quivira. Smithsonian Miscellaneous Collections, 101:1–24.
1959 An introduction to Kansas archeology. Bulletin 174, Bureau of American Ethnology, Smithsonian Institution, Washington, D.C.
1961 Prehistoric man on the Great Plains. Norman: University of Oklahoma Press.
1964 The Great Plains, pp. 193–222, in J. D. Jennings and E. Norbeck, eds., Prehistoric man in the New World. Chicago: University of Chicago Press.

Wendorf, Fred, and A. D. Krieger
1959 New light on the Midland Discovery. American Antiquity, 25:66–78.

Wendorf, Fred, and J. J. Hester
1962 Early man's utilization of the Great Plains. American Antiquity, 28:159–71.

Wendorf, Fred, A. D. Krieger, C. C. Albritton, and T. D. Stewart
1955 The Midland Discovery. Austin: University of Texas Press.

Wheat, J. B.
1955 Mogollon culture prior to A. D. 1000. American Anthropological Association, Memoir 82.

White, Leslie A.
1932 The Pueblo of San Felipe. American Anthropological Association, Memoir 38.

1935 The Pueblo of Santo Domingo, New Mexico. American Anthropological Association, Memoir 43.

1940 The symbol: the origin and basis of human behavior. Philosophy of Science, 7:451–63.

1942 The Pueblo of Santa Ana, New Mexico. American Anthropological Association, Memoir 60.

1949 The science of culture, a study of man and civilization. New York: Farrar, Straus and Co.

1959 The evolution of culture: the development of civilization to the fall of Rome. New York: McGraw-Hill.

1962 The Pueblo of Sia, New Mexico. Bulletin 184, Bureau of American Ethnology, Smithsonian Institution, Washington, D.C.

1964 The world of the Keresan Pueblo Indians, pp. 83–94, in Stanley Diamond, ed., Primitive view of the world. New York: Columbia University Press.

White, Leslie A., with Beth Dillingham
1973 The concept of culture. Minneapolis: Burgess Publishing Co.

Wicke, Charles R.
1965 Pyramids and temple mounds: Mesoamerican ceremonial architecture in eastern North America. American Antiquity, 30:409–20.

Willey, Gordon R.
1958 An archaeological perspective on Algonkian-Gulf relationships. Southwestern Journal of Anthropology, 14:265–72.

1966 An introduction to American archaeology: North and Middle America. Englewood Cliffs, N. J.: Prentice-Hall.

1971 An introduction to American archaeology. Vol. 2, South America. Englewood Cliffs, N. J.: Prentice-Hall.

Willey, Gordon R., and Philip Phillips
1958 Method and theory in American archaeology. Chicago: University of Chicago Press.

Williams, Stephen (ed.)
1968 The Waring Papers. Papers of the Peabody Museum of Archaeology and Ethnology, vol. 58.

Wilson, Clyde
1956 A new interpretation of the wild rice region of Wisconsin. American Anthropologist, 58:1059–64.

Winship, George P.
1896 The Coronado expedition, 1540–1542. 14th Annual Report, Bureau of American Ethnology, pt. I, Smithsonian Institution, Washington, D. C.

Wissler, Clark
1914 The influence of the horse in the development of Plains culture. American Anthropologist, 16:1–25.

1938   The American Indian, an introduction to the anthropology of the New World, 3d ed. New York: Oxford University Press.

1941   North American Indians of the Plains. New York: American Museum of Natural History.

Wittfogel, K. A., and E. S. Goldfrank
1943   Some aspects of Pueblo mythology and society. Journal of American Folklore, 56:17–30.

Woodbury, R. B.
1961   Prehistoric agriculture at Point of Pines, Arizona. Memoir 17, Society for American Archaeology, Salt Lake City, Utah.

Wormington, H. M.
1957   Ancient man in North America. Denver, Colo.: Denver Museum of Natural History.

Wright, Herbert E., Jr., and David G. Frey, (eds.)
1965   The quaternary of the United States. A Review Volume for the VII Congress of the International Association for Quaternary Research. Princeton, N. J.: Princeton University Press.

INDEX